PERIOD STYLE

PERIOD STYLE

JUDITH AND MARTIN MILLER

PHOTOGRAPHY BY JAMES MERRELL
CHIEF CONTRIBUTOR: FREDA PARKER

MITCHELL BEAZLEY

PERIOD STYLE

Judith and Martin Miller
Photography by James Merrell
Chief Contributor: Freda Parker

Edited and designed by
Mitchell Beazley International Ltd,
Artists House, 14-15 Manette Street,
London W1V 5LB

Senior Executive Art Editor **Jacqui Small**
Editor **Alex Towle**
Assistant Art Editor **Larraine Lacey**
Editorial Assistant **Jaspal Kharay**
Design Assistant **Camilla Joerin**
Production **Ted Timberlake**

Reprinted 1990

A CIP catalogue record for this book is available from the British Library
ISBN 0 85533 731 1

Typeset in Bernhard 11/13pt Modern Roman and 9/10pt Modern Italic by Bookworm, Manchester
Colour reproduction by Scantrans Pte Ltd, Singapore
Printed by Printer Industria Grafica SA, Barcelona

CONTENTS

FOREWORD BY JUDITH MILLER 6

THE ELEMENTS OF STYLE
Concealment and Furniture 14
Colour 18
Fabrics 20
Plants and Flowers 22
Collections 24

PERIOD BY PERIOD
Medieval 26
Elizabethan and Jacobean 36
The 17thC Country House 46
The Early American Home 52
English Baroque 60
The Age of Elegance 66
Queen Anne 66
Early to Mid Georgian 72
Mid to Late Georgian 80
American Federal 100
18thC Country 104
Colonial 110
Shaker 122
Baroque and Rococo 128
Louis XIV 130
Régence and Louis XV 130
Louis XVI 133
19th-century adaptations 133
Regency, Empire and Biedermeier 148
Regency 148
Empire 159
American Empire 161
Biedermeier 174
Victorian 176
The Victorian Town House, to 1870 179
Late Victorian 185
Arts and Crafts 210
Edwardian and Art Nouveau 216
Edwardian 216
Art Nouveau 218
Art Deco 222

CREATING THE LOOK
Medieval 34
Elizabethan and Jacobean 44
17thC Country 58
English Baroque 64
Queen Anne/Early Georgian 70
Mid to Late Georgian 88
18thC Country/Colonial 120
Shaker 126
Continental Baroque and Rococo 146
Regency/Empire/American Empire 172
Victorian Townhouse 202
Victorian Country 208
Arts and Crafts 215
Edwardian/Art Nouveau 220
Art Deco 226

DIRECTORY OF USEFUL ADDRESSES 228

GLOSSARY 236

INDEX 237

ACKNOWLEDGMENTS 240

1

The fireplace is a crucial factor in establishing period. This stone and brick hearth, with its row of copper vessels on the mantelpiece, effectively evokes the 17thC.

2

A grand Elizabethan dining hall demands a wealth of portraits in richly carved and gilded frames – not only on the upper walls but also over the timber panelling. This style of dining room was influential in smart Edwardian homes.

I have been involved in the concept, planning, writing and photography of this book for over two years, and it seems strange at last to be embarking on a foreword. As with all such projects, one's ideas develop, constantly adapted by new experience. My understanding of period style has been hugely enriched by what I have seen recently in period-style interiors all over Britain, Europe and America. This book reflects not only the principles I started off with, but also the insights I have discovered on the way.

I have for a long time been interested in how the interiors of houses developed through the centuries, how tastes changed and, most importantly, how we might adapt period styles to our modern way of life. *Period Style* is about our own homes, so it looks squarely at domestic interiors – it is far from being a collection of stock shots of museums and stately houses.

Neither is *Period Style* a dissertation on history. Certainly, the book attempts to understand the past, hopefully in a spirit of empathy; but above all it shows how we can *live with* the past. It is not a book for the purist. Very few of us have furniture, pottery, silver and so on from one period, and it has to be said that this has always been the case. The spirit of the book, I hope, is one of a joyful eclecticism that itself has a basis in history.

If I'd chosen to deal only with the great stately homes, the changes in style would have appeared more dramatic. The rich and powerful could transform the look of their homes whenever the impact of new styles reached them. As travel became fashionable, particularly with the advent of the Grand Tour, changes in style swept through Europe and over to the Colonies. However, I have chosen in this book to deal mainly with more modest homes where change tended to come slowly. Styles ebbed and flowed uncertainly, rather than in a series of cataclysmic changes. Someone furnishing a room in the

opposite

This alcove in Dennis Severs' house in Spitalfields, London, exudes the spirit of the 17thC. The drama is created by the deep green gloss paint which reflects flickering candlelight. The hanging of plush red fabric on the wall and the rugs draped over the table seem to cosset the collection of earthenware pots, pewter jugs, bottles and fruit. The rather severe old portrait is lit from below by a candle shielded by a scallop shell. All paintings were lit from below until well into the 20thC.

3

Oak panelling and oak furniture from a variety of periods are given a lighter feel in this bedroom by the use of colourful textiles and a framed sampler hung on the wall.

4

An Elizabethan open hearth can be furnished with early cooking utensils for authenticity. The dresser offers a chance to display blue and white china. Note the evocative Windsor chair and giant candle – the latter for use as much as display.

1

On a Jacobean staircase, a painted canvas floor cloth framing a Regency sofa.

2

A glimpse of 18thC England.

3

Drapes frame Regency chairs.

18th or 19th century often had to compromise, accepting novelties only as and when they could afford them, or as individual whim dictated – much as we do today.

Still, it is interesting how we immediately can get a feel for a period when we walk into a room. Many things combine to create a distinct ambience – the architectural details, the colours, the furniture, the flowers, the fabrics, even the sounds and smells. Our senses are bombarded by a multitude of stimuli. An example springs to mind from recent experience. On a photo session we visited a splendid medieval priory which was being sensitively restored by the owner, an artist. As we walked into the hall, which was dimly lit and sparsely furnished, the air was slightly smoky, there was a strong smell of frankincense, and religious music filled the vaulted hallway. There was no doubt what period we had walked into. Perhaps not everyone would want to live in such a sparse environment, but I am making this point to show that certain elements – often just a few elements – can be identified as making a strong statement of period.

In attempting to create a period style, sensitivity and tact are needed. Some elements mix easily without disrupting the mood, some don't. It takes a great deal of panache to mix conflicting periods – for example, Victorian romantic with modernistic linear. Such juxtapositions can be done, and we have many examples in this book – but they need careful handling.

In a mixed interior, the ingredients that set the dominant style are not always the obvious ones. Often the key feature is quite small – perhaps one striking sculpture or painting. Elsewhere, the major statement might be conveyed more generally – for example, by the colour of the walls, the density of objects in the room, or the use of wild flowers in profusion all around. Style can be created simply with two chairs and a table cleverly arranged, or a small area of a room dedicated to a collection of period objects. Such approaches allow for comfortable living. Many antique chairs are very uncomfortable, so

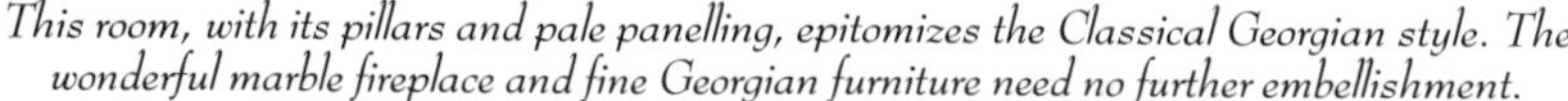

opposite

This room, with its pillars and pale panelling, epitomizes the Classical Georgian style. The wonderful marble fireplace and fine Georgian furniture need no further embellishment.

4

Pedestals with urns help to give emphasis to a 19thC French Empire composition.

5

An American Gothic chair.

6

A Regency table sets the mood.

1

This is a typically Victorian corner, with characteristic heavy fabrics, a piano, a pole screen and a chaise longue.

2

The style of this bedroom was inspired by its 18thC ceiling.

3

An exotic lacquer bed.

you will often want to keep your modern sofas and chairs. The important thing is to make sure that the fabrics suit your chosen style or are absolutely neutral. In New York we photographed a wonderful six-storey house in the Village, owned by Lee Anderson. Everything here was American Gothic – furniture, lights, sculpture, teaspoons – but in the middle of the main drawing room there was a striking anachronism: an upholstered Federal wing chair, made 80 years earlier, beautiful in its own right but quite out of place in this Gothic environment. American Gothic is one of the most visually exciting styles, and Lee's pieces were of the highest quality. But chairs in this style are just not comfortable. So, to sit in the midst of them all, Lee has something that is.

The refined styles of the aristocracy, designed to impress, are difficult to replicate without acquiring pieces of comparable quality and craftsmanship. However, period style need not be expensive to create. Rustic or provincial pieces can be used to evoke the period, rather than top-quality townhouse items. Moreover, as this book moves through the ages we have tried to identify what I suppose you could call "tricks of the trade" – effects that can be achieved convincingly at relatively modest expense.

Magnificent full drapes, for example, can be made from the least expensive fabrics – even Indian muslin. You need not automatically decide on wall-to-wall carpeting – why not try a few rugs on plain floor boards or a stone flag or tiled floor. Rushes strewn authentically on the floor would sabotage the vacuum cleaner, but rush matting is a suitable alternative. Some people might feel that lavender strewn in little piles in the corners of a room smacks of eccentricity. However, lavender smells beautiful and, if an early rustic feel is what you're looking for, this trick really works – and what a conversation piece! Many ideas of this kind will be found in the "Creating the look" sections in this book, in which we look at specific period styles in the

opposite

This warm alcove, with its artistic Victorian set-piece, is in a basement kitchen/dining room in London. The walls are covered with a beige-backed wallpaper with warm rust-coloured sprigs. The lead urns filled with rust-coloured "trees" stand on a large tin flower, bin. The collection of Staffordshire blue and white printed meat plates frame a sentimental Victorian oil.

4

A Victorian wash-stand, shaving mirror and towel rail stand proud beneath a pair of Venetian scenes.

5

A chandelier may be all that is needed to evoke the past.

6

An Arts and Crafts mood prevails.

FLOUR

1

Candlelight is essential for such an early dining room. Note the very simple treatment.

2

Art Deco objects and colours.

3

This room is subtly Edwardian.

context of what can realistically be achieved today. In these sections I have even included a few musical suggestions (not always strictly in period), designed to stimulate further exploration.

There is often much to be said for avoiding the safe option. Take wall treatments, for example. While Georgian styles might seem to demand muted colours, striking walls in bright yellow and blue can look just right. Never be afraid to experiment.

Turning to lighting, I have to admit to an absolute passion for candles. Nothing evokes a period feel like the flicker of candlelight – and it is so flattering! However, having declared my interest, I must say that some ultra-modern lighting can achieve excellent results, while remaining very discreet. Whatever approach you adopt, the lighting has to be considered carefully, as modern rooms are often much smaller than their period equivalents.

I must mention one *bête noire* – white plastic light switches on dark or deep-coloured walls. This dread was not instinctive, but was something that emerged from a photographic trip. On returning home I immediately set about with a paint pot and covered the erstwhile brilliant white switches with deep raspberry paint. Radiators, similarly, can be terribly obtrusive. We have dedicated some space in the book to how to conceal them; and conceal them you must. Paint them, frill them, box them in, but don't leave a stark white box on your wall – unless, of course, the wall is white.

History should be your servant, not your master. Period style, like any other style, has to be something you feel happy with. If you feel like a change, you might like to add some exotic touches throughout the house. Or perhaps choose one room for a totally over-the-top treatment – a tented Empire bedroom or a Victorian bathroom full of stuffed birds. But first immerse yourself in this book. Enjoy it. Decide what you like. Be inspired.

JUDITH MILLER 1989

opposite

This beige and black drawing room has been stylishly designed by Harry Schule. The couch was made in New York in the 1930s and was designed by architect Albert Meyer. At this period architects often designed not merely the building but all the interior fittings as well. The lamps by Arteluce were made in 1957. The Art Deco style blends perfectly with more modern designs. Note the decorator touch – the edging on the curtains echoing the zebra rug.

4

Dramatic sculptures add extra interest to an Arts and Crafts setting, brightened by tulips.

5

A palette of the 1920s.

6

Exotic pillars in a kitchen.

CONCEALMENT AND FURNITURE

Obviously, it is neither desirable nor practicable to copy the living standards of a medieval, Georgian or even Victorian household. We demand greater standards of comfort, better heating, lighting, plumbing and so on than were even dreamed possible in the past. Along with these standards of efficiency come problems of modern-day clutter – radiators, electrical equipment, light switches and the like. In a period-style interior such details may need to be concealed to preserve the historic mood.

The simplest treatment of radiators is to "paint them out", by giving them the same treatment as the wall. This might mean merely painting them the same plain colour, or perhaps marbling, rag rolling or dragging them. If the walls are stencilled, the design should be continued over the radiator, regardless of the ridges. Alternatively, radiators can be boxed in and the front covered in perforated board, a trellis of slats or a metal grille. Again, the box can be painted to blend with the room. Or the boxing could be made to look like a cupboard. A new piece of furniture in the Regency era was the chiffonier, usually in rosewood and often with a brass grille over silk on each door. In a Regency room it would, therefore, be appropriate to disguise the radiator as a chiffonier, graining or staining a less expensive wood to resemble rosewood and leaving out the silk.

1

1 — *The modern built-in wall unit in the style of a Victorian credenza conceals a sound system.*

Built-in cupboards and bookcases can be made and decorated in a style to suit the period of the room. As with boxed-in radiators, cupboards can be matched with authentic pieces of furniture. In an Edwardian house it is perfectly in period to have built-in furniture – seats in niches and inglenooks, as well as fitted cupboards. In an early Georgian setting, it would be authentic to create an arched niche on either side of a fireplace and make matching cupboards below.

In other situations, you can build cupboards that continue the theme of a room. A glass-fronted wall cabinet with wooden tracery in the form of pointed arches would look appropriate in a Gothic interior. Or if you want a cupboard to be totally unobtrusive, it could be disguised behind a smooth panel and decorated to match the walls; or the door might be covered with a mirror and then surrounded by an ornate frame. TV sets and hi-fi systems can be housed in free-standing period-style furniture. Edwardian music cabinets make excellent hi-fi cabinets. The back can usually be cut away to accommodate wires without damaging the piece. Speakers obviously can't be hidden away, and must be positioned for acoustic not

2

2 — *In an 18thC drawing room the radiator has been partly panelled and painted to match the skirting board.*

3 — *An unobtrusive flat-fronted radiator is painted to match wood panelling in a 19thC living room.*

4

3

6

5

4 and 5 — *A lesson in concealment – two decorative treatments that let the heat flow through. One is a string and bead curtain in the living room of Charleston farmhouse, in Sussex (home to the Bloomsbury group), the other a fake 19thC chiffonier in a late Victorian interior.*

6 — *A modern radiator, rag-rolled to match the walls, looks like fluted panelling.*

7 — *An extremely grand brass radiator cover in a French 18thC bedroom.*

7

8

A vanity unit and a cupboard full of bathroom clutter are cleverly disguised as an 18thC display cabinet.

8

9

9

Built-in library shelving is given a Classical feel with pediments and plinths.

10

An interesting built-in cupboard in the style of a Georgian display cabinet.

11

This 19thC-style jib door (such doors are fitted flush into the wall and thus made unobtrusive) opens to reveal a collection of beautiful 18thC glassware.

10

11

14

15

15

The age-old problem solved. Here, a TV is cleverly tucked away inside a late 18thC linen press.

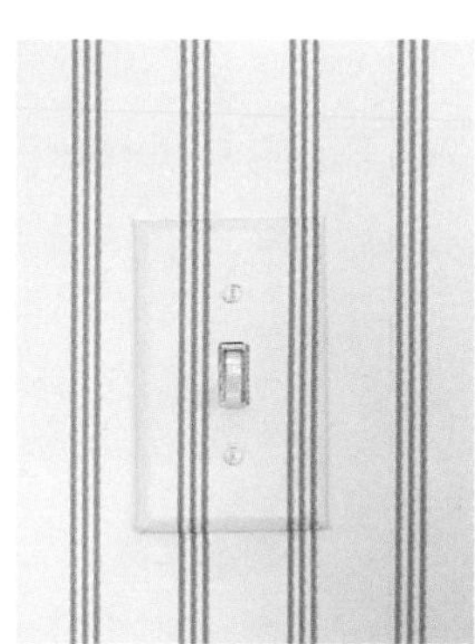

16

12

A pine unit is filled with Art Deco pottery in this modern built-in kitchen.

12

13

13

Here, the top of a pine dresser has been built into a pine-clad wall. The shelves display a wonderful collection of "Mandarin" patterned Newhall porcelain. The chest below is an example of tramp art – a form of applied folk decoration.

14

A modern built-in kitchen in the grand French country house style.

17

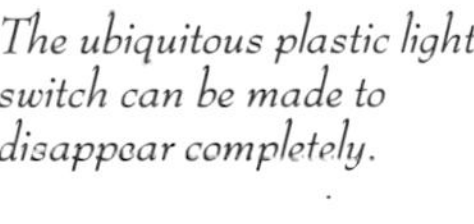

16

The ubiquitous plastic light switch can be made to disappear completely.

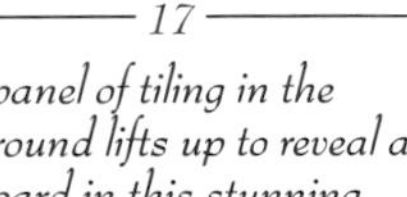

17

The panel of tiling in the foreground lifts up to reveal a cupboard in this stunning bathroom – a homage to Art Deco.

18

This fantasy post-Modernist library proves that the need to store books and papers can stimulate some imaginative solutions.

18

1

1 and 2

Cupboards and shelves can be made to fit in with any style. In picture 1 a collection of tins is displayed on suitably Arts and Crafts shelving. In 2, pretty Georgian cupboards have been simply fronted with white-painted wire and pleated silk.

2

3

3

A less-than-perfect Biedermeier buffet has been cleverly adapted to accommodate a kitchen sink and hob unit.

4

4

An inglenook, fitted out with modern units of solid oak, gives this kitchen a nostalgic country look.

5

A single well-chosen piece of furniture can give a room instant period style. Here, a 19thC Venetian chair from the Andy Warhol collection makes an amusing counterpoint to the New York skyline.

5

6

A mixture of wonderful pieces from the late 17th and early 18thC gives this essentially modern room a real sense of style. The window treatment evokes the 19thC, and the coffee table is an example of excellent modern craftsmanship. There is much to be said for mixing good items from all periods.

aesthetic purposes. The housings can be painted or covered with fabric; however, the discreet yet no-nonsense look of modern high-tech speakers will not be obtrusive in most period settings.

Modern plastic light switches can be an eyesore, especially if attention is drawn to them by a starkly contrasting wall colour. Painting over light switches and sockets or covering them with fabric to match the walls can be a successful strategy. Transparent switches can be bought which leave the wall covering showing through the plate. In a Victorian setting a better choice might be to install brass light switches. Wooden switches painted in a range of colours are also available.

It is in the kitchen that modern appliances become particularly obtrusive. Most firms that supply fitted kitchens offer fascia panels to disguise the dishwasher and washing machine. Dresser-style wooden units can be purpose-made with fake drawers to hide modern technology.

Our modern ways to arrange furniture are different from the practices of times past, and we require certain pieces that did not exist back then. Many early chairs are very pretty to look at but uncomfortable to sit on for any length of time. Modern sofas built along traditional lines look good in almost any period setting, especially when upholstered in an appropriate fabric.

Beds can pose a problem. Until the 19th century, imposing four-poster beds were usual, but in homes today they take up rather a lot of space and are generally very expensive. You can, however, create a four-poster effect by draping a simple framework with fabric, or by fixing poles to the ceiling and hanging curtains from them.

Another way to achieve a period feel in a way that is compatible with modern lifestyles is by using pieces of furniture in a manner that is different from their original purpose. For example, old panelling, church pews, fireplace surrounds, screens and the carved back sections from Victorian sideboards can be revamped and turned into attractive bedheads.

One standard item of late 20th-century furniture that few of us can do without is the coffee table, non-existent until the 1920s. If buying a new coffee table, don't choose a flimsy, apologetic piece or a fancy one. Look for a large plain one in a style that will not date. Pick a wood sympathetic to other furniture or choose a marbled or lacquered finish (the latter would be especially apt for the 17th century). There are also low versions of Regency drum tables that would work well in a house of the Regency period. Alternatively, make your own coffee table by taking a square dining table (non-antique!) and cutting it down. Or place glass or marble on carved stone supports.

6

7

— 10 —

A blackamoor drinks table effectively mirrored in a small hallway sets a Regency seal upon a penthouse apartment.

10

— 7–9 —

There are various solutions to the problem of accommodating a coffee table in a period-style setting. In picture 7 a carved wooden upturned capital is topped with a marble slab. In 8 an oriental effect has been achieved using a 19thC Chinese table base and a piece of plate glass; and in 9 a marble slab is set into a simple lacquered frame.

8

— 13 —

In this country house setting the strong lines of a Gothic chair dominate a simple bedroom. Such interesting furniture will animate plain surroundings.

— 14 —

The choice of colours and the wall cabinet give an otherwise Victorian bathroom an Arts and Crafts feel.

14

9

11

13

— 15 —

An 18thC Italian carved limewood panel puts a modern divan bed firmly in period.

15

— 11 —

A Victorian steel marble-topped table gives a flavour of period to a modern kitchen.

— 12 —

A 1930s radio finds a new life here as a side table.

12

16

— 16 —

An illusion of a four-poster bed can be created with heavy drapes, modern turned posts and curtain tracking.

COLOUR

1
A rich Victorian range of colour and pattern sets off a typically sentimental bust.

2
An applied cornice has been given a handpainted, distressed finish in colours related to the reproduction 19thC wallpaper panels – not a difficult job but certainly time-consuming.

1

2

3
An American Colonial interior of the late 18thC showing the softness of the traditional milk paint – this was raw pigment mixed not with oil or water but with skimmed milk.

3

Two of the most vital elements in setting a mood are colour and pattern. The correct choice can compensate for minor deficiencies such as lack of panelling or cornices and even for major deficiencies of proportion. Colour and pattern can even change the character of a house from one era to another.

One of the periods most readily evoked in this way is Victorian. Rich, dark colours, pattern upon pattern and layer upon layer of textiles create the enclosed, womblike feel of a High Victorian town interior. Lighter and more airy interiors, associated with the country look, are created by setting sparkling white lace, linen, muslin and crochet against white or pastel colour-washed walls.

In some cases, the same colour scheme can evoke more than one period. For example, the medieval era favoured earthy tones – reds, browns, ochre yellows, greens and inky blues obtained from natural dyes. This same palette reappeared four hundred years later when William Morris and the Arts and Crafts Movement looked to the Middle Ages for inspiration.

Today's fashionable paint effects work well in many period situations. The panelling, or even plain plastered walls, in an early Georgian room can be dragged in two closely related tones of the grey, olive green or browns of the time. Rag rolling or sponging can add to the elegance of a mid-Georgian room. Colour rubbed or washed onto a paler colour can help the mellow feel of a country-style room of almost any period.

It is not always necessary to use colour in exactly the same way as it would have been used originally. It is most unlikely, for example, that a late 17th-century room would have been painted bright yellow; but such a colour can give a real feel for the flamboyance of the era.

Different colours have different psychological effects which should also be taken into account in the decorative plan. For example, red tones seem to advance upon the eye, making the room seem smaller and more intimate, whereas blues and greys seem to recede, creating a sense of spaciousness.

In the end, colour choices are so personal – one man's pale green heaven is another's version of hell – that the best advice one can give is to first find a style that you are comfortable with, and then, if you can't pick a colour from the appropriate palette of the age, trust your own judgment and choose a colour you can live with. As with other aspects of period style, the aim is usually to create the ambience of the past, not a strict replica.

4
Colourwashed floorboards have been sanded back to accentuate the grain, making a lovely background for a kelim. This look is typical of the 18th and 19thC.

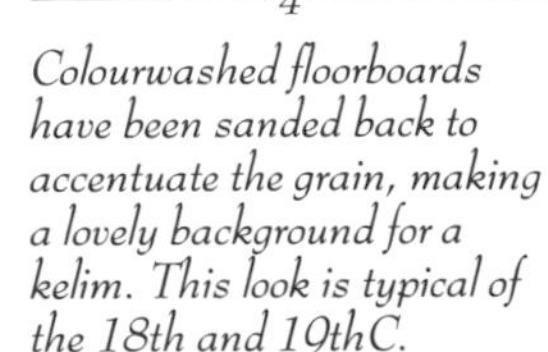

4

5
A trompe l'oeil effect on this floor has been painted to match an 18thC Delft-tiled fireplace.

5

6
This rough plaster wall surface conveys a flavour of antiquity.

7
The illusory power of paint is illustrated by a distressed plaster finish edged with ochre, a marbled skirting board and colourwashed floorboards attractively bordered in blue-grey.

6

7

9

11, 12 and 13

Wood panelling takes kindly to paint, from strong vibrant colours to pale 18thC classical washes.

11

14

This is the palette of Arts and Crafts: natural wood and significant areas of strong matt colour against a background of creamy white. The golden yellow of the gerbera daisies and the blue-grey of the thistles are evocative of the period.

14

8, 9 and 10

Three dramatic wood finishes. The first (8) is panelling dragged in muted colours, the second (9) is a magnificent burr walnut finish that matches the Queen Anne chair, while the third (10) is a Victorian-inspired tour de force.

8

12

15

A Victorian feeling is effectively conveyed by a modern reproduction wallpaper by Zoffany and a painted wooden bed.

15

10

13

16

16

Two-tone dragged rose-coloured walls set off a sparkle of silver crystal and mahogany.

17 and 18

Trompe l'oeil finishes are not for the faint-hearted.

17

18

19 and 20

Stencils can be restrained and formal, as in picture 20, where the design of cricket bats and balls has been applied directly to the wall; or the look may be exuberantly countrified as in picture 19, where a stencilled wallpaper has been used.

19

20

2 and 3

These typical examples of the Victorian fabric-dominated style show that the mood need not be dark and heavy.

1

Fabric draped from a coronet frames this Regency bed, and beautifully evokes the ambience of the period.

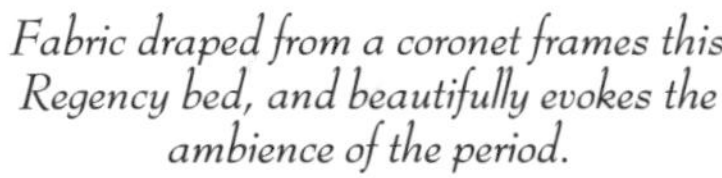

1

7

7

In this tiny dining room, a curtain covers one whole wall and two layers of fabric are draped over the table. The mood is early Victorian.

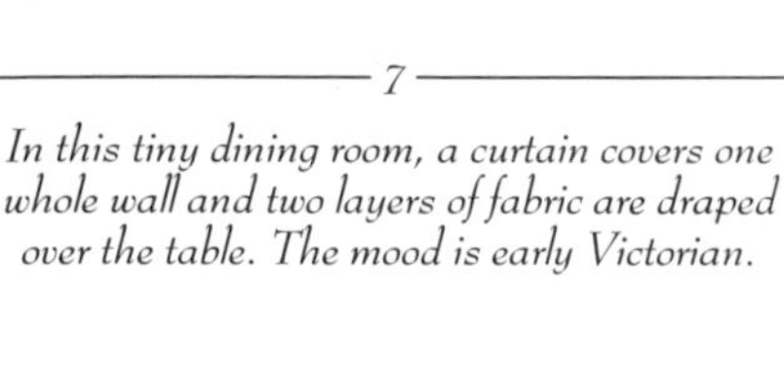

2

6

8

The bedlinen here is made from a fabric that was chosen to match the blue and white porcelain. The overall feel is 18thC.

8

3

4

4

A favourite Art Deco furnishing fabric – uncut moquette.

5

5

In this basement dining/ sitting room a cosy, intimate feeling has been achieved by the dark, earthy colours of the fabrics and the strong patterns of the kelim-covered cushions and table.

6

A Victorian feeling is conjured up with quilted bedspreads, lace tablecloths and embroidered cushions.

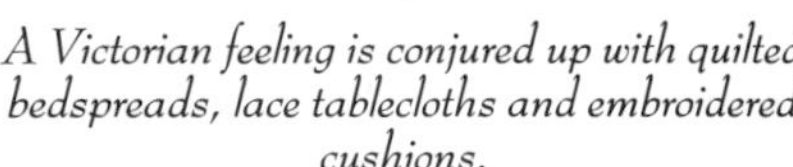

9

10

9 and 10

A medley of pattern and texture in two different rooms of a Victorian house. Box-pleated fabric covers conceal metal filing cabinets.

Traditional fabrics, many of them based directly on historic patterns, others merely historic in inspiration, are essential ingredients in the creation of a period style. As an alternative to wallpaper, they can add luxury and texture that transform the whole mood of the room. Even on a smaller scale, used as curtains, upholstery or bed hangings, period-style fabrics can set the keynote, announcing themes of colour and design that are taken up elsewhere in the room.

To imitate styles in which silks, brocades, damasks and gold braid were used in abundance can be an expensive undertaking. However, lighter, less expensive fabrics are capable of giving a similarly luxurious effect. Even plain muslin, worked into a stylish curtain arrangement, can look extremely effective.

Genuine period fabrics can be acquired at auction but the earliest examples are likely to be of interest only to the most enthusiastic. However, one can often come across Victorian and Edwardian materials. Old lace – whether machine-made or hand-made – is widely available, often as decorative panels that can be set into plain lengths to make a decorative centrepiece.

Pattern and colour are the key factors in contributing to a period mood. Floral patterns have a timelessness that enables them to be used in almost any setting, but care should be taken to match the degree of formality: formal patterns will suit a townhouse style, but for a country style you should choose a looser, more casual pattern, perhaps with country cottage flowers rather than roses or lilies. Vegetable dyes always have a more natural look than synthetic dyes.

There are certain designs that instantly conjure up the past. For example, suitable motifs for medieval, Elizabethan or Jacobean rooms include fleur-de-lys, stylized flowers and heraldic emblems. For Rococo interiors there is a wide range of period-style fabrics that show the design preoccupations of the age – garlands of flowers, knots of ribbons, foliage and flowers, often with a touch of chinoiserie. However, the obvious choices are not always the best ones, and sometimes the most valid approach is to opt for a plain colour rather than a pattern. In a Regency or Empire room, plain, light blue curtains with swags and tails might be exactly right, creating an effect of luxury and sophistication. Even a simple length of fabric draped over a pole can look stylish in some settings: reproduction curtain poles, with decorative finials, are widely available. Deep, rich colours with strongly contrasting plain borders – for example, green edged with red – might be a good alternative for a medieval setting.

Fabric used generously around the bed can evoke the grand ambience of historic bedrooms, with their four-posters and half-testers. Here, the element of disguise comes into play, as the framework of the bed can be very simply constructed: if the hangings are full enough, none of the frame need be visible.

11

— 11 —

Pretty antique lace tablecloths make beautiful curtains in a light, feminine Victorian style. This one has a tie-back made from a lace table runner.

12

— 12 —

An 18thC feeling is achieved here with needlepoint cushion covers and hangings and an extravagant tassel – which was probably originally a tie-back for a large and magnificent draped curtain.

13

— 13 —

The fabric chosen for the windows and the upholstery in this room is a linen, printed in subdued colours to give it a period look. It makes a foil for the Aubusson cushion covers.

14

— 14 —

Victorian cotton towels hang over a pine bathroom rail, framed by floral curtains.

15

— 15 —

A window simply draped in unlined muslin evokes a delicate Victorianism.

16

— 16 —

Antique tassels add a period charm, suggestive of the 18thC Continental style, to an inexpensive cream cotton curtain.

PLANTS AND FLOWERS

1 and 2

Two approaches to topiary: large strong shapes make for a Classical, formal setting in 2 while in the hallway (1) the smaller, more intricate shapes suggest a country house.

3 and 4

Unusual containers add a touch of individuality. Here, a mahogany cellaret (zinc-lined wine storage box) makes a permanent home for a collection of indoor plants (4) and an 18thC oak cradle accommodates vases of daisies (5).

2

3

6

A wonderful display of dried flowers in a 17thC interior. The lead urns contain bunches of lavender, larkspur, hydrangea, poppyseed heads, wheat, barley and cornflowers.

7

Ornamental cabbages in terracotta pots make a centrepiece for a Victorian kitchen table.

1

4

6

Plants and flowers help to bring any room alive, and in a period room should contribute to the overall character. The choices of blooms and foliage, containers and style of arrangement are all equally important. Take the colours of the room into account – for example, bright red flowers might be used to enliven deep burgundy. Bear in mind that foliage is not always green – there are many other shades available, from coppery red to silvery grey.

Exotics have an obvious appeal, but sometimes it is preferable to use humbler flowers, such as buttercups. Roses, of course, have strong Romantic associations. Use lots of twigs to give an interesting structure to your arrangements. You should not be afraid to try out daring experiments. Try to create conversation pieces. The bright splashes of red or white berries can be highly evocative. Fruit too, used in abundance, has appropriate associations of ripeness, and will last for a long time. Dried flowers can be effective but it is difficult to prevent them from gathering dust. When hanging up herbs to dry, make sure that they hang in clumps, not singly.

5

5

A simple jug of field grasses and wild flowers in an 18thC Colonial setting.

For a medieval or Elizabethan house, echo what is happening in the garden. Fill bowls with primroses and violets in spring, dog roses in summer and berries and leaves in autumn. This works well in a country setting of any period style. In a late 17th-century house, copy a practice of the time and have informal arrangements of flowers in blue and white pots around the house. Place a really large container filled with flowers or boughs of greenery in an empty fireplace in summer. Formal rooms in the late 17th century sometimes featured symmetrical arrangements of closely clipped shrubs.

In the Regency, cut flowers and flowering plants really came into their own. Use them in profusion, arranged informally. Victorian houses are the place for jardinières full of aspidistras and ferns.

Small-scale furniture can be used as stands or containers – for example, wine coolers. You could include period objects – candlesticks, figurines and so on – in a floral arrangement.

7

8

9

— 8 —

A Victorian footbath with a leaf motif is filled with a collection of garden greenery. A bunch of long-stemmed flowers peeps through from the back. The flowers and leaves make a good counterpoint to the collection of Victorian parian ware figures.

— 9 —

The glow of massed candles and the vase of dying tulips create an atmosphere of slightly sinister Romanticism in this artist's basement.

— 10 —

A mass of greenery and fine architectural features conjure up a Victorian conservatory.

10

11

— 11 —

A dried flower arrangement inspired by an Elizabethan pomander. The muted colours here convey a distinct flavour of the past.

— 12 —

Wild flowers, artfully arranged on a conservatory table, make a simple statement that would fit into any country style.

12

13

— 14 —

These flowers are cleverly colour-matched to a collection of Art Deco pottery.

14

15

16

— 13 —

A beautiful arrangement of yellow roses, lilies, antirrhinums, white anemones and crab apples lighten a 17thC panelled room. Note how the side light from the window makes the flowers glow with life and how the colours are echoed by the apples and lemons in the 17thC Delft bowl.

— 15 —

A magnificent festive showpiece worthy of a grand setting is created by a profusion of red flowers and berries displayed on a pair of 18thC torchères.

— 16 —

Currants and berries make a Victorian centrepiece, surrounded by a Belleek porcelain flower ring.

Displaying a collection of suitable objects is an excellent way to build up a sense of period, even if you do not want to take on the major project of furnishing a whole room in period style. An informed approach to collecting will help you acquire a feel for the time – and eventually you will probably find that other aspects of the era are affecting your thinking about design and decoration, almost against your will.

One approach is to treat the growing collection as a constant quest for perfect pieces: this is the connoisseur's way, purist and uncompromising. However, you can also use collections as a purely visual strategy for creating a particular mood, in which case the quality of individual pieces is less important than their overall effect. For example, a group of blue-and-white china will make a strong collective statement even if some of the pieces are damaged.

Obvious subjects for collections are ceramics, glass, metalware, silver, prints and paintings but in fact there is no limit to the categories of object you can group together to announce a unifed theme. Anything from tea bowls to carpet cleaners is potentially collectable.

A major decision is whether to display the collection on a wall or on a horizontal surface. Either way, the collection must carry conviction. If you have only a few objects to begin with, avoid the temptation to spread them evenly around the room, as this will dilute their impact. In planning an arrangement, remember to allow room for the collection to grow.

Glazed display cabinets have the advantage of cutting down on dusting, but with some sacrifice of immediacy: behind glass the items may tend to look remote. Porcelain looks good on carved, gilded wall brackets: convincing brackets, made in Florence, have been finding their way into auctions recently, catalogued as authentic. Small Victorian pieces can be aptly displayed in a whatnot. For an earlier period, a group on shelves in a niche can look stunning.

The way things are arranged is almost more important than the contents of the collection. A formal, symmetrical grouping, for example, can suggest the 18th century, even if the items themselves are from a different era.

Small, relatively flat objects, such as cigarette cards, can be unified by being arranged in a single wall-mounted frame, or in a group of frames placed close together. Prints, still relatively inexpensive, look particularly effective en masse in plain frames, in a loose approximation of the historic concept of the print room. At a still more popular level of the market, it would be fun to make your own Victorian scrap screen.

If authenticity is the aim, paintings will tend to be earlier in period than the setting in which they are placed. Remember that paintings should be lit from below, not from above. You could use a picture light fixed to the frame, or perhaps focus a discreet spotlight on the work from floor level.

1

1 *These 18thC creamware plates on cream-coloured panelling show a subtle approach to displaying a collection.*

2

2 *An interesting collection of 18th and 19thC treen on a Regency centre table. Treen is a generic term for small wooden objects, mostly turned, generally associated with tasks of domestic life.*

3

3 *Blue and white vases, densely clustered.*

4

4 *An attic room can be a good place for a collection of miscellaneous exotica. This one includes blackamoors and bronzes, ivories, carved elephants and carpet bowls.*

5

5 *A varied collection mixed in both subjects and style can still have an appearance of unity. What links this group of statues is the medium – marble.*

6

6 *An accumulation of Staffordshire figures and pottery unambiguously and colourfully evokes the Victorian age.*

7

Another distinctly Victorian collection: 19thC majolica vases and Staffordshire pottery window stops (used to keep sash windows slightly open) in the shape of lions.

8

This collection of 18th and 19thC blue and white Chinese porcelain has been glued to gilded brackets to prevent accidental damage.

8

7

9

9

Staffordshire pottery comes in many guises. These ducks, cows, geese, swans and fish make a veritable menagerie.

10

This overmantel mirror provides a reflective background to a symmetrical arrangement of porcelain and tole (painted metal wares).

13

10

11

This fascinating bathroom in Lord and Lady McAlpine's country home sports an amazing collection of stuffed birds, some solemnly perched, some on the wing. The room has the air of a private study – one with an unusual centrepiece in the form of a magnificent Victorian cast-iron bathtub.

11

12

12

A collection of earthenware pots, decoy birds and gardening implements is displayed here against a suitably earthy background.

13

Putting together a collection of everyday objects that are still inexpensive and plentiful, such as these miniature 19thC jugs, makes every visit to an antique shop a pleasure.

14

Silhouettes were a popular art form of the 19thC. Here they are displayed against a strongly patterned chintz, against which few other images would survive.

14

15

16

16

Painted boxes on a painted chest make a feature that is made more vibrant by the sponged pink wall treatment. The chest is a copy of an early 19thC Connecticut piece.

15

Dishes, as well as plates, can be wall-hung. Here, the colour choice unites all the elements of the setting.

MEDIEVAL

1

Grand houses in the medieval period were far from the dark and gloomy halls of our imagining. They were full of colour and life. Robust pieces of furniture and functional utensils were teamed with a joyful profusion of texture and pattern resulting in a vigorous and colourful impression – "style" is hardly an appropriate term here, since it presupposes a greater degree of self-conscious planning for overall effect than was available to most people before about the middle of the 16th century.

For a peripatetic nobleman, constantly on the move from one home to the next, furnishings had to be portable. Possessions were carried in chests and hampers and arranged anew in the current residence. The medieval house was a working environment where master and mistress, children, servants and visitors mingled, and where there was little place for purely ornamental objects. Rooms were sparsely furnished. The less grand the home, the more simply made the furniture. Textiles played a particularly important role. Fat, feather-filled cushions helped to make hard wooden seats more comfortable, and a length of richly coloured fabric softened the hard outline of a plain trestle table. Hangings of tapestry, wool or linen provided an instant form of decoration and an essential means of making a draughty interior more habitable.

Textiles and painted decoration made the somewhat austere interiors of the period glow with colour. Natural dyes and pigments gave rich earthy colours – warm reds, ochre yellows, strong greens and blues – and in particularly opulent homes the paintwork was frequently embellished with gold. Needless to say, the homes of the vast majority of people were small, simple and unadorned timber-framed cottages.

Walls

These were seldom left undecorated – even the wooden or stone mullions of windows were limewashed.

Painting Certainly as far back as the 13th century it was usual to whitewash or colourwash walls, and stone walls were often given a smoothing coat of coarse plaster made from lime, sand and hair. In many cases walls were

2

1 and 2

The medieval illusion can be created by a conscious emphasis on rustic simplicity. This 16thC Burgundian wrought-iron candle stand (1) is a case in point. It is an original but any village blacksmith should be able to copy it. The soft light of church candles creates a period feel, and incense burning in the wrought-iron trays adds to the sensory stimulation.

One of the most common mistakes in recreating an early style is in using a too perfect wall finish. This roughly plastered wall (2) has been limewashed in off-white. (The brilliant white of some modern paints would ruin the effect.) The 16thC wrought-iron candle holder and snuffer covered in wax exude medievalism. Candles made from beeswax give a softer, warmer glow than do paraffin wax candles, they are a lovely honey colour and they even smell right when lit.

1

The medieval look in its pure form is a style in which architectural elements dominate. This medieval priory with solid stone walls, polished floorboards and strongly defined windows is a setting that demands an authentic treatment. A stunning 15thC oak chair with marquetry decoration, a plain trestle table with richly coloured textile covering, a bronze mortar and plain earthenware jugs, all look perfectly at home here.

given a more elaborate finish than a simple coat of colour. They might be marked out with a pattern of red lines to imitate masonry. Individual blocks were sometimes then painted with a floral design – the rose was a popular motif. Alternatively, walls might be enlivened with a painted frieze or heraldic devices relating to the family.

All-over, simple geometric patterns were another option for the medieval house decorator. In a timber-frame building this design would be painted over the structure of the room and the plastered areas in between. It was not always considered necessary to plaster over the beams first to give a smooth surface on which to work.

Often whole rooms were painted with full-blown murals: biblical themes, scenes from histories and romances, hunting or the countryside.

Panelling Simple vertical boards, perhaps moulded to mask the joins, might be of oak or fir. Softwood boards would commonly be painted; green was a fashionable (and expensive) colour in the 13th century and was often embellished with gold. The wainscoting was often additionally ornamented with roundel paintings.

Textiles

Hangings were a very useful, as well as ornamental, addition to a medieval interior, making it warmer and more comfortable. Tapestries were expensive. Not so costly were hangings of woven wool, worsted or linen either in a plain colour or painted with a simple design.

Textiles were used also to cover a table, usually a board on trestles, and to make seating more comfortable. Sometimes an extra-long piece of cloth would be used to cover both seating and an area of the floor for extra comfort and luxury. There was no fixed upholstery until Elizabethan times – at this stage loose cushions helped to soften hard chairs.

Ceilings

Within the frames created by beams or vaulting, ceilings frequently had designs painted on them and the beams, too, might be decorated.

Floors

Beaten earth, hard plaster, wooden boards or red and yellow tiles of glazed earthenware were the choices for the floor. The earliest tiles were encaustic: a wooden pattern was pressed into the clay and then lighter-coloured pipeclay was spread in the hollows, making the pattern very durable. Less expensive and quicker to produce were the later printed tiles. Some tiles were also painted.

Rushes were strewn over earth floors and watered to keep down dust. Matting of plaited rushes ("Egyptian matting") was used to good effect in some great houses.

2

3

2 and 3

Creating a period feel in a room is like creating a theatrical set. It is essential to obtain the right props and then arrange them so that they can speak for themselves. Here, an exceptional 16thC carved oak chair, a simple brass candlestick, old manuscripts and books furnish the stage to perfection.

1

1

Here is proof that the medieval look can be achieved with furniture from other eras – a wonderful modern elm coffer made by Richard Latrobe Bateman as part of a set of six cut in the round from one elm. Its solid form fits well with the Arts and Crafts candlesticks and 17thC crewelwork hanging.

2

Another fortunate mix of period pieces – wooden candlesticks and 15thC panelling live happily with a modern wall hanging by Candace Bahouth based on the 1920s Moorcroft pottery collection arranged on the simple 16thC chestnut table.

2

3 and 4

In these examples old and new rustic oak and fruitwood furniture blend with plaster walls, stone arches and heavy rush matting.

5

This medievally inspired painted Gothic Court collection furniture by Stuart Interiors would fit well into a 19thC Gothic room.

6

Furniture, pottery and fabric from many centuries and countries can be combined if they are based on a common theme. Here a modern copy of a 16thC chest, a 19thC copy of a 15thC Italian folding chair, modern copies of 16thC drinking flagons (called Bellarmines), a modern fabric based on a 16thC original and a late 19thC screen share an undoubted unity of design.

3

4

5

6

1

1

In this spectacular medieval priory all the furniture has been designed with great understanding of the period by Richard Latrobe Bateman. From the folding chair to the wardrobes, the elm coffers and, above all, the magnificent bed, the strength and simplicity of design flows through, in perfect harmony with the vaulted room. The hangings woven by Vanessa Robertson echo the deep reds, pinks and purples typical of medieval interiors.

2 and 3

In the bedroom, a medieval feel can be achieved by the clever use of strong, clear colours and tall canopies without sacrificing comfort or convenience.

2

3

Furniture

At this stage furniture was minimal. Chests were very common. The table would usually be literally a board resting on trestles. There would be benches and stools, with a chair for the head of the household. There might also be built-in benches and a wall cupboard. An open cupboard would be used to display metal tableware.

In the great chamber and/or parlour the great bed had pride of place and trundle beds, chests and coffers and simple stools were ranged around the walls. These pieces would be made from native wood, were mostly of simple planked construction, and were sometimes painted.

Accessories

Vessels for eating and drinking were commonly of wood – smooth-grained sycamore, ash or cherry would be turned to make goblets, trenchers and bowls. Candlesticks were made in a similar way.

Medieval households contained a quantity of pottery – jugs, bowls, dishes, chafing dishes and so on. Brass and bronze cooking pots supplemented simpler iron ones. In the hearth would be iron implements for tending the fire and for cooking. An iron or wooden candlebranch might hang from the roof or stand on tripod feet. Bunches of herbs would hang drying from the ceiling.

1

COLOURS Use rich, natural-dyed colours offset by "unbleached" beige tones and black, and enriched with touches of gold.

WALLS Walls can be off-white or colourwashed. Warm pastels work well. You could divide the walls into "panels" with a pattern of red lines and decorate some of the panels with flower designs or heraldic devices. You might like to use paint to repeat a floor tile design on the walls. You could hang fabric all around the walls like curtains, or use large tapestry or needlework designs or lengths of printed fabric in alcoves or put a tapestry or needlework hanging over a fireplace. Although wallpaper is not strictly correct for this period, you could paper your walls with one of the 19th century designs by A.W.N. Pugin based on medieval motifs such as fleur de lys, trellis and pineapples.

FLOORS Stone slabs or printed earthenware tiles in earthy colours have the right look. Black and red quarry tiles laid alternately in a diamond pattern are another option. As a modern alternative to rushes, choose matting of woven sisal or, better still, plaited rushes.

SOFT FURNISHINGS Tapestry-style patterns and printed designs of heraldic devices or stylized roses have a suitable medieval feel. Woven damasks and plain woollen cloth in rich colours and cotton velvets in mellow, glowing tones also work well, as do many of the designs by William Morris. Curtains were not a medieval feature, but you could hang a single curtain drawn to one side during the day, or a pair of plain curtains.

FURNITURE Plainly constructed chests, benches, box-style armchairs, settles and trestle tables, as well as built-in cupboards and seats in the same style, are the correct choice. Oak, or other native woods, are right for the period, preferably not blackened – this was a Victorian fashion. Wood furniture can be matt-painted in brick-red or dark green, perhaps with detail picked out in gold. You could get away with furniture in old or painted pine if it is simply constructed. Art Deco and Arts and Crafts furniture would fit in well, as would simple modern furniture. Soften hard wooden furniture with fat cushions and soft textile coverings. Unless you are a purist, you will probably want some soft seating. Choose plain-shaped sofas and cover them in a fabric with a medieval feel, or in unbleached calico with a throwover of patterned fabric.

LIGHTING Supplement free-standing or ceiling-hung iron or wooden candlebranches and candlesticks with concealed electric lighting. Rustic-looking electric fittings in wood and metal might also serve.

ORNAMENTS Turned bowls, plates and candlesticks in smooth-grained woods, slipware dishes and drinking vessels and iron fire implements help set the scene. Free-standing embroidery frames and spinning wheels would complete the picture.

FINISHING TOUCHES Hang bunches of herbs from the ceiling as decoration and to scent the air – you might also try burning incense. An open log fire is essential. If you have the right kind of fireplace you should be able to pile the logs directly on a bed of ashes and not worry about a fire basket. Apple logs smell wonderful. Religious music – perhaps plainsong, or works by Allegri or Thomas Tallis – should waft around the rafters.

CREATING THE LOOK

2

1 and 2

Medieval style is uncluttered, even sparse, with off-white or softly colourwashed rough plaster walls. Too fine a finish would kill this warm, human interior. The red and green tiles in this entrance hall are in fact Victorian but the look is absolutely typical of the medieval period.

ELIZABETHAN AND JACOBEAN

1

The interior of a well-to-do English house during the reigns of Elizabeth I and James I was made mellow with carved wood, rich textiles, elaborately framed paintings and the dull gleam of pewter and polished leather.

An unprecedented sense of luxury and comfort reflected both the relative stability of society and the new prosperity of the merchant classes. Interiors were embellished with surface decoration of carved wood and ornamental plasterwork – often in a free interpretation of one of the Classical Orders. Renaissance ideas combined with nostalgia for medieval times resulted in a cheerfully eclectic mix of Classical and Gothic decoration on furniture, panelling and plasterwork, with motifs including caryatids, Doric, Ionic and Corinthian columns, acanthus leaves, egg-and-dart mouldings and, in particular, strapwork – which imitated cut leather.

A pride in possessions was expressed by paintings, rich hangings, intricate embroideries, tapestries with leafy woodland motifs or imitations of oriental carpets (known collectively as turkeywork). Open shelf buffets – which at that time were called court cupboards – were used for the display of plate. There was a proliferation of well-made furniture in new designs and with new functions. The innovation of fixed upholstery suggested a concern for comfort. Much of the wood was vigorously carved.

Walls

Panelling This was widely used to line rooms. Hardwood panelling – usually pale honey-coloured oak – would often be a simple arrangement of undecorated square or rectangular panels set in a moulded framework.

2

3

1

This small corner combines the features most prevalent in an early 17thC grand house. It is important to realize that these homes had wonderful rich textiles in strong colours. Plain walls were often painted – note the three-tone blue. You may have to have colours specially mixed.

2

Elizabethan panelling was of a glorious honey colour, not the dark, overpowering panelling favoured by the Victorians. Tapestries and hangings can still be found at auction or in specialist shops, but they can be very expensive to restore, and early tapestries do need to be well looked after. It is worth looking at late 19thC examples.

3

Parham House in Sussex belies the impression that Elizabethan houses were dark with low ceilings. These rooms have a wonderful light and airy feel. The black and white marble floor, while probably 18thC, is in keeping with the rest of the room.

1

1

This wonderful 17thC carved refectory table with a simple bench and a set of 17thC chairs is set on solid oak floor boards against a backdrop of dark wall panels. The effect depends on the coloured patination of the various woods. There are very few totally authentic tables around: most of those that come up for sale have been made up from old wooden floor boards or even railway sleepers, but they can look good. Don't dismiss 19thC or even modern reproductions as long as they are well made. Do look for a good warm colour, as stained and polished oak can be dark and dead.

2 and 3

Panelling took many forms in the late 16th and early 17thC. Old panelling can still be acquired from specialist dealers or architectural salvage yards but do ensure that it will fit the room. Some firms also produce reproduction panelling – look for depth of colour and good strong carving. In this early period, chairs were still reasonably rare, joynt stools and benches being the norm; however, most people find these quite uncomfortable, so for comfort's sake look for any plain 17thC chair and add tapestry cushions or stuffed leather seats.

4 and 5

Plain floor boards do add to the general Elizabethan feel, but they are not always practical. Instead of using rushes on the floor, choose one of the many types of rush matting. This period again demands candlelight. However, well-concealed modern spotlights can be used to pick out details. Rush lights were one of the earliest forms of lighting. Basically, they consist of a wooden base, sometimes beautifully turned, sometimes adjustable, with a rush dipped in grease, the pith being the wick. Wrought-iron chandeliers with simple decoration are perfectly in keeping. Original chandeliers can be copied by any proficient blacksmith. Ensure they are not too perfect, as a little unevenness gives a better impression of age.

2

3

4

5

1

1

If you are buying reproduction furniture, it is essential to buy faithful reprductions and to check for good deep colour and sharp clear carving. Everything in this shot is a modern copy by Stuart Interiors, from the reproduction 17thC Derbyshire chairs to the delft plates.

2

This superb room at St Mary's in Bramber, Sussex was painted for the visit of Queen Elizabeth in 1585. It is an exceptional example of early trompe l'oeil, executed by an itinerant Flemish painter-stainer. The coffer is genuine 16thC, but the chair is a 19thC copy of a 16thC model – obviously much less expensive than the genuine article. Of the two pewter tankards, one is old, one is brand new.

Panels were sometimes carved with a variety of motifs, and the more elaborate linenfold, which was carved to imitate softly draped linen, was a popular alternative. Plain panelling might be relieved by a carved frieze or might incorporate a carved fireplace mantel supported by caryatids or Classical columns with a panel depicting an allegorical subject above it. All panelling in its original state would have been much, much lighter than it is today – what we see has been darkened by age or by Victorian wood-stain.

Detail might be picked out in coloured paints or inlay. Softwood panelling was almost always painted – perhaps to imitate a hardwood.

Painting The plaster in unpanelled rooms was frequently painted and sometimes divided horizontally into dado, infill and frieze. Walls and woodwork might be painted to resemble more desirable and expensive materials such as walnut, marble, stone or fabric hangings. Walls might also be covered with geometric patterns, often interspersed with flowers.

Wallpaper The earliest known English printed wallpaper dates from 1509. At this time papers were designed as separate panels. By about 1600, linked repeat patterns were printed. Designs of shields, vases, flowers – motifs which also appeared on plasterwork – were usually printed in black on white. Additional colour might be added freehand or by stencilling.

Paper was sometimes pasted directly onto the wall, but was more often pasted onto linen and then attached to wooden battens, or just nailed to the wall with copper tacks.

Textiles Patterned tapestries were popular status symbols for the rich. As these were not usually custom-made to fit a particular room, they would often overlap the wall and be taken around corners: it was quite usual for a tapestry to extend across a doorway, which might have been a little inconvenient but did help to keep out draughts. The hangings on the bed might match those used for the walls. As in earlier times, walls in less grand houses were hung with painted cloth.

Ceilings

In the grander houses, beams would now be concealed by decorative plaster ceilings. Elizabethan plaster ceilings are usually composed of fine-ribbed, often geometric designs. In the early 17th century, broad, flat bands of strapwork were common. Repeat patterns were cast from reverse moulds; details were usually modelled by hand, and painted.

Floors

Wooden floors were common, particularly for upstairs rooms. They might be of oak or elm – both very hardwearing – or of imported fir. Boards were generally much wider than today, but floors would often be made up of boards of different widths. During the reign of James I, parquet floors or coloured stone paving became fashionable in grander houses, and flagstones began to be used at about the same time.

Furniture

There was more furniture in the home than previously, and it was more luxurious and comfortable. Oak was the first choice, but beech, walnut and chestnut were sometimes used. For the rich, the medieval practice of painting and gilding the wood continued; even oak might be painted red, blue, green or black. It is difficult to know what the original colour of unpainted oak furniture would have been. While it was certainly waxed or oiled, and sometimes limed to darken it to a mid-brown (unlike the pale limed oak of the 1920s), we can be fairly certain that it was not stained black as the Victorians would have us believe.

Some pieces – especially tables, beds and cupboards built to impress the guests – were large and heavy, featuring rich carving in an amalgamation of Renaissance and Gothic motifs or with strapwork decoration.

The most important piece of furniture was still the bed. The wooden canopy which in medieval times had been suspended from the ceiling was ousted by the four-poster. Before the 16th century was out, this in turn was superseded by a bed with a carved headboard supporting the canopy at one end and two posts supporting it at the foot. An alternative type of bed had a very light framework, but elaborate hangings.

As in medieval times, stools and benches were the most usual type of seating. Some joined and turned chairs were also made. Around 1600 a new type of armless chair made its appearance: the back-stool or

2

1

2

3

4

"farthingale" chair (named after the cumbersome skirts of the period) had both seat and back upholstered in turkeywork, leather or cloth. This was the first time that fixed upholstery appeared.

Tall cupboards with doors, called presses, were used for storing clothes, linen, books and valuables. Better-quality chests were joined rather than planked. There was also a type of chest with a drawer at the bottom. Three-tiered open court cupboards, perhaps incorporating a drawer, were used to display plate. Food was stored in ventilated closed cupboards built into or hung on the wall. In households where a room was specifically set aside for eating, frame tables on fixed supports were usual. In humbler households and for servants, trestle tables were the norm.

A fairly common piece of furniture was the versatile bench table; the hinged back could be swung over to turn bench into table.

Accessories

Table covers and cushions added to the comfort and, along with tapestries and hangings, helped give a soft luxurious appearance to an interior in which there were large expanses of wood.

Pewter was widely used for plates, spoons, drinking vessels, candlesticks and so on. There were also some beautiful objects made in silver – salts , ceremonial cups and flagons engraved with designs based on Flemish and German originals.

Glass vessels, for most people, were made of thick, green, cast Wealden glass, although the rich enjoyed delicate Venetian glass, or imitations of it made in England by migrant workers from Italy.

Pottery was often of mediocre quality and would be used for tableware only by the poor, though good, cheap black-, green- and yellow-glazed ware was available. The rich might have stone-glazed wares imported from Germany, Islamic pottery or Chinese porcelain, perhaps mounted in silver.

Clocks were very rare until the end of this period. Early on there were brass-cased table clocks and iron wall clocks, later brass-cased lantern clocks were hung on the wall.

5

1

Period interiors have a special feel about them when most of the elements come from the same era. This 17thC Flemish needlework armchair blends perfectly with the 17thC furniture and panelling. (The tablelamp is made from a 17thC candlestick and a pleated parchment shade.) The design of the textiles is typical of the period, with roses, irises and carnations worked mainly in pink, indigo and blue-green. The original vegetable dyes keep their freshness, whereas the more modern aniline dyes tend to fade. Some fabric companies produce reasonable machine-made copies of early fabrics, particularly flamestitch. It is also possible to find hand-woven examples, but these are expensive. An alternative, particularly for a cushion or stool cover, is to buy an early pattern with, if possible, vegetable-dyed wool and embroider it yourself.

2

The solid wooden look of an Elizabethan bedroom can be enlivened by the use of fabrics. Crewel work is particularly effective. Early crewel work is difficult to find, although most major auction houses now have textile and costume sales and most major cities have specialist textile dealers. There are also modern reproduction fabrics – good ones will echo the deep natural colours of early textiles.

3

Some of the hand-stitched silk draperies on this spectacular Elizabethan bed at Parham House in Sussex are traditionally ascribed to Mary Queen of Scots but could equally have been worked by her sister-in-law, Marie de Medici. The textiles comprise cream satin embroideries worked in about 1585; the Mary Queen of Scots needlework on the coverlet, back and canopy and the top testers; and the curtains and mattress valences of Hungarian point flamestitch, worked c. 1615.

4

An Elizabethan or Jacobean look can be created with a tapestry or a length of fabric with good strong colours hung on plain walls. Archways can also be hung with tapestries, which serve a dual purpose of adding colour and cutting out draughts quite efficiently. The Regency low chairs flanking the fireplace are from the Maharaja's Palace in Hyderabad, but they seem at home here, as does the Great Dane on his woven blanket.

5

The main factor that gives this room its turn-of-the-century feel is the rough, off-white plaster work and the tapestry hanging. The bed head is a later copy, and the furniture rather mixed in date and provenance, but the overall feel remains early 17thC.

1

The Great Hall in Parham House in Sussex embodies the essential elements of the Elizabethan interior – bleached oak panelling, pewter plates, 17thC leather buckets and portraits of the highest quality.

COLOURS Deep jewel colours – reds, blue, greens, glowing yellows – are a foil for oak furniture.

WALLS If you are lucky enough to have wood panelling, consider stripping off any dark varnish and waxing the wood to a mellow gold. This will make rooms considerably lighter and less sombre. You could also install softwood panelling and paint it a strong (blue, red or green), or grain it to imitate a hardwood. As in a medieval house, you could hang walls with fabric – woodland tapestry-style fabric would work well. Wall papers would have been used by this time, so you could choose a simple mono-print of shields, vases or flowers.

FLOORS Wood flooring – polished boards or parquet – or stone paving suits this style.

FURNITURE Oak is the most usual wood for furniture of this period and there is a fairly wide range of suitable styles to choose from. Look for pieces with quite elaborate turning and carving – stools, benches, chairs, court cupboards, press cupboards and chests. Wood furniture can be painted if you wish. This is the right setting for upholstered, low-backed "farthingale" chairs covered in leather, or fabrics with the appearance of needlework or Oriental carpeting. Look for 19th-century "Elizabethan" reproductions; they are less expensive than the real thing and, in general, very well made. Avoid crudely carved "Jacobethan" hybrids.

SOFT FURNISHINGS Tapestry and tapestry-style fabrics, velvets, damasks and Jacobean-style crewelwork help to build the picture, and so do Oriental rugs used as tablecovers. As in a medieval house, curtains are not authentic to this style but are a necessity for most people. Choose plump cushions with tassels at each corner to soften hard seating.

LIGHTING See Medieval, page 35.

ORNAMENTS Display pewter plates, candlesticks and dishes and dark green or fine-blown glass and green, black or yellow glazed pottery. Silver and Chinese porcelain or Islamic pottery is correct for this period, although they would have been available only to the rich. Oil portraits work well in this style of interior, adding to the richness of colour and texture. Add bowls of sweet-smelling pot pourri and pomanders to give the authentic scent of the age. Then all you need is a crackling log fire and some harpsichord music, madrigals or a Gregorian chant on the the hi-fi. Such details always help to create an authentic ambience.

CREATING THE LOOK

2

2

Superb wood carving embellishes these Jacobean chairs and the "melon bulb" legs of the Elizabethan draw-table. The leather ale-flask and horn beakers provide added authenticity. A similar composition could be achieved with 19th C reproductions.

THE 17thC COUNTRY HOUSE

1

Several distinct influences from overseas affected the decoration of English rooms in the middle years of the 17th century. These gradually percolated through from town to country and provincial homes. From France came a fashion for decorating whole rooms *en suite* – with hangings, table covers, upholstery and so on all matching.

Inigo Jones' visits to Italy allowed him to observe Classical architecture, as well as the buildings of the 16th-century architect Andrea Palladio, at first hand. His more correct interpretation of the Classical Orders was expressed in a new concern for overall proportion. Although Jones' work was largely confined to the Court circle, his ideas did gradually spread.

Trade between Britain and the Protestant Low Countries resulted in a cross-fertilization of ideas on furnishing and furniture-making, contributing toward a plainer style of furniture.

Early in the century chinoiserie and so-called "Indian" styles became popular in aristocratic circles thanks to the importation of a whole variety

1

This corner of a landing is an excellent example of 17thC period feel. The bronze bust of Charles I and the Carolean open armchairs, set against light panelling, give an instant feeling of the age.

2

There is more to creating a 17thC country look than merely buying the right furniture: there are also the colours, textures, sounds and scents to consider. Here, the warm glow of fruitwood chairs and the rich patination of an oak table are intensified by the dull gleam of pewter, the flickering light of the candles and the generous profusion of flowers and fruit.

2

of items from the Far East. Among them were lacquerwork furniture, boxes and screens which inspired "japanned" pieces by English and Dutch craftsmen.

Walls

Panelling This usually entailed small units of equal size covering the entire surface. Inigo Jones, with his strong emphasis on Classical proportions, sought to change that, and his work is well illustrated by his Haynes Grange Room, now in London's Victoria and Albert Museum. This room, inspired by the Pantheon in Rome, has no skirting: pine boards run from floor to cornice, punctuated by Corinthian pilasters. More pilasters, topped by pediments, flank wall niches, fireplace and windows.

Meanwhile, in the homes of the less wealthy, traditional softwood panelling might be grained to simulate expensive hardwoods such as walnut, or marbled or tortoiseshelled, or decorated to resemble lapis lazuli. Alternatively, it might be simply painted over with a pale colour.

Venetian-style paintings might be incorporated into the panelling of a room.

Wallpapers These were often printed to imitate expensive textile hangings: there were damask patterns and Irish stitch (flamestitch) designs as well as florals. Papers were printed to look like wainscot panels, marble and turkeywork.

Textiles Any interior of any standing, if not panelled, would be decorated with hangings. These might be of silk damask, brocatelle, worsted or woollen cloth or more commonly a much cheaper, coarser fabric, woven with a repeat pattern; this pattern is known in England as Dornix.

Such fabrics were woven in narrow widths, which meant that they could be seamed together to fit a particular room; sometimes two colours would be alternated. The complete hanging would then be surrounded by a border, and joins covered with a galloon or a silk or metal lace. Hangings of gilt or embossed leather were also fashionable, the designs often showing Moorish or Islamic influence.

Tapestries continued to be used for walls, bedhangings and so on. It was not usually

possible to fit tapestries to a room quite so neatly as other fabrics, because they were bought ready-made. Sometimes, however, the very grand would have rooms designed to take an existing set of tapestries.

Windows

Curtains were still not common and their role was simply to keep out sunlight. This function might also be served by a "sash" – a frame with paper, linen or silk stretched over it.

Where curtains were used, they were not treated lavishly. As with bedhangings, a single curtain would be hung from a pole on rings and drawn to one side when not needed.

Floors

Strips of rush matting, like hangings, might be tailored to fit the room. The standard type of matting was thick and heavy and held the dirt but there was also a finer, lighter, more decorative type imported from Africa. By this stage oriental rugs might well be seen on the floor rather than on the table.

Ceilings

Under the influence of Inigo Jones, fine plasterwork designs in geometric patterns started to appear on the more expensive ceilings. The squares, ovals or circles were sometimes filled with paintings.

Furniture

Life was definitely becoming more comfortable. The most usual type of chair was upholstered, and was based on the back stool of earlier times. Larger versions with higher seats and arms were used for the most important member of the household or for a visitor. Often such "great chairs" would have matching footstools, and the same basic design was used to make couches. Upholstery fabrics included turkeywork, velvet,

1

The 17thC look is created here by an interesting ensemble that illustrates how styles from different periods and different countries will mix quite happily. Key elements are a German 16thC oak table, a stark portrait and a William and Mary walnut chair.

2

Naive animal paintings are typical of the era. These candlesticks are 17thC Italian. The early 18thC provincial dresser harks back in style to the 17thC.

3

This exotic corner has been created with a solid Charles II chest and a screen made from a 17thC Dutch oil painting.

4

Good 17thC furniture calls for simple arrangements.

5

Wrought iron, plain woods and a naive painting on a stark white wall – an embodiment of 17thC country style. All the furniture here is original.

2

3

4

5

1

2

2

The sitting room of the home featured on these two pages is a comfortable and relaxed interpretation of 17thC style, which includes a modern settee and a glass central table.

3

A set piece of typical 17thC groupings – note the way the paintings are hung, the grouping of the Qianlong "laughing boy" figures and the straightforward arrangement of the late 17thC chairs and the William and Mary double lowboy.

3

1

A magnificent collection of mid-17thC French walnut furniture on a white Amtico vinyl tile floor – an interesting juxtaposition that works remarkably well. The collection of Kangxi porcelain is arranged in the typical 17thC Dutch manner. Remember that when buying Chinese porcelain for such a display it is not necessary to buy absolutely perfect pieces, but do look for a good rich colour of blue.

leather, and plain cloth, depending on the pocket and taste of the owner.

Provincial homes might have the old-fashioned heavy oak, panel-back chair which continued to be made well into the next century. There were also simple chairs, with or without arms and often painted red, green or black, which had turned members and rush seats. Both rush seats and solid wooden ones might have down-filled cushions with a tassel at each corner.

The gate-legged table and the chest-of-drawers made their appearance in the middle of the 17th century. In the dining room, as well as the necessary table and chairs, there would be a cupboard or buffet for plate, possibly with each open shelf covered with a linen cloth.

The bedroom continued to be the most important room in the house, and the bed might well be fitted with hangings matched to those on the walls. Dressing tables began to be seen. These would have floor-length table covers or carpets with a small top-cloth of linen.

Lighting

Rooms were still lit by candles – or with simple oil lamps. Table candlesticks in the larger houses would be of brass and in the humbler ones of pewter. Candles were also carried in wall sconces, backed with a brass, tinplate or mirrored plate to reflect the light.

Accessories

Brass and silver were increasingly used for domestic implements during this period – fireplace furniture, chandeliers and so on. Trumpet-based brass candlesticks are typical.

4

4

In a corner of this sitting room stands a pair of absolutely authentic 17thC Venetian chairs which have been re-covered in a modern flamestitch fabric.

THE EARLY AMERICAN HOME

Not surprisingly, the early colonists built, furnished and decorated their houses to resemble those that they had left behind. Although wealthy English people settled in Virginia, settlers came mostly from small towns and rural areas of Germany and the Low Countries as well as Britain, and were able to bring little with them except tools; therefore, houses and furniture had to be made with materials that were to hand. In the early days, settlers had to find what shelter they could, but by the middle of the 17th century it was fair to say, of New England at least, that "the Lord hath been pleased to turn all the wigwams, huts and hovels the English dwelt in at their first coming, into orderly, fair and well built houses, well furnished many of them." These houses might be of timber, brick or stone.

Despite regional variations, a large proportion of the interiors of the time reflected the English influence. "Well furnished" they may have been, but to modern eyes they would be utilitarian and lacking in comfort.

Walls and floors

The boards which made up the structure of the house might form the interior surfaces of the rooms as well. In the better houses, walls might be plastered and whitewashed, or clad with vertical boards which helped to keep the house warmer. In the Hart Room of New York's Metropolitan Museum of Art – an authentic re-creation of the period – three walls are plastered and whitewashed, while the fireplace wall is clad with boards decorated with a light moulding at the joins. Floors would be nothing more than bare wooden boards.

Furniture

Settlers were not often people of fashion, and in any case new ideas were slow to travel across the Atlantic. Locally made furniture of native woods, often oak, reflected the styles current in Europe a few years earlier.

Chests, which could be used for both storage and seating, remained necessary pieces of furniture from the earliest times. These chests often had carved decoration, with different regions favouring different patterns.

Trestle tables were common where rooms had to serve several purposes – including sleeping. For the same reason, fold-up tables and frame tables with detachable tops were popular. Small occasional tables served a number of purposes. Another useful piece when space was at a premium was the hinged-back chair, sometimes with a drawer under the seat, which converted into a table.

Stools and benches were the usual seating, but three types of chair were made locally. The first two both had turned members and wood or rush seats: the Brewster armchair had a double row of spindles in the back and more spindles below the arms and under the seat, while the Carver was quite a simple affair with a single row of spindles in the back only. The third, or Wainscot, chair was an imposing piece with a panelled back and wooden seat.

Later, toward the end of the century, the more comfortable "Cromwellian" chair – the type of back stool preferred by Cromwell, with upholstered back and seat – made its appearance.

Court cupboards and press cupboards to store household goods and to display plate and pottery were important items in any household, and toward the end of the century they became very elaborate showpieces.

Accessories

Textiles were used to bring comfort and colour into rather spartan interiors. Well-padded cushions in woollen cloth, ornamented with large tassels, softened the wooden or rush seats of chairs. Examples of the art of patchwork and quilting were displayed throughout the home.

An abundance of suitable clay made it possible to make pots, pitchers and so on for general household use; these were often embellished with slip or sgraffito decoration. The shape and decoration varied from place to place. The Pennsylvania Dutch made particularly attractive wares with naive designs of birds, animals, flowers and leaves. Pewter was also used for household objects, and craftsmen worked in silver from quite early on.

1

This 17thC room from a house in Wilmington, Massachusetts, is absolutely authentic, from the solid simple furniture to the off-white walls to the hint of concern for creature comforts evidenced in the padded seat cushions.

2

This room from New Hampshire is from the very early 18thC. It is panelled with feather-edge boarding that has been painted. Early paintwork had a streaked effect – this wasn't deliberate, but was due to the composition of the paint – so a perfect modern finish would look quite wrong. The panelling itself is easy to copy. The banister-back chairs are perfectly in period, as are the delftware plates which are contemporary English copies of Chinese porcelain originals. Horn beakers, while you wouldn't want to drink out of them every day, nor put them in the dishwasher, contribute to the mood and are still quite inexpensive at auction.

1

2

1

1

This authentic painted dresser dates from c.1700 but it is a country piece, and country furniture tended to lag several decades behind the times. If you want to give furniture an antique painted effect, then this is the model from which to draw inspiration.

2

This is a room in a Victorian terraced house with a distinct 17thC country look about it. The mood has been achieved by clever use of colours, a couple of ingenious 17thC carved panels teamed with a modern American paper frieze, solid-looking furniture and a faded Persian carpet. The spongeware on the dresser dates from the 19thC, but it fits in perfectly, as do all the other simple country hand-worked pieces.

3 and 4

Here are two other views of this delightful room, which is full of conversation pieces. The eclectic collections are all on the theme of hand-crafted country pieces.

2

3

4

1

2

1

This wonderful 17thC country furniture is enhanced by the choice of paint colour and textiles. The wardrobe has been created by hanging a pair of 19thC patchwork quilts in place of doors.

2

Against the excellent background colours, this Elizabethan four-poster gets its country feel from the mix of fabrics. The crewel work hangings are original but 19thC copies would look as good and some modern Indian fabrics would give a similar effect. Patchwork always looks right for country styles of any period. The ottoman is covered with a kelim – you could use a damaged kelim in this situation.

3

The essence of the style is conjured up in all the elements here – the colours, the original painted dresser, the brightly coloured 19thC spongeware, the earthenware, the rushlight holders, the samplers, the naive painting, the prints and the chandelier – which is a modern copy of a 17thC original.

3

1

1

This room gives an overall impression of 17thC style while retaining elements of modern comfort – a perfect compromise. A large tapestry dominates the room, Chinese porcelain is much in evidence, and the modern carpet is mostly hidden by a Persian rug. Of course, coffee tables were not a feature of 17thC homes, but they do seem to have become an essential for modern life – this clever solution comprises a sheet of plate glass resting on a quartet of cast lions.

This is a relaxed style that is suitable for beamed cottages and or houses of modest pretensions. The style can be easily adapted to bring the same homey feel to buildings of other eras.

COLOURS Slightly faded colours suit this style – almost as though the rich Elizabethan fabrics had been exposed to sunlight for some time.

WALLS Paint these white or in a soft shade to complement other colours in the room – peach, cream or apricot suit this mellow style.

FLOORS Polished boards, sisal matting or flagstones have the right feel and can be topped with oriental rugs in faded tones of pink, turquoise, blue and beige.

CREATING THE LOOK

FURNITURE Pieces at this time were well-made, but less heavily ornamented than Elizabethan and Jacobean pieces. Supplement fine original or reproduction pieces with appropriately styled pine furniture that has been given a distressed paint finish. Gate-legged tables of the 1930s can work just as well as original 17th-century ones.

2

3

2 and 3

Two views of a 17thC set-piece on a perfect mid-17thC dresser. A mass of candles in holders of all different shapes and sizes is interspersed with delft, earthenware, saltglaze, leather and bronze (which could all be reproduction) and brought to life with generous displays of flowers and fruit.

SOFT FURNISHINGS Printed Jacobean design, flamestitch patterns, embroidery, old-looking velvets and faded silks work well.

LIGHTING See Medieval, page 35.

FINISHING TOUCHES Brass candlesticks would look good with the mellow polished furniture. There was a growing interest in all things Eastern at this time, so lacquerwork boxes and screens would be appropriate.

Music to set the mood would include Vivaldi's *The Four Seasons*, Bach's *Brandenburg Concerts 1-6*, and Vaughan Williams' delightful *Fantasia on Greensleeves*.

ENGLISH BAROQUE

1

The Baroque feel of this magnificent dining room is mainly achieved by the deep turquoise panelled walls, the ornate cornice and the gilding. Panelling at this period was more prominent, with more panels, especially on doors. Rooms often contained niches, for porcelain or busts. The chairs and table here are early 19thC, but their sturdy form fits well with this style in this setting.

1

2

Dennis Severs has turned his City of London home into living history. This ground floor receiving room is an authentic re-creation of the Restoration period. Note the dark painted walls and floor, the low level of light, and the paintings lit from below by candles shaded with scallop shells. It is worth remembering that all paintings were bottom-lit – and were painted with this in mind – until the advent of electric lighting.

The emergence of the flamboyant English Baroque style coincided with the restoration to the English throne in 1660 of the equally flamboyant Charles II after 11 years of staid and serious Commonwealth.

The version of Baroque that developed in England under Charles II and matured in the reign of William and Mary (1689-1702) came partly direct from France but more strongly via Holland.

The Baroque is a style of theatrical grandeur, of swelling curves and massive forms. Rooms now looked very different from those of previous eras. The basic shell was often rather sombre, but the effect was offset by the glowing jewel colours of painted ceilings, tapestries and upholstery and by the gleam of silver chandeliers, silver-decorated furniture and mirrors.

Queen Mary had developed a passion for oriental porcelain and blue-and-white Delftware while living in Holland, and she started a craze for collecting these pieces when she came to England as Queen. Displays of blue-and-white wares became as typical a feature of an English room, and later of an American parlour, as they were of a Dutch one.

The greater sophistication and comfort of the William and Mary style reached America just as the era was ending in England. The American version lasted roughly until the mid-1720s.

Walls and ceilings

The rooms of great houses were often panelled in oak. This was the high point of wood carving in England, with craftsmen like Grinling Gibbons and Edward Pierce creating naturalistically carved fruit, birds, flowers and animals. Motifs were frequently carried out in pearwood or limewood, then applied to oak panelling. Pine woodwork was frequently painted to look like marble, rockwork or a finer wood such as walnut.

Plasterwork During the Restoration great advances were made in plasterwork with the development of a harder, quick-drying plaster, *stucco duro*, which made it possible to create elaborate naturalistic motifs similar to those found in wood carving. By the end of the 17th century, however, elaborate plasterwork was giving way to the new vogue for painted ceilings.

Hangings for walls These were now often decorated with a fringe along the top and bottom and down the edges. Leather hangings were particularly popular for dining rooms because they did not absorb smells.

1

2

1

Brightly coloured walls, although in period, would not have done such justice to this William and Mary corner table.

2

Choosing a suitable fabric for early upholstered furniture is not easy. Flamestitch designs tend to work on any early chairs.

3

This corner of Dennis Severs' receiving room (see p.60) houses just a fraction of his fine collection of 17thC Restoration artefacts. This is not an age of pristine refinement – there should be ashes in the grate and candlewax dripping over candlesticks.

4

A grand panelled room has been painted in tones of light burgundy. It makes a striking background for the 17thC lacquer chinoiserie side chairs and the massive 18thC blue and white vases and covers. Symmetry is the essence of English Baroque in the grand manner.

3

4

Wallpaper Hand-painted papers from China were considered the height of fashion. Block-printed papers were locally produced in rolls.

Windows

Curtains began to take on a more important role. They were often hung in pairs in the 1670s and soon rod and rings were disguised by a pelmet, which became the chief focus of decoration.

Floors

Parquetry was sometimes used in grand settings. Persian, Turkish and Savonnerie carpets were now commonly seen on the floor. Turkeywork was used for carpets as well as for upholstery, and there were serge "German carpets".

Lighting

Rooms were brighter at night than they had been, since people tended to burn a greater number of candles. Candlestands had come into fashion, and chandeliers were hung quite low.

Furniture

Walnut ousted oak as the fashionable wood at this time, and pieces were often inlaid with marquetry. There was a passion during the Restoration for decorating furniture with silver; indeed, some pieces were completely encased in silver. Oriental lacquer was extremely fashionable, and screens were sometimes cannibalized to make cabinet furniture.

American William and Mary furniture

The same basic shapes of furniture came into fashion in America. Some pieces were imported and were then copied by local craftsmen. On the whole the native product was more restrained than the original models.

Corner cupboards and occasional tables were in demand to display collections of imported ceramics, and bed hangings were elaborate.

Accessories

The fashion for tea, coffee and chocolate required new types of pottery and silverware. Forks became usual in fashionable circles. The Restoration was a very prosperous time, and silver was used for all manner of pieces.

Owing to advances in English glass, glass goblets were ousting silver for wine – which must have improved the taste considerably.

— 1 —

Sometimes even a hallway or an alcove can convey an immediate sense of period. This late 17thC chest on stand is in a hallway facing the front door.

— 2 —

An alcove on a stairwell houses a period piece – a late 17thC chest, framed by a suitable swag of fabric over the window.

1

— 4 —

This dining room has elements from many periods but its basic feeling is English Baroque. The chairs are 19thC copies of 17thC style – always a good buy, as early chairs are expensive and tend to be too fragile for everyday use. The rococo carved and gilded wooden brackets are originals; however, quite good modern Italian copies are not difficult to find.

2

— 3 —

This is a harmonious blend of authentic antiques with well-made, properly researched reproductions. The bureau is a country piece from the early 18thC, the chair is a modern reproduction William and Mary, the tyg (drinking vessel) is dated 1709, and the slipware candlesticks are new.

3

4

WALLS Large oak panels framed with moulding or pine panelling painted to look like marble or walnut are both authentic treatments. If you can't afford the real thing, you could divide a plain plastered wall into sections edged by mouldings and then give each "panel" a suitable *faux* finish. Another approach would be to use pine panelling painted with a distressed finish – one tone rubbed or dragged over a very similar one works well. You could cover panels or whole walls with damask or moire stretched onto battens, covering the nails with fringing in the manner of the time.

Yellow is a pleasing background for collections of blue-and-white porcelain. Chinese hand-painted wallpapers would also suit the style.

FLOORS Use oriental or Savonnerie-style carpets on parquet or polished boards.

SOFT FURNISHINGS Suitable fabrics include damask, moiré and silk. You might use a linen-weave with a block-printed chinoiserie design. You could hang curtains from rods and rings or top them with a fringed pelmet.

FURNITURE Walnut is the wood for this era. Choose narrow high-backed chairs with scrolled legs and carved tops. Barley-twist legs are also right for the period. Chair seats and backs might be caned or covered in needlework or cut velvet. Swing toilet mirrors on box stands are very characteristic. Choose chests-on-chests raised from the floor on turned legs. Victorian furniture called "Elizabethan" was really in the style of William and Mary: this would certainly be less expensive than original pieces. Look too for lacquered chinoiserie pieces and screens.

LIGHTING Candlelight was still the only form of illumination. Silver candlesticks, chandeliers and wall sconces are correct, but you can compromise with silver-coloured reproduction electric fittings, or better still install concealed uplighters with soft peach-coloured bulbs.

ORNAMENTS Blue-and-white Chinese vases and jars massed on shelves over a fireplace, on tables, on top of cabinets and on wall brackets give a feeling of the age. An abundance of silver is characteristic, and lacquered boxes would reflect the fascination with the Orient.

FINISHING TOUCHES It was fashionable to display a large piece of oriental porcelain or Delftware vases on the stretchers under a cabinet. For a similar effect place a large vase or ginger jar under a side table and match it with a collection of blue-and-white jars and vases on top.

The music of the Baroque period is a bit of an acquired taste – try Pachelbel's *Canon*, the various song collections of Purcell and his *Funeral Music for Queen Mary*. There is a CD, *Baroque Favourites*, which includes works by Pachelbel, Purcell, Vivaldi, Bach, Mouret and others.

CREATING THE LOOK

5

5

A perfect set-piece of English Baroque style: a 17thC Portuguese table adorned in the appropriate manner with Kangxi and Qianlong porcelain, set against a wall of brilliant yellow.

THE AGE OF ELEGANCE

1

Queen Anne occupied the English throne for just twelve years at the beginning of the 18th century. This was a time of transition from the flamboyant English Baroque to the Palladianism of the Georgian era. Interiors became plainer and both furniture and metalwork styles were simpler and more elegant.

QUEEN ANNE

Despite the fact that no great innovations were made in architecture or the decorative arts during Queen Anne's short reign, the period has become synonymous with all that is desirable in elegance, comfort and good taste. This was the time of a domestic, understated English style typified by a rather gentle, domesticated Queen.

The era is characterized by a greater simplicity, with the emphasis on first-class materials and workmanship. The beauty of a piece of furniture derived from its shape and from the figuring of the wood and simple veneering, rather than depending on marquetry, carving and ornament. The same applied to silver and to brass: decoration was often limited to simple engraving and "cut-card" appliqués.

The Duchess of Marlborough, friend and confidante of the Queen, summed up the commonly held desire to "have things plain and clean, from a piece of wainscot to a lady's face".

AMERICAN "QUEEN ANNE"

The quiet elegance of the "Queen Anne" style spread to America but was not current until well after the Queen's death. The second quarter of the 18th century is the age of "American Queen Anne". As in England, the most characteristic features of the style were its overall elegant simplicity and the cabriole leg, which appeared on chairs, sofas, tables, low- and high-boys and so on.

The Dutch influence was still very much in evidence. Hand-painted Delft tiles were imported from Holland and often used to decorate fireplaces. A type of large painted cupboard, typical of the New York area, was based on a Dutch style but had grisaille decoration instead of the fine woods and ornate carving of the original.

1

The 18thC was the age of elegance and opulence – or rather of opulent effects achieved with imagination and flair rather than by an ostentatious display of wealth. This four-poster has been created from a divan, using floor-to-ceiling posts, lengths of moulding and masses of fabric, tassels, bows and braids. Even the fancy scrolls are simply the cardboard centres of kitchen rolls, covered in fabric. The fine collection of Chinese porcelain is in fact a motley assortment from many periods – some of the pieces are quite badly damaged.

2

Subtlety is not a vital ingredient of early 18thC interiors. This corner is delightfully overdone, with rich fabrics everywhere and a mirror with a crewelwork overframe: crewelwork applied to a plain frame can achieve a convincing effect. The collection of items on the table, including feathers, vinaigrettes and brushes, all add to the sense of profusion.

3

In the same bedroom as that depicted in the larger picture (2), an early 18thC chest-on-stand, framed by an unusual display of blue and white porcelain on gilt brackets, stands out against the pale blue walls. The interesting display on top of the chest has been kept firm by glueing various pieces together; obviously this is not recommended for fine, early porcelain.

2

3

1

The plain panelling in this room has been painted a wonderful warm shade of deep chestnut, which is ideal at night-time and very cosy in winter, but could be rather dark during the day, particularly if the room is north-facing. The scallop shell candle shields are an inventive touch. The magnificent garlands are made of nuts threaded through chicken wire and varnished.

2

The elegant lines of early Georgian furniture look particularly good in a context of pale yellows.

2

3

4

3

This wonderful example of an early 18thC walnut dining chair covered in red damask shows the superb craftsmanship of the period. The style has been much copied, both in the 19thC and today.

4

These Queen Anne style chairs are an unusual addition to a Regency country kitchen where rustic chairs or settles would have been more orthodox. The chairs have been painted, which makes them look less formal, and they fit in very well. The paint also hides the fact that the chairs were bought as singles, not as a set.

5

6

7

5

In this New York apartment on Park Avenue, beautiful pieces of Queen Anne walnut furniture create the style. The placement is absolutely right, as symmetry was very much a theme of the age. The flower watercolours are also in period – these are originals, but there are some very good prints around.

6

An early 18thC silver table, authentically crammed with 18th and 19thC silver boxes, makes for a pretty, feminine interpretation of the style. The casual bunch of sweetpeas sets it off perfectly.

7

The mixture of 17th and 18thC furniture sits well in this 16thC interior, the choice of fabric helping to create a sense of harmony. If you can't find or afford original needlework, there are plenty of good copies to be found.

1

COLOURS Hues were quite strong and dark in the early Georgian interior. Paints were limited to olive greens, browns, greys and off-whites, and the colours of printed fabrics were mainly reds, browns, purples and blacks. Silks and velvets added rich reds, greens, blues and golds.

WALLS If you are lucky enough to have an early 18th-century house with its panelling intact, you are halfway to creating an authentic "feel". If not you might consider having plain pine panelling installed to divide the walls into three areas – dado, infill and cornice. Incorporating cupboards, arch-topped niches and fireplaces into the panelling is correct for the period. Panelling can be grained to simulate a more luxurious wood, or it can be painted – grey, brown or olive green are suitable colours. An imperfect "dragged" paint effect in two closely related tones works well.

If you do not wish to go to the expense of having a room panelled, you could simulate panelling by applying moulding, then painting in an appropriate colour.

FLOORS A large rug is a better choice than a fitted carpet – an oriental design works well. Originally a rug would have been placed on top of plain, scrubbed boards. This is not a popular choice today: instead you might prefer to sand, seal and polish your floorboards, or perhaps darken them with a wood stain, coloured varnish or gloss paint. If you do not have a wooden floor, or want a warmer look, you could cover the floor with sisal matting and use rugs on top. Also correct is floor cloth, canvas painted with a geometric pattern.

SOFT FURNISHINGS Damasks and velvets suit this style, as do coarser cotton fabrics with a block-print design in black, dark red or brown. Brightly coloured printed fabric was not readily available at this time.

Shuttered windows can be left uncurtained in a room in this style, but the effect of this can be rather bleak. A better choice is to hang full-length curtains from a pole or, as would have been fashionable at the time, to cover the "workings" with a pelmet.

Self-coloured woven damasks based on 18th-century designs are widely available and are a good choice for upholstery. You might like to copy the practical Georgian habit of covering fine upholstery with slip-covers in an everyday fabric. Striped ticking, which can be bought in a number of different colours, looks most attractive when used for slip-covers. Alternatively, you might like to use it for the actual upholstery.

FURNITURE Choose pieces with the cabriole legs characteristic of this time – dining chairs, upholstered wing-chairs and sofas, writing tables, dressing tables, chests-of-drawers, as well as chests-on-chests, dome-topped bureau-cabinets and bureau-bookcases. These may be in walnut – characteristic of the Queen Anne period and early reign of George I – or mahogany which replaced it. In a less formal setting choose more robust "country" pieces in oak which have the same, although heavier, lines.

Georgian furniture is expensive, but you can pick up single chairs at auctions and make up your own sets. Reproductions made in the 19th century look better than modern ones, as they will have acquired a certain patina of age. If you want to mix in modern furniture – which can look stunning if done with sufficient conviction – choose pieces with a fine, elegant line. Bauhaus-inspired pieces can look good in a Georgian setting.

ORNAMENTS Pictures in gilt frames – portraits, landscape paintings and hunting scenes – suit rooms in this style. Hogarth was beginning to make a name for himself by the late 1720s and prints of his *Beggar's Opera* and *Rake's Progress* also help create the mood.

Genuine 18th-century porcelain and pottery is very expensive, but a collection of pottery with simple blue-and-white patterns reminiscent of the delftware of the time makes a good substitute. Use an informal vase of flowers to fill a fireplace opening in summer. Mirrors played an important role; look for small wood-framed mirrors with arched tops.

1

This room is coloured with confidence – elegant and opulent. The nut garlands, ornate ceiling, pilasters and candles make a major contribution to the mood. Candles give out considerable heat as well as light. Ladies used fans to screen their faces from candles and firescreens to obscure the hearth. This was partly to protect their eyes from the glare but also to prevent their thick wax make-up from melting.

2

Another view of the same room. Authentic touches include lavender swept into the corners, and oranges and cloves in dishes. Tea-making was by now a major social ceremony, and here we have all the artefacts, including early English porcelain cups and saucers.

CREATING THE LOOK

2

LIGHTING Don't light rooms too brightly – candles would have been the only source of illumination at the time. Use them where you can with candlesticks in brass or silver according to your pocket. Electrified chandeliers are produced, but give a much brighter light than candles ever did. Electric table lamps give attractive pools of light: choose classic candlestick or oriental ginger jar shapes. Supplement these with wall-lantern styles and mirror-back sconces. Dimmer switches for centre lights or table lamps help in creating the right atmosphere.

FINISHING TOUCHES Whether or not you decide to panel a room, it is worthwhile building in an arched niche on either side of a fireplace, with panelled cupboards underneath. Originally such niches would be used for a bust or statues but today they might display porcelain.

1

A well-researched early Georgian smoking room recreated in Dennis Severs' City of London home. The placement of the furniture (the chairs are modern copies) takes its cue from the period painting over the mantelpiece. This is a dramatic room, not for people of refined tastes. The main focus of attention is on the artfully arranged collections of drinking vessels, bottles and bowls.

1

2

This close-up of the room shown on the opposite page reveals a streaked, nicotine-coloured finish to the walls. Note the attention to detail here — the mantelpiece display that sets the scene so perfectly. Many of these items can be purchased quite inexpensively in provincial auction sales and even car boot and garage sales.

While the wealthy homes of Europe were awash with Rococo swirls, England was going very much its own way. The gracious and elegant Palladian style of the middle years of the century was inspired by a reappraisal of the work of the Italian architect Andrea Palladio and his English disciple Inigo Jones.

A wall in a typical Georgian Palladian room would be divided into three – the dado, the infill, and the frieze and cornice – corresponding to the division of a Classical column into base, shaft and entablature. The same principle was applied to the fireplace. Mouldings played an important part in these rooms. They were used to create the friezes and cornices, to decorate the coffering of ceilings and to ornament doors, windows, fireplaces and large furniture. Repeat designs include dentil, egg-and-dart, Greek key, acanthus leaf, Vitruvian scroll and bay-leaf garland.

Symmetry and balance were the keynote of such a room: a niche with a statue or bust on one side of the fireplace would inevitably be balanced by another on the other side. The newly fashionable combination of console and pier glass would be symmetrically placed. Rooms were still formally arranged, with furniture set back against the walls.

Interiors contained less wood than formerly. Principal rooms in fashionable houses came to be decorated with plasterwork instead of wood panelling. Floors covered with large carpets were becoming more and more usual and for the first time curtains played a major role in decoration. One of the great changes was in the colour of wood furniture – it was now rich brown mahogany instead of golden walnut.

Strong colours were usual in a Palladian interior. It was not until the middle of the century that paler colours became fashionable.

In the 1740s, signs of the asymmetrical Rococo style, typified by the S-curve, began to influence Georgian interiors. It did not permeate the style of whole rooms. Rococo motifs might sometimes be incorporated into plasterwork. More often, however, Rococo elements were seen in smaller decorative pieces – in girandoles, mirrors and brackets, in furniture decoration and in silver and porcelain articles. Typical motifs were the small shells which might be found in rock pools, lightly drawn acanthus leaves, ribbonwork, plants and flowers, festoons and waves.

At the same time chinoiserie, another style fashionable on the Continent, was becoming the rage in England.

The mid-18th century enthusiasm for everything Chinese had little to do with China, but was a Western vision of an exotic, little-known country, Cathay – a sort of willow-pattern-plate world. Chinoiserie pagodas, pavilions, dragons and mandarins worked well with the asymmetry and writhing lines of Rococo and were often combined with them, particularly in plasterwork and carved wood. There was a great deal of chinoiserie furniture – cabinets topped by pagodas and so on – and the style was sometimes adopted for whole rooms to charming, if slightly dotty, effect.

1

The early Georgian era still had a rustic feel about it, especially in ordinary middle-class homes where a fireplace full of ashes and broken clay pipes would have been a common sight, and would not have been thought untidy.

1

Gothick was another style that came into fashion. A purely English phenomenon, this was about as close to the real medieval world as chinoiserie was to China. It manifested itself in mock ruins and quirky garden buildings as well as in interiors and, occasionally, whole houses. It called for Gothick objects and, of course, appropriate furniture. Window tracery, pinnacles and crockets appeared on otherwise standard Georgian cabinets, bookcases and chairs.

2

2

A touch of whimsey on the wall of the same room. A lot of the fun in creating period styles comes from scouting about to find small items from your chosen period and arranging them as a set piece on a shelf, a mantel or a wall.

Walls

Wood panelling started to wane as a fashion in grander homes. Instead, the walls of principal rooms were decorated with stucco. They might also still be hung with textiles – silk damask, velvet and so on. The fabric was usually nailed to battens and the nails hidden by decorative fillets of carved and gilded wood, gilded or painted papier mâché or gilt leather.

Wallpaper, like textiles, was frequently used for ladies' apartments. Flock wallpaper became very fashionable.

Ceilings

Coffered plaster ceilings, ornamented with Classical mouldings and complemented by classically inspired cornices and friezes, were usual for this period. Often they were gilded. Ceiling and wall decoration might be executed in papier mâché.

Floors

In grander houses floors were often carpeted, so that it was not necessary for the floor itself to be decorative: scrubbed bare boards were adequate.

As well as oriental rugs and Savonnerie ones imported from France, there were patterned Axminster carpets. Wilton cut-pile carpeting would be joined in strips to make large carpets and then finished with a complementary border.

Much less expensive was a type of carpeting that had no pile and was reversible, known as "Scotch" carpet or "listed" carpet. It was woven from strips of cloth and could be used as runners or joined to cover larger areas. Another inexpensive floor covering was floorcloth – canvas painted with a simple geometric design.

Windows

Curtains were now a usual feature of a room, softening the outline of windows. If textiles were used to cover walls in the room, the curtains would usually be of the same fabric; in a bedroom they would frequently match the bed hangings. Festooned and draped curtains were by this time more fashionable than simple paired arrangements.

3 and 4

Here are more examples of an early Georgian mantelpiece and tablescape that go a long way toward creating the feel of the times. The delftware items here are English copies of the extremely popular Chinese porcelain of the period – note the naive quality of decoration. These pieces, which are perfectly good enough for this type of display, are somewhat chipped and battered and therefore quite affordable.

3

4

Furniture

Large pieces of furniture, such as bureaux and bookcases, show a strong architectural influence in their design and ornament. Console tables are very characteristic of this time. They were supported by brackets at the back and by a single front support, which would usually be an elaborately carved and gilded affair; typical subjects were eagles or dolphins. The tops were usually of marble or scagliola (imitation marble).

The name of Thomas Chippendale is particularly associated with the mid-1700s. Although his workshop was relatively small, his book of designs, *The Gentleman and Cabinet-Maker's Director*, was highly influential.

The wood usually chosen for chairs and cabinet furniture at the beginning of George I's reign was walnut. Then, in the 1720s, mahogany – a wood hardly seen before in England – began to be imported. Mahogany was stronger, less affected by worm and more suited to carving than walnut, and the trees were bigger, making it possible to cut larger planks.

5

This is a convincing example of panelling painted to emulate a grained wood effect. Again, small-scale still-life set-pieces on the mantelpiece and side table, are all-important in establishing the appropriate atmosphere.

5

The cabriole chair leg which came into fashion in the reign of Queen Anne continued to be popular for some time. The graceful curve of the leg affected the shape of the whole chair, which was more curving than before. The knees of such chairs were often carved with smooth oval cabochons; seat rails might be ornamented with lion or satyr masks. Cabriole legs were finished with different types of feet at different times, but the most enduring was the claw-and-ball foot. Cabriole legs were also used on tables.

From the 1730s chairs became squarer-looking, and had wider, squarer backs with a bowed top rail reflecting Hogarth's "waving line of beauty". The upholstery of seats, backs and arms was square-edged to suit the general shape of the chair, unlike the stuffing of French upholstery which gave a domed outline. Loose covers in striped or checked linen were used to protect expensive upholstery fabrics, and were removed only for very special occasions.

The wing chair continued to be popular until the middle of the century, when it went out of fashion. There were folding dining tables, with flaps supported on swing legs. At first these tables were oval, but later they were more usually rectangular, which made it possible to place several together to make a long table.

Tea tables continued to be fashionable and might be rectangular or round, often with a gallery around the top. There were also special small stands for kettles.

Accessories

Busts, costly porcelain figures and delftware displayed on wall brackets and chimneypieces were very much in vogue.

Tea caddies were an essential part of the English tea ceremony: containers, often of silver, were stored inside a decorative box which was usually locked. This was opened up with due ceremony and the tea mixed and made at the table. Landscape paintings and portraits depicting the sitters in their homes became popular.

2

2 — This interesting interior combines rich drapery with simple matt painted walls, country chairs and plain stained floorboards. The oak gateleg table is actually Edwardian but painted a Georgian green. The candelabrum is a modern copy.

3

3 — A Georgian feeling is re-created here with comb-effect painted panelling acting as a backdrop to typical furniture of the period. The chairs are originals.

4

4 — Strong matt green painted panelling and black painted floorboards create an effective background for a fine portrait and a beautiful chair. The window drapery here is purely ornamental – internal shutters keep out the light.

5

5 — An elegant display of rusticity can be consistent with the Georgian look. Painting the insignificant table the same colour as the panelling is a clever idea.

1 — The look in this dining room is typical of a middle-class home of the period. Carpets would not be appropriate, but rugs could be thrown over the varnished floor.

1

Shutters dispense with the need for curtains in this dramatic wine-red sitting room – the perfect setting for the Georgian furniture. Nothing is over-manicured or over-done: this is a comfortable, lived-in room. The oak child's chair is a genuine country piece but looks quite at home in these elegant surroundings.

1

2

This relaxing sitting room with rough, painted walls and decorative drapes has a distinctly Georgian feel. The shutters and window frames have been painted with an interesting two-tone streaked effect. The chandelier is 18thC in style.

2

3

This homely little corner, painted in two shades of green, has a Georgian ambience despite the radiator.

4

This bed, in a very small room, has been constructed to fit in with Georgian-style panelling – the book shelves cut into the walls are an interesting feature, and very convenient for bed-time reading.

3

4

5

The three-tone paintwork gives added prominence to the panelling in this comfortable, intimate room. The arrangement of pictures is typical of the period – note the run of prints on the right and the plates "hung" on a strip of fabric that can be glimpsed in the Chippendale mirror.

5

1

1

No one would guess that the location of the sitting room shown here and in picture 2 is an apartment on Park Avenue, New York. The style of Chippendale furniture featured here is often referred to as "Chinese Chippendale", and is regarded as some of the finest English furniture ever produced. Elaborate curtains with intricate pelmets are very much part of the late Georgian style. On a practical level, it is worth having roller blinds behind the drapery, as drawing such curtains tends to ruin the form.

2

The pilaster, cornice and door frames are all applied mouldings. The dramatic colour scheme is a bold alternative to the safer, if more boring, pale green or magnolia paintwork so often associated with this type of setting. Note how the comfortable modern seating blends in with the overall period effect. In this appartment, each major room is in a different period style – you can glimpse the Art Deco room through the open door.

2

By the end of the 1750s there was a reawakening of interest throughout Europe in the Classical world. Excavation at sites such as Herculaneum and Pompeii built up a more authentic picture of life in an ordinary Roman household and revealed that interiors were decorated in a much less rigid and more flowing style than had been previously thought, with painted decoration as valid an element as mouldings and stucco. This evidence, together with the discovery of many well-preserved everyday domestic articles, had a great impact on late 17th-century interior design.

The most important figure in developing the English version of Neo-classicism was Robert Adam, who dominated interior design in the years 1760-90. An aspect of Adam's vision new to English decorating was his concept of an interior and its furnishings as a coordinated whole. In an Adam room the design of floor, ceiling, walls and furniture is all closely related. The Neo-classical style of Adam is much lighter and more elegant than the Palladian. He aimed "to transfuse the beautiful spirit of antiquity with novelty and variety".

Neo-classical motifs used in painting, plasterwork and furniture include acanthus and laurel leaves, festoons, guilloches, medallions, urns, rams' heads, tripods, gryphons and curling arabesques, sphinxes and lyres, the husk, anthemion (honeysuckle) and palmette. Many Adam rooms are in the "Etruscan" style – painted with figures based on Greek red-and-black figure pottery (it was thought at the time, erroneously, that these pots were made by the Etruscans).

Colours generally favoured by Adam were pale green, blue, and pink, although some colour schemes remained surprisingly strong; the breakfast room at Osterley Park, Middlesex, for example, has bright yellow walls with blue papier mâché borders and white woodwork.

Delicate plain furniture, either painted or in satinwood decorated with marquetry and inlay, is typical of this time. Pottery and porcelain shapes were plain and elegant based on Antique models.

Walls and ceilings

The architectural elements became less dominant in Neo-classical rooms – cornices, friezes, mouldings and relief decorations were now noticeably shallower and more delicate.

The ceiling was the most important feature of a room, according to Adam. It might be decorated with plasterwork and/or painting, and the design on the ceiling was often echoed (not exactly copied) by that which appeared on the floor. Plaster decoration for both walls and ceilings was the distinctive feature of many rooms and was very often white.

Walls might be painted a single plain colour and decorated with a border. The wall above the dado was sometimes divided into panels ornamented with scrolling acanthus foliage, perhaps with specially commissioned small paintings incorporated into the design. Alternatively, a white stucco dado rail, border and frieze, and roundels and rectangular panels of Neo-classical motifs, might be set against a single-colour background.

For more modest interiors, Josiah Wedgwood sold Black Basaltware tablets – cameos and medallions copied exactly from Roman and Greek

1

This panelling, taken from a 1790s house in Colchester, Connecticut, shows the influence of the Classical period, particularly in the broken pediment and the coloured niche. The chair is a superb example from Philadelphia, c.1760.

2

A classic late Georgian feel suffuses this room, with its pale lemon walls, niches, archways and Adam-style fireplace highlighted in white. The Regency stool and the modern armchair are quite in keeping, and the collection of mid-18thC creamware is absolutely right. To create a Georgian interior, it is not necessary to start with a Georgian room – all the architectural features can be purchased and applied to blank modern walls and ceilings.

3

A dining room in the Classical tradition with a good beige background colour, applied pilasters picked out in beige and cream and a trompe l'oeil detail above the door. The table, chairs, glassware and creamware plates are all in style, and there is no conflict with the Regency chiffonier, as this period saw the birth of the Regency style.

2

1

originals – for "inlaying in the panels of rooms . . . or as pictures in dressing rooms".

Walls might also be hung with fabric in the same way as in Palladian houses, or papered, perhaps with a Neo-classical pattern.

Floors

Flooring materials were much the same as in the previous period. In grand houses decorated by Adam, the design, whether marble or carpet, would usually echo that of the ceiling. Two carpet factories – Moorfields and Axminster – produced carpets in competition with the Sȧvonnerie carpets of France. Both produced Neo-classical designs for Adam rooms. Painted floorcloth was still used extensively.

Windows

Pairs of curtains were in fashion during this period, often topped with a festoon pelmet; these pelmets might also be used alone to decorate the top of a window. Venetian blinds were occasionally seen.

Furniture

The shapes of the Neo-classical period were simple and delicate, with straight legs. The preferred wood was satinwood – except for the dining room – and often decorated with marquetry and inlay. Much furniture was painted; in Adam houses, panels painted by Angelica Kauffmann were inserted into tables and commodes.

Eating and drinking was a serious business in Georgian England and one of the most important rooms in the house was the dining room. The

3

1

furniture for this room – mainly a male domain – was mahogany. Adam is credited with inventing the sideboard – a marble-topped table with an urn on a pedestal at either side. Both urns and pedestals were designed to hold all the necessities of a dining room – knives, plates, water, bottles of wine and so on. Later on in smaller, less grand rooms the pedestals were combined with the table.

Adam designed the key pieces of furniture in most of his interiors – pier tables and the mirrors to go over them, commodes to stand against a particular wall. Elegant semicircular tables and commodes are typical of Adam. He also designed decorative pieces such as girandoles, urns, *torchères* (candlestands) and so on. Adam furniture was frequently gilt or painted and gilded to carry through the theme of the room for which it was intended.

Chippendale designed in the Neo-classical style and made furniture for Adam houses, but the names associated most closely with furniture for less grand homes of this period are Hepplewhite and Sheraton. Their books of designs influenced numerous furniture makers.

The typical Hepplewhite chair has a shield back decorated with Prince of Wales feathers, urn or triple lilies. Some Hepplewhite furniture is carved and painted or japanned. He also favoured elaborate marquetry decoration.

Sheraton chairs usually have square backs with upright splats. He designed some delightful small pieces of furniture – for example *bonheurs-du-jour* (writing desks for ladies) and a version of the flap-sided Pembroke table. Many pieces are inlaid or have painted decoration.

Accessories

Josiah Wedgwood realized the importance of the new Classical fashion very early on, and he produced Creamware for the table in simple Classical lines which complemented the interiors and furniture designs of the day. He also produced Jasperware and Black Basaltware which imitated different types of stone. The shapes and decoration of many ornamental pieces of Jasperware and Black Basaltware are based exactly on those of antique Roman and Etruscan (Greek) vases. Among the pieces made in Jasperware were copies of the famous Roman glass Portland Vase of the 1st century BC.

Worcester and Derby porcelain in classical shapes, often decorated with landscape views, is typical of this period.

Matthew Boulton, metalware manufacturer and friend of Wedgwood, supplied Adam with ormolu decoration for doors and chimneypieces. He also manufactured some very fine pieces in Blue John stone mounted in ormolu.

Romantic porcelain figures by Meissen, Sèvres, Chelsea and Bow were also fashionable.

1

Georgian style works well with the muted tones of pale green. Panelled walls give the impression of a late Georgian interior, but the furniture here spans the Queen Anne and early Georgian periods. Simplicity and symmetry are the keynotes. When you have such exceptional pieces of furniture, drapes can be quite understated.

3

2

Of all period furniture Georgian styles are the most adaptable – as much at home on a vinyl floor as on a Persian rug. Georgian chairs of totally different designs work together very well, so you can buy them as singles, which is much less expensive than buying a set.

3

Plain white painted panelling from c.1700 sets off the impeccable details of this fine Chippendale furniture. The panelling could be copied using pieces of dado rail. The painted floor cloth is perfectly in period.

4

The Georgians valued proportion and light much more than their predecessors or their successors. Here, white painted windows and shutters accentuate the light and airy feeling so typical of the style.

1

— 1 —

Fabrics play an essential role in setting a style. Here, the drapery and the Georgian-style bookcases give an immediate feel of the age. Marble fireplaces, either authentic or reproduction, can be bought from architectural salvage companies or auction houses.

— 2 and 3 —

The clean, simple lines of a modern apartment can provide an excellent setting for fine 18thC furniture. Here, the overall Georgian feel is helped along by pale colours and Classical shapes. The glass Albrizzi table, itself a classic piece, contrasts well with the Thomas Chippendale chair, one of 18 made by the designer himself for Brocket Hall.

2

3

4

5

— 4 —

This 18thC butler's tray makes an excellent drinks stand. The pile of old books is in fact an artfully disguised ice-box. Note how the flooring changes from boards to brick as you pass from drawing room to dining room – Georgian furniture looks good on either surface.

— 5 —

A peaceful Classical Georgian mood created in a room with all the original architectural features of the period. Pale colours are very much part of this look.

1

COLOURS You can choose between a pale palette of creams, greys, pale greens and yellows or stronger colours such as rich pinks and blues, turquoise, even tangerine. Both look right in a Georgian interior.

WALLS These can be divided into dado, infill and frieze with mouldings creating the divisions and panels. They can then be decorated with paint, perhaps using two closely related tones for different areas. Broken paint finishes – rag rolling, dragging or sponging – suit this style of room. You may decide to offset coloured walls with white plasterwork and mouldings; this works particularly well if you decide on a pale wall colour.

Hand-painted Chinese wallpapers are correct, or you could choose one of the less expensive printed papers based on 18th-century chinoiserie or other patterns. Wallpapers imitating damask, silk, printed cotton and chintzes were fashionable in the 18th century, and there was a vogue for flock wallpaper. Give an authentic finishing touch by adding a gilt fillet border around the edges of panels or other areas of paper. Alternatively, walls can be covered with fabric stretched onto battens with braid covering the nails around the edges.

SOFT FURNISHINGS Suitable fabrics range from damasks, moirés, and velvets to simple block-printed patterns and multicoloured designs of birds and flowers. It was customary to have curtains in the same fabric as that used on walls. Festoon curtains are right for the period, as are pairs of curtains, topped by elaborate swag-and-tail pelmets.

FURNITURE Less costly than the real thing are pieces made 100 or so years later when there was a revival of this style. Commodious wing chairs combine comfort with formality, and modern sofas with uncluttered lines will complement true or reproduction Georgian shapes. It is possible also for a skilful hand to blend frankly modern furniture with period pieces. For example, a simple chrome and glass table can set off straight-legged Chippendale-style chairs to stunning effect.

FLOORS AND LIGHTING See page 71.

ORNAMENTS Mirrors play an important part in this type of room – both as decoration and to reflect light. Choose designs with asymmetrical rococo decoration. Look for mirror-backed wall brackets, known as girondoles, in rococo or chinoiserie style. Hang prints in formal groupings and balance one group with another.

FINISHING TOUCHES Copy a Georgian trick and buy sheets of printed garlands and ornaments to creat *trompe l'oeil* "plasterwork" details, ribbons, tassels and other decorations.

Paste prints to the wall in formal arrangements and frame them with monochrome stencilled "frames" to make your own version of a period print room.

"Hang" small decorative pictures on lengths of gathered fabric, topped with bows. This is particularly effective with oval portraits.

Cover the chain supporting a chandelier with a tube of gathered fabric.

Decorate the centre of some wall panels with a large stencilled design of an urn or a Wedgwood-style cameo.

From well-concealed speakers, the strains of Bach's *Orchestral Suites* might be a good choice, or Mozart's *Symphony No. 40,* or Haydn's *12 London Symphonies*.

1

Classical pillars used to create an imaginary division in a room are a feature of the Adam style. The symmetry is also carried through in the fireplace, overmantel mirror, rug and flanking display cabinets. Georgian furniture, over the long period of its development, was of consistently high quality and craftsmanship: this means that early Georgian pieces can be in total harmony with those of late George III. Here, the whole gamut of styles is represented from a chair of c.1725 to a Sheraton table.

CREATING THE LOOK

2

A modern electric table lamp, proportioned along Classical lines, its stem taking the form of a plinth-mounted column, looks just right among exquisite furniture in this corner of a pale, panelled Georgian drawing room.

1

2

3

— 1 —

Walls of sunshine yellow make a good background for blue and white porcelain and mahogany furniture. There is no need to sacrifice comfort for style – wing chairs are luxurious and perfectly in period, and modern sofas on simple, traditional lines harmonize well. The coffee table problem (they didn't have them, we need them) is here solved with a sheet of plate glass and a quartet of gryphons in support.

— 2 —

In any modern interpretation of the Georgian look, due attention must be paid to both comfort and colour. Here, moden seating, upholstered in neutral shades, blends attractively with the panelling and the drapes. Polished floorboards with Persian rugs are a colourful option.

— 3 —

A lesson in Georgian symmetry – a well-balanced display of good furniture against pale stripes.

4

4

The antiqued stained wall finish in this room is reminiscent of early painted furniture and conveys a real 18thC feeling. The green on the walls has been matched to the kelim rug on the floor. Note the hessian carpeting – a good alternative if you want to use rugs on a plain surface and your floorboards are less than wonderful.

1

2

1

This room is dominated by large windows and their attendant drapery: the rich, plush, padded curtains bunch casually on the floor. The stripes on the walls are created by careful application of a two-tone dragged paint finish.

2

This corner of a late Georgian room in the Geffrye Museum, London, is authentic in every detail. Note the large wall panels surrounded by carved egg-and-dart mouldings, the way the architectural details have been picked out in white, and the fact that the decoration on the furniture is inlaid, not carved. The contemporary prints work as well as paintings and are certainly more affordable.

3

A good way to treat a Georgian interior is to apply a suitable paint colour above the dado rail and white below, down to the floor. This way, you have a rich warm background for paintings and collections, and a white background to show off the elegantly carved legs of Georgian tables and chairs.

4

The skilful wood-effect paint finish on the panelled walls and the highly polished floorboards superbly complement the patina and inlaid decoration of this exquisite Georgian table.

5 and 6

This wonderfully simple Connecticut farmhouse exudes Georgian country style at its best – generous chintz curtains, bare polished floorboards, beautiful mahogany furniture, simply framed naive portraits and a profusion of flowers.

3

5

4

6

1

2

1

A Georgian chest of drawers combines function and beauty in a way that typifies the period. A new chest of drawers would be worth only a fraction of its original price the moment you got it home, and might even fall apart within five years or so if the workmanship were not up to standard. However, a Georgian original would last many lifetimes and would certainly increase in value.

2

A simple late Georgian chest flanked by two lovely chairs and a symmetrical arrangement of prints – the essential Georgian statement.

3

In this bedroom, the striped walls and the simple lines of sofa, chairs and table are unmistakably Georgian in feeling. The distinctly Victorian bed adds a stylish dash of surprise and shows that it is perfectly acceptable to mix period styles.

4

This is a New York apartment. The Georgian style has been achieved with a couple of original pieces of furniture, clever use of fabric and a good sense of detail. The Empire-style bed canopy introduces a note of contrast.

5

Obviously, the concept of a Georgian bathroom equipped for modern convenience is a contradiction in terms. However, if you are trying to conjure up a period mood among present-day porcelain and plumbing, carry through the colours and the draperies used in the bedroom and choose perhaps one item of period furniture. This pretty piece is a late 18thC Pembroke table adorned with a collection of small porcelain pieces and silver boxes.

6

This bedroom shows how well Georgian can work as a feminine style – the pale colours, quilts and sprigged fabric are in sharp contrast to the dark rich tones of the furniture.

3

4

5

6

1

1

The period feel of a dining room can depend to a large degree on how you "dress" it. This table is c.1800, the chairs are c.1880, but the overall Georgian look is due to the 18thC engraved glass and the Copenhagen porcelain dinner ware.

2

Beautiful late Georgian furniture and silver are shown off against a background paint mixed to match the ground colour of a Sèvres porcelain rose Pompadour figure.

3

A strong, attractive wall colour makes this excellent George III sideboard really glow. The pair of George III knifeboxes show the Georgian flair for combining practicality with elegance: they provide a convenient solution to the problem of storing cutlery.

4, 5 and 6

Reproduction Georgian-style chairs work well here in three completely different settings. In the dining rooms shown in 4 and 5 it is colour that sets the keynote. In the third example (6), fabric is the source of inspiration.

2

3

4

5

6

1

2

1

Hallways are intended to create a strong first impression – here, stripped pine, peacock blue walls, a plain stone floor, a collection of decoy ducks and various other paraphernalia create a Georgian country feeling.

2

Walls the colour of crushed raspberries help to enliven the formal atmosphere of this symmetrical marble-floored hallway. The orange tree sentinels add to the symmetry and also add an outside/inside dimension.

3

A strongly Classical interior reflects the transition from late Georgian to Regency. The painted floor echoes Classical designs, and the walls are painted to imitate stone. The urn shapes and the subject matter of the painting are consistent with this return to Classicism. This ensemble has been created not in a grand Georgian mansion but in the hallway of a New York apartment.

3

The War of Independence interrupted the flow of new ideas on interior design and furniture from Europe to America. Consequently, it was not until the 1790s that Neo-classical influences began to be seen in America.

Houses were now more spacious, with lofty ceilings and large windows which often extended down to the floor in the French manner. These well-proportioned interiors were well suited to the modified version of the Neo-classical style current in America in the Federal period, which spans the years from 1790 to about 1810. Toward the end of the period, influences of the incipient Greek Revival style could be seen.

Walls and ceilings

These were more simply decorated than in Neo-classical rooms in England. The ceiling would probably have a central plaster rose. French scenic wallpapers were popular, giving rooms a spacious feel.

Windows

Formal swag-and-tail or draped pelmets in silk were seen in Federal-style rooms, used often over simple muslin or fine cotton curtains.

Floors

Hand-knotted pile carpets produced in Philadelphia in the 1790s were made in strips which were joined. "Ingrain" or "Scotch" carpeting might be used to cover whole rooms. Painted floorcloths, sometimes with patterns imitating Turkey or Savonnerie carpets, were widely used.

1

The simple expedient of placing one good period piece in a hallway can set the tone for the whole interior. This small Federal-style settee shows the influence of Sheraton.

1

2

This warm, matt-painted dining room embodies the essence of Federal style – note the stencilled floor and the painted display cupboard. The Sheraton-style fancy chairs date from c.1820. The flexible dining table is a Federal double D end – in this photograph the two D ends have been placed together to form an oval and the centrepiece is being used as a sideboard to the left of the picture. The colonial brass chandelier is a reproduction. The painting, dated c.1795, is a naive work from the Hudson River School. The porcelain is a mixture of English Newhall and Chinese export – all from approximately the same period.

3

The Deer Park Parlor in the American Museum in Bath is a typical late 18thC interior from Baltimore County, Maryland. You can see the strong Adam influences in the proportions and mouldings, especially in the fireplace surround. The furniture with its inlays and veneers shows the influence of Sheraton and Hepplewhite. The bookcase is from Boston and is made of mahogany and pine with bird's-eye maple veneer and border details of rosewood. The wallpaper, with its motif of ears of corn, is a French paper made specifically for the American market, which by now was of great significance commercially.

2

4

A simple wallscape redolent with Federal detail. Note the stencilled floor (handpainted by the owners), the matt-painted panelling, the original painted Sheraton fancy chairs, the William IV cut crystal, marble and glass lustres (slightly later but they fit in well), the Hudson River school painting and the beautiful Federal tiger maple and bird's-eye maple card table – probably made in Massachusetts around 1790.

5

A pleasing mix of English and American furniture is shown in this house in Southport, Connecticut. The two corner chairs are English, c.1790, the tripod table is American and the wonderful paired Pembroke tables are from Baltimore. The mirror on the right is Queen Anne, the one on the left, American Federal.

6

An American interior decorated in turn-of-the-century style. The stunning drapes are not for drawing but for decoration only, their fanciful headings echoing swirls atop the mirror. Mahogany furniture looks magnificent against a background of neutral colour.

4

5

3

6

1

Furniture

The pattern books of Hepplewhite and Sheraton with their modified versions of Adam style were widely used by furniture makers in America. Frequently, elements from different books of design were merged together.

The United States had no great national centre of fashion and culture comparable with Paris in France and London in England. This resulted in furniture with widely different regional characteristics. The best painted and japanned pieces came from Baltimore; inlays in light wood and areas of painted glass are a feature of furniture from this area. Typical of New England was the Martha Washington, or lolling, chair, based on earlier French and English open armchairs.

New pieces at this period included the tambour desk, sometimes with a bookcase on top. Many new types of table and sideboard were being made.

Accessories

Shapes of silverware exhibited the straight sides and symmetrical curves of the Neo-classical style. In the Metropolitan Museum's American Wing a Federal tea service has the pieces in urn and helmet shapes with eagle finials. Candlesticks would be of simple column shapes. Presentation pieces were fashionable and again would usually be based on antique models.

The popular tableware designs of Wedgwood were imported from England. Trade with the East was now flourishing, enabling oriental porcelain in Neo-classical shapes made for the Western market to be a usual feature in an American Federal room.

Ornamental chandeliers and candelabra decorated with glass drops were imported from England to complement the formal style of decoration. Multi-branched candelabra frequently had cut and engraved glass shades.

2

3

4

1

This stencilled bedroom in the American Museum in Bath is an excellent example of the wall and furniture decoration popular in the early years of the 19thC. A journeyman artist would have painted this – arriving with his dry pigments and paper stencils, he would have mixed his paints with skimmed milk and decorated the house in exchange for board and lodging. The small chairs would have been bought from a "Yankee peddlar" who distributed goods from the back of a wagon. The canopy bedstead which dominates the room is authentically hung with handworked lace and dressed with an embroidered quilt.

2

Canopy bedsteads were popular well into the 19thC. Lace hangings give the bed a light and airy feeling, as do the simple country flowers and the plain white walls. The patchwork quilt is a distinctly American touch which can be copied using one of the excellent modern patchwork quilt kits.

3

This exceptional American walnut bed, c.1780, with drapes that accentuate its linear style blends perfectly with the pair of English mahogany commodes and the French lyre-back chair, all from the closing years of the 18thC.

4

This late 18thC canopy bed is in a lovely small country house in Connecticut. The simple country chest is c.1800, and the bench is a seat from a horse-drawn sleigh. The country feeling is unmistakable – polished boards, unlined curtains and a simple rug are all that is required to set the scene.

18THC COUNTRY

1

If you do not have the time or patience for ragging or dragging your walls, you can use one of the many ragged, dragged or sponged-effect wallpapers. This one is by Osborne and Little. The plain floor boards and painted furniture all add to the country feel. The old coffer was repainted in a naive style in the early 20thC. As a general rule, don't ever strip any furniture with original paintwork, just enjoy its lived-in looks. The chair in the foreground is late 18thC French provincial.

1

2

2

Broken paint finishes are an important part of any early country style. The two-tone vanilla sponged effect, which here extends over walls, doors and architraves, produces a suitably faded appearance. Bare polished boards are perfect for this style.

3

An early country kitchen is no place for fitted units, but this practical arrangement is a good compromise. These dresser-type units have been cleverly distressed with a streaked paint finish that complements the walls. The country mood is further reinforced by rustic antiques.

In country and provincial districts, styles in furniture and decoration were more informal than in cities. Even when urban fashions filtered through to country areas, they tended to appear in a more robust form than originally. Change for fashion's sake was not common. Wood panelling, for example, remained popular in the country long after it had lost favour in town. Furniture was chunkier and sturdier with less refined decoration, in keeping with a more rustic setting. Shapes originally intended to be made in walnut or mahogany might well be translated into oak.

In general, the 18th-century country style followed the basic principles of symmetry and balance of the Georgian interior, but the whole feeling was more mellow, more lived-in, more rustic.

Walls and ceilings

Drawing rooms and dining rooms of the grander country dwellings were generally lined with wood panelling which was sometimes painted in pale, sunny, country colours. Other rooms would have limewashed walls of brick or stone or rough plasterwork and exposed beams — just as in country cottages.

Floors

Humble homes, and the humbler rooms of larger homes, would have floors of stone or tiles, or polished wooden boards strewn with rag rugs, rush matting or painted floorcloths. Grand drawing rooms would be carpeted with maybe the addition of an oriental rug.

Windows

Again, simplicity was the keynote here. In winter, thick fabrics which kept out both light and chilly draughts hung from wooden poles, alternated in the summer months with lightweight linens.

Furniture

Of course, some of the fine furniture of the Georgian period found its way into grand country homes, but in general provincial centres were making robust and simple variations on forms that were more appropriate to country life. Typical of the 18th-century country interior are the provincial ladderback chair and the simple oak sideboard.

The early years of the century saw the advent of one of the most useful pieces of furniture ever devised — the kitchen dresser.

FLOUR

1

1 and 2

Two views of the same room in which good late 18thC/early 19thC furniture is accentuated with appropriate fabrics, rush matting and plain walls. The door curtain gives the room a cosy feeling and also cuts down draughts. Around the inglenook fireplace bare bricks add to the atmosphere, and the ladderback chairs with tie-on cushions look invitingly comfortable. Originally, a log fire would have crackled in the open hearth. The wood-burning stove is a 19thC invention: modern, efficient copies are virtually indistinguishable from the real thing.

2

3

4

5

3

Fitted kitchen dressers convey an immediate sense of period. The benches and simple plank-top table add to this effect. The butcher's block is perfectly in keeping and combines country style with practicality. The look is simple – bare boards, stripped pine and an interesting use of colour. Wild flowers and weeds in simple containers complete the picture.

4

An inviting breakfast room with a distinctive 18thC feel benefits from the warmth and practicality of a modern Aga cooker backed by a collection of period tiles. Early tiles can still be bought quite inexpensively in odd lots at auction sales. Collections of kitchen-related items such as pots, kettles or jugs will give such rooms visual focus.

5

This is the scullery of the room shown in picture 4. Its practical pine units are shown off against a patterned terracotta wallpaper, and pine shelving displays collections of blue-and-white porcelain and pottery. Old ladderback chairs can be bought singly and painted and stencilled to make them look like an old and matching set.

1

An early country atmosphere has been created in this modern kitchen by a clever use of old pine and simple uncluttered lines. The chair, which is French, actually dates from the mid-19thC as does the Dutch painted table, but their simple forms make them look much earlier.

2

Dressers are actually very practical, providing worktop space and plenty of storage. Although they look bulky, they don't take up a large amount of space, as they are wide and tall rather than deep.

3

This airy kitchen has been given an 18thC feeling by the matt creamy paintwork, stripped pine and polished floorboards. The terracotta colour makes the chimney breast a focal point.

1

4 – 7

These kitchens would fit happily into an 18th or 19thC period home, and still meet the requirements of a 20thC cook. In picture 4 the ladderback beech chairs and the sturdy pine dresser make for a strong early feel. The colourful pottery collection in 5 is Victorian. The early 19thC French provincial pine armoire in 6 displays a collection of modern pottery based on early designs. This piece, with the check wallpaper and the slate floor, evoke the no-nonsense solidity of the period country style. In 7 the Pennsylvania "Dutch" chairs and dresser in the American Museum in Bath show how the Americans' imaginative use of colour transformed these traditional shapes. The painted tole ware on the dresser features scenes from the New World. These strong earth colours are a valid alternative to the pale faded look of the English country kitchen.

2

3

4

6

5

7

1

Colonial style and English 18thC country style have many features in common: simple rustic furniture, usually made of oak, yew or fruitwood; an absence of clutter; simple panelling; open fireplaces; and plain wall finishes. One of the differences lies in the palette of colours the Americans were using: strong matt "earthy" colours, while certainly found in Europe at this time, became a key feature of the American Colonial home. Note the locally made decoy ducks and the way in which the stone hearth meets the floorboards.

1

2

Strong earthy colours are set off by a roughly plastered whitewashed wall. This looks very effective here because the rough plasterwork is obviously deliberate – unless done with conviction, this effect might give the impression that the decorators were due back next week. This room has four doors, each painted a different, but complementary colour on both sides.

By the early 18th century, America had begun to find its feet as a nation, and this self-confidence, this sense of a national identity no longer dependent on the old world, found expression in the American Colonial home. Interiors were now positively "American" in feeling – light, airy, uncluttered and colourful. There was pride in local craftsmanship, and although many furniture styles were based on English designs, the American interpretation was unmistakable. American flora and fauna found their way into textile and stencil designs and there was a growing market for home-grown artefacts and ornaments – for simple glazed pottery, carved wooden bowls, fine paintings and drawings by local artists. With scarcely a backward glance at Europe, America was setting a style that was all its own.

Walls

From about 1700 interior walls were plastered and painted. Some quite sophisticated panelling was also being used which might even be painted in flat colours – blue was a particular favourite – or even crudely marbellized.

Furniture

Rooms were uncluttered, this feeling was considerably helped by a fair amount of built-in storage. Fireplaces were often flanked by cupboards with doors that matched the panelling of the walls. There were corner cupboards for storing plates and display cabinets were quite common.

The furniture of this period was quite refined and beautifully crafted. Many pieces were made using English designs, generally after their English vogue had finished. These adopted styles were much simplified and varied considerably from one part of the country to another, depending on the woods that were locally available.

Typical chairs of the period were simple wooden armchairs, sometimes with upholstered seats, although a few fully upholstered wing chairs were to be seen. Slant-fronted desks and highboys were very popular, and were made in considerable numbers in American furniture workshops.

Floors

The simple plank floors of the early American home were now often stencilled or covered with painted floorcloths or rugs of woven flax.

Lighting

Chandeliers and oil lamps replaced tin sconces and simple candle holders of earlier times. Candlesticks were quite often made of brass, as were the fire implements and irons.

Windows and draperies

Most homes had shutters on the inside of windows, and often on the outside as well. In the very best rooms, simple curtains in plain fabrics were used – they were sometimes swagged, but never elaborately.

Beds were generally covered with quilts or simple coverlets, but in grand houses the master bed might be draped and covered in printed or embroidered fabric.

2

1

The success of this delightful house depends to a large degree upon the use of colour, a beautiful blue teamed up with a milky white. Walking through the house occasions a series of sensory surprises. Contrasting colours, interesting groupings of furniture and objects seen from different angles create an exciting environment. Attention to detail is an important factor, as always. A country house style demands a profusion of country flowers, not stiff, formal bouquets, and paintings should have a simple painted wooden frame or none at all.

1

2

Often the most powerful expressions of period style can be made in a very simple way. This strongly defined stairway has been painted in three tones of blue, and it nicely frames the magnificent early oak chair set against it. The oriental rug adds warmth and visual interest.

3

A wonderful object lesson in the use of colour. The exterior timber-clad walls and the door have been painted a surprising shade of purple – reminiscent of mulberries and cream – revealing inside a hallway of warm terracotta and glowing wood.

2

3

1

2

1

This kitchen achieves a period feeling without any sacrifice of modern convenience. The colour of the architraves, surrounds and practical modern units contrasts with the stark white of the walls and the open shelves. The stone sink with brass taps is a striking feature – both items can be obtained as modern reproductions.

2

The matt moss-green paint on the woodwork and corner cabinet here is a traditional type of paint with a milk base. Note that the interior of the open-shelved cabinet is painted a different colour – this is an authentic treatment. The doorway frames a perfect example of a mid-18thC Colonial dining room. The banister-back chairs are uniquely American. The balusters were first split – each one being therefore a half-round – and then the two halves were stuck together and turned as one piece. When the chair was assembled, the turned sides were placed on the outside of the chair-back, so that the inside was smooth, for sitting against.

3

This wonderful 18thC Rhode Island keeping room has been lovingly restored by Stephen Mack, whose knowledge and feel for period interiors has been developed by his work in dismantling and rebuilding period structures under threat of demolition. The room has many of the elements that help to create a warm country feel: the wide floor boards, the plain walls, the pottery, the 18thC country furniture, the wild flowers, the herbs hung up to dry, the wrought-iron cooking implements, the simple turned wood and wrought-iron chandelier. The 17thC Dutch painting is an interesting reminder that early colonists brought some of their treasured possessions with them. Note the white milk paint, flaking slightly, on the planked walls.

3

1

This is an uncluttered style. The simple, firm lines of the 18thC ladderback elbow chair are set off by the tasseled cream muslin summer drapes. The country look is reinforced by the natural wooden floor, the off-whites, and the terracotta-coloured panelling. The simple ceiling is nothing more elaborate than the underside of the floorboards and joists of the room above.

1

2

By keeping the walls stark white and bringing colour into the room via the painted woodwork and the wonderful 19thC quilt, this room has been made to appear larger than it actually is. The bed was designed to allow sea chests to fit under it, providing useful storage space. The basket in the window, now used for dirty washing, is an original feather basket in which down and feathers were collected for stuffing into mattresses and pillows.

3

Waking up to wonderful views is an added bonus for the owner of this Rhode Island home. The lack of curtains gives the bedroom a simple, country feeling. Of course, such an approach is feasible only where windows are not overlooked and are sufficiently well-fitting to keep out draughts. The slant-top desk dates from the 18thC and still boasts vestiges of its original red milk-painted finish. (Painted pieces are much more valuable if left alone, however tatty the paintwork.) The banister-back chair is also an 18thC original, as is the quilt over the luxurious feather bed.

2

3

Overleaf

1

The choice of paint is tremendously important in re-creating an 18thC Colonial home – the colonists had only natural dyes and pigments to work with, whereas modern paint technology is geared to perfect colour consistency and a perfect finish. This is a corner of an 18thC country bedroom, complete with open fireplace – a romantic addition to any bedroom.

2

These two sea chests provide excellent storage space while lending their rustic charm to the Colonial house. The rough-planked, white-painted wall is totally in keeping. It is interesting to glimpse through, on the right, to the much more sophisticated chest-on-chest, and on the left to the wonderful early stone sink and rich-coloured units in the kitchen. Notice how good the open shelves look in this context.

3

This 18thC blanket chest with its original paintwork is an excellent example of the delightfully unsophisticated furniture of mid-18thC North America. The contemporary hog-scraper candlestick and the later onion-type lantern all add to the air of New England simplicity.

4

Note the wonderful contrasting earthy colours here. The matt paintwork looks even better when scuffed with use.

5

Stark white paint throws coloured woodwork into relief and shows off the simple lines of 18thC furniture, artefacts and painting to good advantage. Here, the wooden floorboards are softened by a Persian rug, and at night the room is softly candlelit. This house is not entirely a period piece, as it is wired for electricity and the points have been cleverly cut into the floorboards – look carefully at the floor area under the leg of the little tripod table.

1

2

3

4

COLOURS These very simple, undecorated styles rely for their impact on the beautiful patina of old wood. Yellows, off-white, pale cream and vanilla would be suitable colours. A distressed look is definitely preferable to perfect finishes, and matt effects are more apt than gloss. Strong colours are not out of place – for example, pinky red or blue.

WALLS Dragged paint finishes, or sponged-effect wallpapers, are in keeping, emulating the coloured limewashes of the period. Around an open hearth, you could opt for an area of bare bricks or stones.

FLOORS Rush matting or bare wood floors with simple rugs (such as rag rugs) would convey the right mood. In the kitchen, you might opt for flagstones or plain rustic tiles.

FURNITURE Keep furniture simple; if you can't afford the real thing, modern furniture made from old pine is acceptable. Staple items of furniture would include simple chests of drawers, and Windsor and ladderback chairs. In the kitchen, dresser-type units should be chosen in preference to built-in units, and the table should be utilitarian bare wood – scratches and other marks will add to authenticity. Benches make an ideal companion to a kitchen table – or better still look for discarded church pews. Pieces with Rococo curves might work if sufficiently rustic in style.

LIGHTING Simple wrought-iron and wooden fittings can be found in present-day versions. Candlelight glittering on surfaces creates a suitably mellow atmosphere. Also of interest are tin lanterns with star-shaped holes, which give out a subdued but scintillating light.

WINDOWS Follow the contemporary practice of alternating between lightweight summer curtains (perhaps thin muslin) and heavier fabric in winter: of course, the heavier would not be necessary if you have shutters. Tassels may be used, but nothing too elaborate. An alternative choice would be simple blinds in a plain material – perhaps with subtle festoons.

BEDS Beds should be simple in style, although that does not preclude a modest form of hangings. Quilts are essential in bedrooms, adding a touch of colour and homeliness. Kits are now available for making your own quilts to historic designs. Alternatively, a random patchwork of colour and pattern will fit in well and will also contribute a perfectly authentic touch.

FINISHING TOUCHES Chests, fruit and wild flowers in baskets, bunches of herbs hung up to dry, naive paintings (particularly of animals), earthenware bowls and carved decoy ducks are just a few suggestions for accessories. Open-hearth fires should be furnished with all the accompanying paraphernalia – andirons, cranks and so on. A possible choice of music to conjure up an 18th-century country mood might include Handel's *Water Music Suites* and *Royal Fireworks Music* and Mozart's *Flute Concertos Nos. 1 and 2*.

1

1

The success of the beautiful home in Stonnington, Connecticut, shown in both pictures here, is due to the combination of sophistication and simplicity. Here, the rough-plastered walls, the polished floorboards and the simple chequered rug, are teamed with fine-quality 18thC American country furniture and an oil painting framed in simple style. The carved duck is an evocative accessory.

CREATING THE LOOK

2

2

This view shows the 18thC style at its most harmonious, with every element working towards the general ambience – light muslin drapes, simple 18th and 19thC country furniture, naive paintings in unadorned frames, rough walls, timber ceiling and pierced tin chandelier. The flowers reinforce the mood.

1

Led by an Englishwoman, Ann Lee, the Shakers were one of a number of Utopian sects which migrated to the New World. They arrived in 1774, and within a decade had established their central community in New Lebanon, New York. In their heyday, the first half of the 18th century, as many as 6,000 Shakers lived in communities as far west as Ohio.

The communal ideals of the Shakers led to a desire for uniformity of style throughout the many communities. Changes in living arrangements, even a decision as trivial as wearing braces rather than belts to support trousers, had to be approved by the central community at New Lebanon. Everything they *did* make and use, however, was of the highest quality. No kind of work was more valuable than any other, whether it was ploughing or weaving or making chairs. The Shaker creed exhorted each member to "put your hands to work your hearts to God." Work was a form of worship – the appearance of Shaker goods should be as pure and simple as Shaker prayers. Most Shaker goods reached their final design form between 1820 and 1850, when Shaker vitality and population were at their height.

The interiors of Shaker dwellings were kept light, plain and simple. Storage was often built-in, and the clever Shaker designs for walls of cupboards and smoothly-fitted drawers have never been bettered. Tables and benches were unadorned and beautifully proportioned; many ingenious serving and sewing counters, desks and chests of drawers held necessities for indoor work. Objects that might clutter the room – hats, cloaks, tools, chairs and clocks – were hung on pegboards high on the walls. Walls and furniture were often painted in cheerful shades of red, blue, green and yellow. Figured woods were sometimes used for furniture making, and chair seats were made of cane, wood splints or multi-coloured fabric tape.

The Shaker ladderback chair – harmonious and lightweight – is eloquent testimony of the sect's sensitivity to good design. This was widely appreciated. Until as late as the Second World War, many Shaker goods were sold nationwide by catalogue.

1

The Shakers made restrained use of subtle colour, as seen in this room. This bottle-green blanket box is topped by a trio of storage boxes. The Shakers piled their boxes in this way to remind themselves that life's purpose was to climb the "steps to heaven".

2

2

A yellow-painted 1840s ladderback chair is hung tidily away on a peg. The three-drawer chest, dating from the mid-19thC, is a typical Shaker piece, and the interesting-looking object sitting on the chest is a beautifully crafted bonnet block.

1

2

3

4

5

1

A naive country portrait of an inspiring Shaker elder in a maple frame is virtually the only ornament in this calm Shaker bedroom. The ladderback rocking chair is a typical Shaker piece, and the skirting board has been painstakingly painted with a feather in a faux marbre finish.

2

The "curly" or tiger maple ladderback side chair and tripod table date from c. 1850. The design of the candlestick was first seen c. 1750 and was still being produced in the 1920s. The sewing basket is mid-19thC. Note the wide planking and the soft but strong colours on the walls.

3

Tiger maple beds in the Shaker tradition sit well with the simple country surroundings of plain white walls and polished boards. This bedroom exudes an almost monastic calm and sense of order.

4

A later Shaker cupboard with its original red paintwork dates from c. 1870. The child's chair is a little earlier. Chair rails for hanging chairs well out of the way were a common feature of all Shaker homes – they made it easier to clear the room for prayer meetings.

5

This is an example of modern built-in cabinetmaking in the true Shaker tradition. It takes up a whole wall of the bedroom shown in pictures 1 and 3 – a place for everything and everything in its place.

1

1

This re-creation in the American Museum, Bath, shows the calm, spiritual feeling of a Shaker interior and the emphasis on furniture and objects that were stripped of ornament, made with patience and expertise – and spotlessly clean. The effect is impressively refined, in the spirit of Mother Ann Lee's exhortation to her followers: "do all you work as though you had a thousand years to live and as you would if you knew you must die tomorrow."

Shaker design can radiate a sense of refuge from the noise and overstimulation of everyday life. For this reason it is prized by collectors the world over. Shaker furniture is shown to best advantage in surroundings which, while not necessarily as ascetic as a Shaker community, aim for a tranquil purity.

COLOURS To emulate the Shaker style, colours should be clear and soft but never drab. White backgrounds will show off the purity of Shaker-style furniture, but a blue-grey colour also works well. Use accents of strong colour here and there – for example, the rich hues of natural timber. The grain of wood should be in evidence. Avoid brightly printed chintz, which will look incongruous.

CREATING THE LOOK

FLOORS Polished wood floors scattered with rag or hooked rugs will complement fine Shaker furniture.

WINDOWS Bare windows are the authentic choice. However, for privacy you might like to add a roller blind or simple white muslin drapes. Avoid pelmets or any kind of decorative trimmings.

FURNITURE Except for commercial items such as boxes and chairs, genuine Shaker antiques are extremely rare. Most are in museums or private collections. However, many modern craftspeople have adopted principles akin to those of the Shakers and are producing Shaker-style furniture of great beauty. Fine cabinetmakers can be found to make single pieces of furniture to order. On a less rarified plane, several furniture companies are reproducing Shaker designs in good materials at popular prices. Even the tradition of the Shaker catalogue persists – unfinished, handsome pieces of furniture may be bought assembled or in kit form to be made up at home.

FINISHING TOUCHES Beautiful utilitarian objects should be proudly displayed, rather than tucked away. A collection of treen would be very much in keeping. Wild flowers would be in sympathy with the general ambience. An antique stove in the main room, or a reproduction stove, will help to reinforce the mood. A chair rail with pegs, in the Shaker fashion, is a good method of storage and an interesting showcase for a collection of objects. Other styles of light, well-proportioned accessories, perhaps Scandinavian or oriental, might coexist well with Shaker designs, provided that they are in a suitable type of wood.

2

2

A Shaker chair from the 1850s made of tiger maple. The feet of the chair have small titler buttons for added support. These were normally made of wood but by the early 1850s the Shakers had patented the pewter titler button.

3

3

A serene, uncluttered Shaker bedroom. At the same time as the Shakers were sleeping in rooms like this, the Victorians were hemmed in by patterns upon patterns, drapes upon drapes, and a clutter of furniture. The rocking chair and rag rug date from c. 1830.

BAROQUE AND ROCOCO

1

The dynamic Baroque style developed in Italy but reached its most influential form in France under Louis XIV. Shells, acanthus leaves, volutes, garlands and scrolls were all used, as in Italy, but tempered with Classical restraint. In the reign of Louis XV the Baroque gave way to the more frivolous Rococo characterized by swirling, asymmetric forms. Both these styles, as well as the more severe Louis XVI style, were adapted enthusiastically in the later 19th century.

1

Styles from different countries of Europe can be mixed without disrupting the overall harmony. Here, an 18thC French marble fireplace is surmounted by a late 18thC mirror and flanked by Italian torchères that have been made into lampstands. The marble figure is ancient Roman.

2

A wider view of the same room reveals a good example of Classical influence combined with the flamboyant French taste of the period. This suite of 18thC French furniture still has its original covering. The wall-hung tapestry was produced by English weavers and embroiderers at the Mortlake workshop, c. 1700.

2

1

This dining room, cleverly created in a hallway, makes excellent use of mirrors and drapes. Note how the drapes look all the more opulent for lying in swathes upon the floor. The strongest influence in this room is the set of 17thC Venetian chairs, abetted by the Fortuny fabric on the wall in wonderful shades of green and gold. (There is a very good equivalent in the Laura Ashley Designer Collection.) The light fittings are Italian – the Italians have always produced stylish chandeliers and candelabra, and still produce good copies.

2

18thC Continental taste is here epitomized by the window dressing, the Venetian glassware, the decorative flower painting on the panels and the massive Classical urn. The little topiaries are a whimsical touch, bringing with them a reminder of the beautiful garden beyond the window.

1

LOUIS XIV, 1643-1715

Several figures are important in the development of the Louis XIV style. The first was the King, who from the time he actually took control in 1661 showed a close interest in the decoration and furnishing of his palaces. The second figure was his minister Colbert who set up the Manufacture Royale des Gobelins to provide all the decoration and furnishings for the royal residences. The third influence was the designer and painter Charles Le Brun, the first director of the Gobelins. Versailles became the centre of court life and here Le Brun created a grand and opulent setting to reflect Louis' power and prestige.

Louis XIV Baroque is typified by rich, rather sombre colours and heavy forms. Early on, only the most costly materials were used for furniture, and many pieces were made in solid silver. Alternatively, heavily carved and gilded wood was chosen. From around 1683 the style became less heavy. About this time there was a financial crisis, and the silver furniture was melted down and replaced by Oriental lacquer and finely veneered furniture, intricately inlaid with tortoiseshell and brass. The craftsmen who carried out this work were known as ébénistes, and the greatest of them was André-Charles Boulle.

RÉGENCE AND LOUIS XV, 1715-74

During the last few years of Louis XIV's reign there was a move away from the Baroque grandeur and formality that had been so much a feature of his court, toward a lighter style of decoration which was to be influential throughout Europe. Under the regency of the duc d'Orleans this trend accelerated. The *Régence*, or Early Rococo period (1710-30), is a time of transition between the solemn Louis XIV style and the full-blown Rococo of the Louis XV style.

Rococo was all about pleasure, and decorative motifs and themes reflect this – love making, music, the countryside. Humour was another key element. Motifs included chinoiserie, turquerie and singerie (monkeys in human dress), often deployed to mildly comic effect.

Women, especially the witty and talented Madame de Pompadour, were playing an increasingly important role in social life at this time. Female influence was reflected in a more intimate, informal approach to design. Rooms became smaller; hence, smaller pieces of furniture were needed. Mirrors played a large part in these Rococo interiors. As well as the mirror over the fireplace there would frequently be matching pier glasses over console tables. Mirror glass might be used to screen a fireplace in summer, as well as on window-shutters: these were concealed during the day and slid across the windows at night. So many reflective surfaces gave a spacious airy look to rooms and made the most of the available light. To add to the effect, candelabra might be an integral part of the mirror frame. Bracket clocks, decorated with ormolu and Meissen figures, were a feature of many rooms, and the animal tapestries of Oudry were very popular. The paintings of Jean Antoine Watteau and works by François Boucher typify the spirit of the age.

2

1

2

1

A mixture of pieces of different nationalities looks unified against a plain, uncluttered background. The 18thC Swedish commode is surmounted by an 18thC oil painting by Karl van Loo and framed by 18thC French chairs with old tapestry cushions. The porcelain on the commode is 18thC Chinese export porcelain, which was produced in designs more elaborate than those preferred by the Chinese themselves.

2

French 18thC furniture is generally beautiful, expensive and fascinating to collect – most good pieces are signed by the ébéniste. This wonderful 18thC French commode was obviously made by a modest ébéniste as it has no signature, but it is undoubtedly of top quality. The chair is by Georges Jacob (1739-1814) who was the leading French cabinetmaker working in the Neo-classical style in the years preceding the French Revolution.

3, 4 and 5

The owners of this New York apartment are serious collectors of 18thC French furniture, paintings and porcelain. The wall colour has been matched to the ground colour of a pair of rose Pompadour cupids elsewhere in the room. The carpet is an 18thC Tabriz which is perfectly in keeping with the Continental look, as is the imported marble fireplace. More modern is the Monet in picture 3 – and the view from the picture windows.

Cabinet furniture of this period is characterized by fine veneers and ormolu mounts. There were several new types of commode, including the *encoignure*, a type accommodated in a corner cupboard and generally used in pairs, and the commode en tombeau, or *à la Régence*, which had three drawers, one above the other, and short legs.

Chairs with caned seats and backs came into fashion, usually with tie-on squab cushions shaped to fit seat and back. These chairs were made with and without arms, were curvilinear in form and had wide seats designed for comfort. There was also a new style of more comfortable upholstered chair: typical of the *Régence*, it had an exposed frame of carved wood and cabriole legs, strengthened with stretchers.

LOUIS XVI (1774-1785)

Even before the end of Louis XV's reign there was a reaction in France, as elsewhere in Europe, against the frivolity of the Rococo. This resulted in a backward look to the grandeur of Louis XIV's reign and a revival of interest in the Classical world. Furniture shapes became more severe – for example, the bombe shape popular in the Rococo became flattened, and curving legs were replaced with straight, tapering ones. Decorations changed too: the writhing, asymmetric designs disappeared, replaced by Classically inspired motifs. Pieces were sometimes decorated with porcelain plaques.

Porcelain and silver acquired the more restrained shapes and decorations inspired by the ancient world. The paintings of Jacques Louis David on improving subjects such as *The Oath of the Horatii* were more appropriate to this style than the light-hearted works of Watteau.

19TH-CENTURY ADAPTATIONS

Domestic interiors of the 19th century were deeply affected by a spirit of nostalgic revivalism. Inevitably, and especially in France, fashionable designers were drawn to the lavish furnishings of the age of the Sun King and his successors. Throughout the century there was a strong leaning toward Classicism of one sort or another, and this could be Grecian, Renaissance, Louis IV-Baroque, or Neo-classical.

From the 1830s the most popular style was the Rococo, or Louis XV. Louis XIV also remained fashionable and the two styles, which should have been quite distinct, often became confused – even in France! Around 1860 these idioms were joined by another Louis style – Louis XVI – which frequently added to the confusion. Decorating in the various Louis styles involved using a fair amount of gilding. Gilt mouldings made from papier mâché or plaster-of-paris, in designs to suit the particular style of the room, were fashionable. These richly decorated Louis styles were expensive and therefore available only to the better off. They were taken up by the wealthy throughout Continental Europe and in England.

On the whole, fashionable French houses were less over-full and cluttered than English ones, although the same type of rounded, deeply padded and sprung furniture was popular. The typical fat, comfortable,

3

4

5

often ugly chair of the day was irreverently known as a *crapaud* (toad).

Wallpaper began to be mass-produced in the 1840s, and by the 1860s it was normal for most rooms to be papered. Designs ranged from the simplest of printed patterns, through to "satin papers", which had a shiny surface, and flocks. The most luxurious were the wonderful scenic wallpapers – the French led the field in the manufacture of these.

Parquet flooring, topped by a carpet, was very fashionable.

The French were considered by a contemporary writer on the subject to "have the best taste in the management of curtains". There were numerous, elaborate methods of draping windows in keeping with the various styles of decoration. These frequently involved elaborate pelmets and cornice decoration. A very simple type of window treatment, which would probably be more acceptable today, was to hang a pair of curtains from an elaborate pole and loop up the sides.

1 and 2

Drapery can make a very strong statement in a room. In picture 1, the generously bunched curtains have a strong Classical feel about them, helped along by the painted and gilt furniture. In picture 2 the interest is focused on the sunburst tiebacks and the plain fabric leading through to a pattern. Generous swathes of curtaining need not be made of expensive fabrics – choose artist's canvas, muslin or lining material, but opt for lots of it.

2

1

3

This room is dominated by a Renaissance figure in carved wood and given extra drama by the clever use of mirrors – large mirrors were typical of this era, as was the placing of sconces (these are Louis XVI) on mirrors to double their effectiveness. Note how the wing chairs and the gilt wood chair blend well with the neutral-coloured modern sofa.

4

The Gilt Room at Chilston Park Hotel, Kent, has been created using 19thC copies of earlier French furniture. The fabrics, which are totally in keeping with the gilt wood furniture, are modern copies of traditional designs. Notice the height of the bed – most early four-posters were this high, and the occupants needed a four-poster stool, like a small set of steps, to climb into bed.

5

A Venetian bed dating from 1810 is swathed in a bedspread of approximately Venetian hues. The chairs, which are Florentine, date from 1780.

6

This very small bedroom has been given a dramatic treatment with bold drapery and interesting paint finishes. Note the Classical columns framing the door and the gilt curtain roses used as door handles.

3

4

5

6

1

2

3

4

1

This dramatic room gives a strong overall impression of French 19thC design with its mirrors, chairs and chandeliers. Key features are the festoon blinds, the massive Chinese vase lampstand and the collection of blackamoor figures.

2

Another view of the room shown in picture 1. The walls have been hand-painted with a marble-effect finish, and the gesso fittings conceal wall lights.

3

The unusual tablescape here displays a good collection of French 19thC gilt wood and gilt metal objects on an 18thC English gilt wood table.

4

Goods and chattels have been carted back and forth over national boundaries for centuries, so there is nothing unusual in this grouping of French Louis XVI-style gilt chairs, a 17thC painted Italian cassone and the Hispano-Moresque plate.

5

Flowers play an important role in the decoration of Kenneth Turner's living room. A floral artist, he understands how a profusion of flowers can set a mood, point up a colour scheme and perfume the air. A mass of lavender, like an indoor bush, fills the stone urn on the left. Also adding to the mood are the wonderful fabric on the chairs, the candles, the baskets, the dramatic busts and the bare floor.

1

This dramatic dining area is in fact a tiny lean-to off the kitchen. It has been given elegant proportions with mirrors and trellis work. The unmistakably Regency chairs are totally at home with the overall 19thC Continental feeling. The late 19thC gilded wood figures are copies of earlier styles, the table has been made from an Italian candle-stand, and the chandelier is a modern Italian copy. The floor is of vinyl tiles but laid in the classic black and white style popular from the 18thC.

2

A hallway in the grand late 18thC style has instant impact. The blackamoor figures are almost lifesize, the candelabra are extravagant and the marble-topped commode provides an exuberant centrepiece. The Zoffany wallpaper in two tones of yellow/gold provides a suitably grand background.

3

Here we have almost the same elements as in picture 2, but the feeling is much lighter, much less grand. All the pieces are later, 19thC examples, but the blackamoor figures still give an appropriately exotic feel.

4

The French pier table to the left of the fireplace here displays a wonderful example of the Rococo shell motif.

5

This fireplace is dominated by bronze groups, bronze and glass lustres and early 19thC fire implements. The shapes look very strong against the stark white background.

1

2

3

4

5

1

2

3

— 1 —

All the pictures on these two pages are of a classic William and Mary country house with a distinctly Continental air. The use of ornate drapes, Aubusson carpets on polished floorboards, Rococo furniture and indoor topiaries all add to the Baroque feel.

— 2 —

These Imari and Chinese blue and white plates are a typical wall decoration of the period. If you decide to emulate it, remember that the plates need not be in perfect condition – they could even be modern copies – but they should be arranged symmetrically. The proportions of 18thC rooms seem to demand symmetry, but if you do want to go against the grain you will not get away with a half-hearted attempt – it will have to be a very positive statement.

— 3 —

The two shades of yellow on the panelling provide a sunny background to 18thC English glassware displayed on a profusion of wall brackets. The series of modern flower paintings was commissioned by the owners and based on the flowers growing in the gardens – rather in the manner of an 18thC patron of the arts! The topiaries add a scent of box hedge and an intriguing inside/outside feel to this main drawing room.

— 4 —

The ornate Rococo settee, magnificent swagged curtains and massive Kang Hsi vases with covers flanked by topiary sentinels are saved from overkill by the plain polished floorboards and the plainly painted walls. The vases on wall brackets reinforce the mood.

4

1

2

1

A convincing 19thC Continental feel can be achieved by the acquisition of one good piece. This mid-18thC French Boulle bracket clock is an excellent example. It is based on a style created by André Charles Boulle (1642-1732), who was chief cabinetmaker to Louis XIV. Boulle work, as it is known, is brass and tortoiseshell inlaid into ebony in dense scrolling patterns. Most of the other items in the picture are 19thC French and are still relatively inexpensive to acquire at auction. The tiles on the wall are 19thC Chinese, and were bought for next to nothing in a job lot from a London sale room. The wall finish is a marbled paper by Colefax and Fowler.

2

The Aubusson carpet sets the scene in this main drawing room in Plas Teg, North Wales. The walls are covered in a pink and gold striped brocade and the stone fireplace is a 17thC original. The giltwood wall sconces and stool give a very French feel and are totally in keeping with the Regency sofas in satin and moire.

3

A Classical French cameo in a Park Avenue apartment. The 18thC French carved fruitwood marble-topped table is flanked by a pair of 18thC chairs. The engravings are originals from Versailles (well-framed and mounted copies would look just as good). On the table sits an 18thC sandstone urn. The whole grouping is perfectly set off by the pale cream walls.

3

1

2

1

A Continental cameo in a classic Regency house is created with a pair of 18thC Italian limewood folding chairs and an Italian specimen marble-topped table supported by gilded cherubs. (Specimen marble tables have tops inlaid with as many different types of marble as the maker could lay hands upon – they are surprisingly expensive at auction.)

2

A wonderful mix of styles in a beamed Sussex cottage. The Louis XV (mid-18thC) chairs – there are many good 19thC and 20thC reproductions of this type – are placed on an unostentatious carpet of sea-grass matting. A 19thC German painted coffer hides a tape deck and attendant paraphernalia, and Chinese baskets conceal the speakers.

4

3

3

An excellent collection of French 18th and 19thC furniture and a Chinese lacquer cabinet-on-stand is teamed up with collections of bronzes, gilt and wood to create a perfect 18thC Continental ambience, with a strong Chinese influence. Modern convenience and comfort are not forgotten: a modern sofa in neutral upholstery blends in perfectly, a coffee table has been created from cast gilt columns and plate glass, and the radiator has been cleverly and beautifully boxed in. In the foreground are the components of a typically French piece of furniture, the duchesse brise; this is a chaise, a chair and a stool which can be used separately or pushed together to make one piece.

4

This pleasantly light and airy room has discreet modern roller blinds at the window which supply the necessary privacy while allowing the shape of the window to be seen to good advantage. The burr walnut table in the foreground is Charles X. The French giltwood furniture was made in the 1920s in the Louis XV style.

1

You can create something of the feel of these rather grand styles by placing appropriate pieces of furniture – real or reproduction – in a setting that makes appropriate use of fabric and colour. All the Louis styles will take an immaculate finish but a look of faded charm is equally appropriate, especially on gilding. An effect of luxury is important to these styles, but this can often be created through judicious use of pattern and colour rather than expensive materials.

COLOURS Strong colours – dark rich reds, greens and blues – or more delicate pastel tones will work equally well: the choice is a matter of individual taste. The bright pastel colours of Sèvres porcelain have a place here – *bleu céleste* (turquoise), *jaune jonquille* (yellow) and *rose Pompadour* (rose pink). One possible approach is to confine strong colours to fabrics and accessories, leaving wall colours more subdued. For the later period, also suitable are colours associated with the Etruscan style – terracotta offset by cream or pale shades of blue or grey. White and gold rooms flatter the charming, rather whimsical furniture and *objets* of the Rococo style.

FABRICS Rich fabrics suit these styles – velvets, heavy silks, damasks. Woven designs of flowers, pastoral subjects and animals will blend well. Particularly for a Louis XVI mood, choose *toile de Jouys* fabrics, printed with a scene in a single colour on a white ground: these are available in modern reproduction. Consider using embroideries and tapestries, or modern fabrics in designs by Fortuny. Bed hangings, generous and ceremonious, are a vital ingredient.

FURNITURE The two basic options are, on the one hand, the rectilinear veneered style; and, on the other hand, the more extravagant bombe shapes associated with Louis XV. The styles can be mixed for a more eclectic look. Imaginative versions of Baroque and Rococo furniture were made in the 19th century, and such pieces can still be acquired inexpensively. Gilded or painted pieces are appropriate to the look, although for a provincial version of Baroque or Rococo you might choose furniture in natural woods.

WINDOWS Window treatments should be relatively elaborate, with swags, drapes and pelmets. Remember that formality is not necessarily inconsistent with softness. Asymmetrical curtain arrangements are appropriate to the Rococo or Neo-Rococo mood. A Regency or Empire window treatment would also blend in well with these styles.

FINISHING TOUCHES Porcelain vases displayed on wall brackets will reinforce the mood. Ornate mirrors also help, and will spread the light from candles. Classical trappings (for example, busts) are in keeping, as are paintings (especially portraits) in elaborate gilt frames, or perhaps architectural drawings. Oriental touches will complete the picture – for example, a luxurious Chinese carpet, and some choice pieces of blue and white china. Roses, in quite formal arrangements, would be the obvious choice of flowers. Appropriate music for these romantic styles might include: Fauré's *Pavanne for Orchestra*, Debussy's *Clair de Lune*, Chopin's *Ballades, Preludes and Nocturnes* and Johann Strauss II's *Viennese Waltzes*.

CREATING THE LOOK

2

1

Drama and exuberance are the keynote of this style. Here, even the walls have impact with their strongly streaked finish, and the tablecloth cascades generously to the floor. Note the size and placement of the urns and candlesticks – timid gestures have no place in such a scheme.

2

The feeling of an 18thC European interior is captured here in the inspired choice of fabrics. Hannerle Dehn, who designed the room, has hand-painted many of the fabrics herself. Elsewhere in the room is a stool that has retained its original 17thC fabric, but such finds are increasingly rare. Note the dramatic effect of the flower arrangements, and the Classical busts on pedestals which always fit well into this period.

REGENCY, EMPIRE AND BIEDERMEIER

1

This is a perfect Regency cameo created in an alcove off a passageway. All the elements are here – the gilded leg of the console table, the black cast sphinxes, the simple urn with white flowers, and the unmistakable lines of a standard Regency chair. The whole arrangement has a distinctly Classical feel.

1

2

The plain walls here serve to accentuate the strong lines of the Swedish Empire style. All Empire styles have a lot in common and therefore they mix together well. This console table is Swedish, c.1820, and the portrait is of the Swedish King Carl Johan XIV – in Sweden this style is often referred to as the Carl Johan style. The pair of sphinxes is in period, as is the Italian sarcophagus on the table – a souvenir from a Grand Tour long ago.

Life in the English Regency period, which in its broadest sense stretched from the late 1790s until the late 1830s, was more intimate and informal than previously. Rooms, often with a bay window, were smaller and had lower ceilings, and the arrangement of furniture was much more casual. Instead of being ranged around the room, pieces were grouped close to the fireplace. Family and friends would gather around a circular table to talk or play cards. Interiors were much better lit than before: the new, efficient oil lamps enabled several people to share a table for reading or writing.

Regency rooms were on the whole light and graceful with fairly plain walls in a clear pale colour. There would be a narrow frieze, and the ceiling was usually plain or decorated with a small central garland with a chandelier hanging from it. Fabric was used in abundance – swathed and draped over pelmets and sometimes festooned between the legs of chairs.

Regency taste had turned away from the late Adam style and the spindly elegance of Hepplewhite furniture. A new late Neo-classical manner was in vogue. This placed the emphasis on a much stricter Classicism of form and shape rather than on mere ornament – as had been the case with Adam. Late Neo-classicism had much in common with the French Empire style which existed alongside it.The major influences were the civilizations of Ancient Greece and Egypt. Furniture based on ancient models was rather heavy and solid-looking – although the typical Regency chair with sabre legs, based on the *klismos* depicted on many Greek vases, is very graceful.

As in France, the rage was for Egyptian motifs, inspired by Napoleon's Egyptian campaigns. This influence was manifest in table supports in the shape of winged lions, monopods and sphinxes and in motifs such as palmettes, lion-masks and paws, scarabs, obelisks and even crocodiles.

Two non-Classical styles – chinoiserie and Gothick – were to a lesser extent enjoying a popular revival at this time.

Walls

Paint The large plain surfaces were frequently painted a single colour and might then be decorated with a discreet repeat pattern, either stencilled or painted freehand.

Very much a feature of the Regency is the *faux* finish – a painted surface imitating marble, wood grain, bronze or porphyry. This might be used on furniture as well as woodwork, fire surrounds and the like.

Textiles Walls might have fabric stretched over them – silk damask, lustring (glazed taffeta), tabouret (half-silk in a plain colour) or wool. Rooms sometimes had fabric draped from the ceiling, like a tent.

Windows

An abundance of drapery – sometimes elaborately looped and swagged and heavy with fringes – decorated the tops of windows, usually over embroidered sub-curtains. Where several windows were grouped together along a wall, one continuous drapery would be festooned along the top. After 1819 fabrics were lighter, and designs more fanciful – many of them printed. Flowered chintz was popular.

1

Floors

The same types of flooring were used as in the Georgian period. Carpet was even more fashionable than before: popular patterns included hexagons and florals. Brussels weave, woven like Wilton but with looped instead of cut pile, was an innovation.

Furniture

Although mahogany was still popular, it is rosewood that typifies the Regency. Other woods used for veneers were maple and the more

1

All the pictures on these two pages are from Plas Teg, a striking Jacobean stately home in North Wales. Here, a strong Regency feel is conveyed by George IV gilded chairs covered in satin and moire – and helped, of course, by the pedestal table and the striped brocade on the walls.

2

The beautiful lines of a classic Regency chaise longue set the scene in this sitting room. The carpet is a priceless Aubusson – a fragile and rare piece that not many people would wish to walk upon – but a less expensive later carpet would blend in well. Lighting is always a problem in a period interior, but here the appropriate soft glow has been achieved by wiring an alabaster urn with a simple bulb holder.

3

3

Regency and Empire interiors are typified by symmetry and Classical inspiration. This meticulously balanced arrangement makes good use of ornate candelabra.

exotic zebra wood. Ormolu decoration was replaced by inlay and galleries in brass.

The sofa table, in front of a sofa, was intended to hold books, tea things, sewing and so on. Like the Pembroke table, it had flaps, but it was larger and the flaps were on the short ends instead of the long sides. Sheraton quartetto tables, in nests, came into fashion, as did combined work-and-games tables. Round pedestal tables (loo tables) were popular.

Sideboards with flanking pedestals topped by urns, in the style introduced by Adam, were still seen, but more common was the bow-fronted type developed by Hepplewhite and Sheraton.

The chiffonier, which could be used instead of a sideboard, was new. It was a pedestal cupboard with a shelf or shelves behind a pair of doors; these might be of solid wood or they might have centre panels filled with brass wire backed by pleated silk.

On chairs with two or more backrails the top one was sometimes carved to resemble rope. Such "Trafalgar" chairs are said to have been a compliment to Nelson.

A more informal lifestyle resulted in more comfortably upholstered chairs. Rooms, except for dining rooms, were arranged for conversation in groups.

Lighting

Wax candles continued to be widely used, and *torchères* were very fashionable. The new designs of oil lamp had a significant effect on daily life.

Accessories

Plant stands reflected the fashion for enjoying flowering plants indoors.

Over the fireplace, a large oblong mirror was preferred to a picture. Another popular style was the round mirror surmounted by an eagle.

1

2

3

4

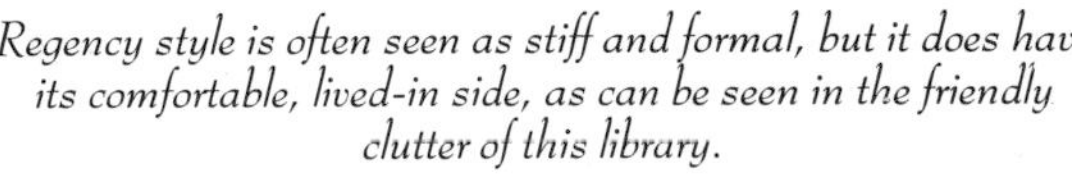

1

An ebonized Regency console table – with the requisite urns and candelabra – surmounted by a massive gilt mirror.

2

A bedroom in Plas Teg, North Wales, which has exceptional marquetry panelling with inset mirrors. In front of the mirror stands a pair of Regency chairs and a games table.

3

Regency style is often seen as stiff and formal, but it does have its comfortable, lived-in side, as can be seen in the friendly clutter of this library.

4

A Regency ebonized chair and table in a wonderfully warm setting created by marquetry panelling.

5

Another view of the library shown in picture 3 reveals a sensational late 18thC desk and an incredible Egyptianesque chair. Both are slightly battered and distressed; nevertheless they demonstrate the superb workmanship and design of Regency furniture and the tremendous interest in all things Classical.

5

1

2

1

This small dining room in a terraced cottage in Kings Road, London, has all the elements of Regency style: the typical convex mirror of the period, the side cabinet with a pair of cornucopiae, the elegant table and chairs and the "marble" floor – effective even though made from vinyl sheeting.

2

This was a period of opulence and grand style, so you should not be afraid to use interesting colours and extravagant drapes. Large Persian carpets on polished boards are more authentic than wall-to-wall Wilton. The fireplace in this room owes its dramatic effect to a marbled paint finish – marbelling is not difficult, it just requires patience and a good book on the subject. The porcelain on the tea table is authentic early and mid 19thC, which can still be found quite inexpensively in job lots in country sale rooms.

3

Regency style comes into its own in large, grand spaces. The strong lines so typical of Regency furniture are particularly suited to rooms that boast high, decorated ceilings, impressive columns and mouldings. This grand dining area, once a hallway, is notable for a symmetrical arrangement of superb elements – an original double pedestal dining-table and chairs (with two carvers), a niche displaying fine porcelain and intricate wallpaper whose stripes emphasize the room's proportions.

4

A formal Regency setting is here given a leafy, country feeling chiefly by the choice of wall colour and curtain fabric. This room has a Classical Georgian symmetry about it – a foil for the beautiful chairs which are perfect examples of their type, with their exuberant scrolling arms and wide sabre legs in the characteristic style.

3

4

1

2

1

This room in Parham House near Pulborough in West Sussex was given its present cream and gold decoration at the end of the 18thC. The marble relief on the fireplace, the French Empire clock in a partly bronzed ormolu case and the reflected pillars all show the period's fascination with Classicism.

2

A Regency mood can be created by judicious use of black paired with either gold or yellow. The period also saw the introduction of many fine mirrors, either in the form shown here or the very typical convex mirror with gilt frame, adorned with an eagle or other decorative theme.

3

4

5

6

7

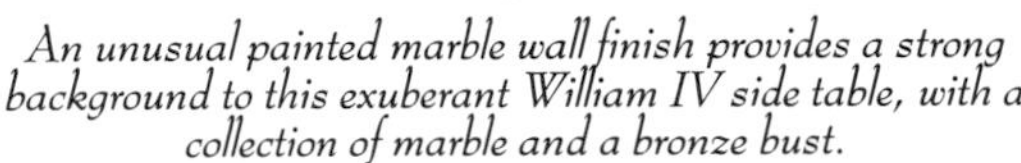

3

An unusual painted marble wall finish provides a strong background to this exuberant William IV side table, with a collection of marble and a bronze bust.

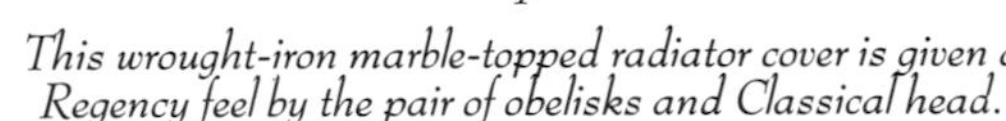

4

This wrought-iron marble-topped radiator cover is given a Regency feel by the pair of obelisks and Classical head.

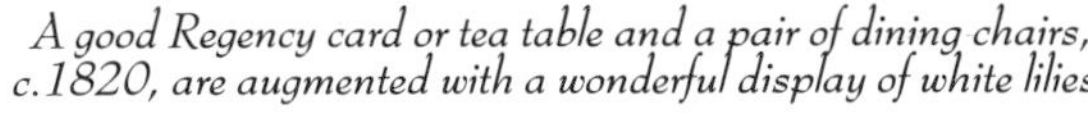

5

A good Regency card or tea table and a pair of dining chairs, c.1820, are augmented with a wonderful display of white lilies.

6

These marvellous black and gilt Regency chairs set the scene in a hallway with faux marbre blocks on the wall and an imitation black and white marble floor.

7

A collection of 19thC treen (turned wooden items) sits on a Regency tea table, making an evocative composition.

The French Empire style which arose in France in the 1790s has been described as Napoleon's propaganda vehicle. Fashionable throughout Europe, the style is typified by interiors luxuriously draped with brilliant-coloured silk, rather like grand military tents, and furnished with rather massive plain-shaped pieces of furniture generously decorated with ormolu and gilt.

In France, as in England, this was a Classical period. There are, however, other strong influences on Empire style. A note of antique grandeur was overlaid with motifs celebrating Napoleon's military prowess. Egyptian motifs became important after his campaigns in Egypt. Decorations included the sphinx and winged lion, Greek caryatids, the swan (Josephine's emblem was the black swan) and the Imperial eagle. Other motifs include stars, palmettes, lotus flowers, medallions, trophies of arms, and the Napoleonic bee.

Walls

Fabric Walls were frequently hung with plain or simply patterned silk; popular colours were bright yellow, brilliant green and crimson. Fabric was sometimes peated onto the walls but usually was draped in a tent-like fashion. The join between walls an tented ceiling might be covered with a pennant-shaped pelmet.

Wallpaper France made the best wallpapers at this time, often designed to imitate fabric. Designs to match curtaining and upholstery fabric were quite usual. Strips of paper, made to look like furnishing borders, were often pasted around the room.

Scenic papers, showing views of cities – Paris, London, Constantinople – and illustrations from literature, were very fashionable.

Dados and chair rails were usual, although in tented rooms they would be hidden by swathes of fabric.

Windows

Pull-up curtains were not fashionable at this time. Instead, pairs of curtains, often muslin, would be topped with elaborately swathed, silk draperies, fixed permanently in position. Sometimes a plain blind matching the silk drapery could be pulled down behind.

Furniture

Furniture shapes were basically simple and geometric, usually adapted from antique designs, often incorporating a sphinx, Josephine's swan, winged lion or caryatid. The Napoleonic Wars made it difficult to obtain exotic rosewood and mahogany; instead, furniture makers used native woods such as burr maple, beech and walnut.

Sabre legs were used on many chairs, and there were stools based on the Roman folding stool. The use of animal forms for furniture legs, borrowed from Ancient Egypt, was common on console tables, gueridons (circular candlestands on a plinth) and so on. Day-beds might be single-ended *chaises longues* or have high backs in subtly varying styles.

Lighting

The new oil lamps were a flexible and efficient form of lighting, but wax candles were still preferred in elegant society, especially for grand occasions.

Accessories

The Sèvres factory had developed a formula for hard-paste porcelain. This was decorated with rich colours, often with touches of gold; sometimes pieces had blobs of enamel to represent gems. Shapes were based on Greek, Roman and Egyptian precedents or on cylinders and spheres.

The finest metalwork was by Pierre-Philippe Thomire. He made bronze mounts for fine furniture, clock cases for Sèvres, large urns delicately modelled with foliage and figures, and candelabra.

1

This room in a flat in central London has a strong French and Swedish Empire feel to it – styles closely linked to the English Regency look but with their own peculiarities. The sofa is Swedish, c.1810. The armchairs from the same period are French: they are inlaid with gilt decoration and are covered in a French silk fabric with a very formal air. The curtain fabric is a design called the "Napoleonic Bee" which is still available in ivory, green, red and bright blue. The commode on the right is French, c.1810, as is the chandelier.

2

These classic Regency black and gilt pieces give a modern bathroom an early 19thC flavour. It is not advisable to place an antique too close to a working radiator – firstly it diminishes the amount of heat produced and secondly it could seriously damage the piece, by destroying glue in the joints, raising the veneer and cracking surfaces.

3

Exquisite black and gilt Regency pieces such as these, with their fine delicate lines, bring a sense of period to a more modern setting of a marbled wall with faux bois skirting.

2

3

1

1 and 2

Here and on the next few pages we see the epitome of the American Empire style in Richard Jenrette's house on the Hudson River in New York State. Every effort has been made to recreate this exceptional house as it once was, replacing all the original pieces of furniture: this has involved Mr Jenrette in years of research and travel to other continents. All the furniture is American and was made between 1800 and 1820, much of it for the Livingstone family who once owned the property. The sense of perfect Classical proportion is everywhere, accentuated by urns and busts (picture 2). The octagonal study (1) has walls that have been painted to resemble stone, and a strongly patterned carpet, specially designed to recapture the opulent lines of the period.

2

The American version of the Empire style succeeded the lighter and more delicate Neo-classical interiors of the Federal period after about 1810. Gradually American Empire developed into the Greek Revival style, which flourished from about 1820 to 1840.

The shift toward greater opulence came first with furniture. The delicate lines inspired by Hepplewhite and early Sheraton designs were replaced by more massive shapes. Pieces were often ornately carved and decorated with gilt, brass inlay and ormolu.

As in Europe, ancient styles and decorative motifs – Greek, Roman and Egyptian – were taken as models and inspiration, but American designs stopped short of the extremes of elaboration sometimes found in Europe.

Early furniture was richly decorated with carving, gilt and ormolu. Later, less expensive painted or stencilled decoration became fashionable. In the last part of the period the rich carving and elaborate decoration disappeared, large expanses of beautifully figured mahogany or rosewood being considered decorative enough in themselves.

Two rooms in the Metropolitan Museum of Art's American Wing illustrate the early Empire and later Greek Revival styles.

The first room is set up for a card party. Decoration and furnishing are altogether richer and more imposing than in previous periods: the materials are mahogany, marble, electric-blue Chinese silk, gilt, ormolu and crystal glass. The mahogany chair and sofa shapes are based on the Roman *currule* stool with its x-shaped base; a pier table in rosewood, mahogany and marble has gilt swan supports terminating in dolphin feet at the front; and the card table is inlaid with various woods, including rosewood, and with brass, and has carved and gilded supports – the front one taking the form

1

2

of a winged female figure in a proud, heroic posture.

To add to the richness of the room, the upholstery fabric is glowing blue silk and the woodwork, including the cornice, is in mahogany. The Classical theme is continued with a marble fireplace, doorcase and window surround topped by a frieze and an Aubusson carpet with a design of hexagons and stylized flowers. Not in the least Classical, however, is the French scenic wallpaper, of a type very popular in the Federal period.

The second room represents a parlour of around 1835 and the whole decoration is in typical Greek Revival style. Plain plastered walls painted a creamy beige are offset by white Ionic columns, pilasters, doorcase, deep cornice and woodwork. The Brussels carpet completely covering the floor is a glowing dark red with a design in shades of gold. The parlour suite that furnishes the room is upholstered in red rep decorated with a gold centre medallion and border. All the furniture is of mahogany and in the late style; its broad simple curves are unadorned by carving or by ormolu. On the round table is the simplest and most discreet gilt decoration.

Lighting was more efficient by this period: the room contains a tall table oil lamp and a pair of double-branch Argand lamps. Both are classically inspired, the first with a column base, the second with oil reservoirs in the shape of Greek amphorae.

1

This upstairs landing in Richard Jenrette's house (see page 161) makes a perfect setting for a New York bookcase and an octagon table and chairs – all American pieces made between 1800 and 1820. The owner has ensured historical accuracy in every detail, down to the carpet runner on the stairs and the Persian rug on polished boards on the landing.

2

The early years of the 19thC are a particularly intersting period in the development of the American domestic interior, encompassing as they do American Empire, American Classical and Late Federal styles. Many of these influences are apparent in Richard Jenrette's house. In this hallway, as elsewhere in the house, he has achieved a wonderful feeling of unity – all the elements mesh together. The generous sweep of the staircase is emphasized by the deep green carpet and the decorative stair rods. The inlaid wooden floor is copied from a floor in the Tsar's Palace in Leningrad.

3

The stark white architraves and marble skirtings here are distinctly Classical, and lead the eye into the drawing room with its strongly patterned carpet. The mirrors are both excellent examples of early 19thC craftsmanship – the pier tables with mirrored bases are called "petticoat tables" because the ladies would check their hemlines before going out to make sure that not a hint of ankle was showing. Lilies are the perfect flower for this style of interior.

1

2

3

1

This is the dining room of Richard Jenrette's house. The furniture for this room was made mainly in New York. The chairs are by Duncan Phyfe, probably the most famous of all American furniture makers: he worked in New York producing designs based on Sheraton, English Regency and French Empire styles. The room has a Classical symmetry accentuated by the painted panels and arrangement of the pictures.

2

In the drawing room is an exceptional collection of Duncan Phyfe furniture re-upholstered in a fabric design called "Napoleonic Bee" – a French Empire pattern which is still being made today. Over the fireplace is a painting of George Washington, and the mantelpiece boasts a Washington clock.

3

Marbled walls make a perfect backdrop to beautiful late Federal furniture, characterized by its delicate lines and inlay work.

1

2

3

1

Alongside the formal Colonial styles of the early 19thC, a country version developed. Here, simple polished boards and white walls with strong matt colours on skirtings, architraves and doors make for a more relaxed way of life. The patchwork quilt partially covers an early 19thC daybed. The simple but effective drapes add colour and style.

2

A lovely country Colonial bedroom has as its centrepiece a good 19thC bed with its original quilt. At the window, summer drapes of unlined muslin make the most of light and air. The simple Queen Anne maple side chair is earlier – c.1760-90.

3

This Empire work table shows how the refined lines of Sheraton developed into more massive forms. The natural figuring of mahogany was by this stage considered decoration enough. Note how the below-dado panelling, the skirting, the fireplace, the architraves and the door are painted a single strong matt colour to contrast with the white above.

4

This guest bedroom in Richard Jenrette's house is decorated in its original colour scheme of deep mauve and yellow. This unusual combination sets off the fine Federal bed, Empire chest and the églomisé mirror typically surmounted by an eagle.

1

2

3

4

1

This hallway in a Park Avenue apartment in New York is given a dramatic Empire feel by the painted stone effect on the walls, the mahogany door with gilt detailing, the pair of early 19thC hall chairs, the Classically inspired painted floor and, of course, the alert pose of Filagree, the dalmatian.

2 and 3

This magnificent early 19thC American house in Connecticut has beautifully painted figured wood-effect panelling and black marble-effect skirting boards, which make a dramatic setting for a Biedermeier inlaid cupboard and a pair of matching side chairs with typical ebonized back splats. In front of the Classical-style fireplace, two Empire sofas face one another.

4

Glimpsed through the doorway here is an American Classical sofa dating from c.1835. Most of the elements are from approximately the same period, although they differ in stylistic influence. The sofa is flanked by a pair of Federal cherrywood candlestands, the lamp bases are Chinese export ware, the Regency pedestals in the hall are reproductions and the urn-shaped wooden containers on top of them are late 18thC English knife urns without tops.

1

2

3

4

1 – 3

All the photographs on these two pages are of Kenneth Hockin's tiny studio apartment in the Village, New York, which he has transformed into an Empire haven. The large chest (1) is really a transition piece between Empire, with its Ionic columns, and early Victorian. The mood is set by the obelisk, the Napoleonic prints and the Empire chair. Note the clever use of a colour accent on the picture rails. In picture 2, the wallscape of black and gilt has an unmistakable late American Empire feel. The American marble-topped console table by Joseph Meeks is laden with distinctly linear articles that accentuate the Empire theme – French Empire clock with obelisks, lamp and candlestand, flower vases and plant. The Regency convex mirror is given added style by a pair of tassels. The tub chair is William IV.

4

The dining room of the apartment is actually the hallway. The melon yellow walls were inspired by an American Empire room-set in a museum. The old pine cupboard was found discarded in the street. The glassware is American flint glass. Notice how the subject matter of the painting above the cupboard has been echoed by a real still life, and how much more effective two small vases of sweet peas are than one.

5

This view of Kenneth Hockin's studio apartment shows how a single strong visual image – in this case a portrait of Napoleon – can set a period scene. Helped by the miniatures around it and the little bedside cabinet piled with boxes, it totally dominates the bright, modern sofa.

COLOURS Strong bright colours are typical of this style – brilliant green, yellow or crimson, offset with gold.

WALLS A fairly simple treatment is appropriate, with large plain surfaces painted a single pale colour. You could add a border design – painted freehand or stencilled – with a simple Greek or Egyptian motif.

Hanging fabric on the wall loosely to create the effect of a luxurious tent is an appropriate strategy. Pictorial wallpapers are a good choice for an Empire-style room. Or choose a design that imitates fabric – edged with braid, this would give a tented feel to the room.

FURNITURE The heavier, rather grand pieces are expensive. Fortunately, sabre-legged chairs, bow-fronted sideboards and drum tables are also typical of the time. Originals of these designs are more affordable, and good reproductions are available.

Day beds are typical of this style; they were made in a wide variety of designs. Hang fabric from a corona above a double-ended daybed to create a tent-like impression.

LIGHTING Oil lamps – as wall lights, pendants and table lamps – were available, so there is a wide choice of fittings to choose from. Rooms were more brightly lit but did not approach present-day levels of illumination; so keep background levels low and concentrate on creating pools of light.

FLOORS Large carpets in rich colours with rather stylized repeat motifs of laurel wreaths, hexagons and the circular designs known as paterae would suit a Regency or Empire room.

SOFT FURNISHINGS Pairs of lightweight curtains in a simple muslin are right for this era, but top them with grand, elaborately looped swags decorated with imposing fringing. Behind the curtains you might like to have a plain roller blind in the same fabric as the pelmet. Where there are several windows close together, continue the drapery across the whole series. Damasks and plain silks are suitable, as are designs with stylized laurel wreaths, swans and the Napoleonic bee. Flowered chintz is a correct choice for a late Regency room. However, avoid the strong contrast of "Regency stripes", as these are a fashion of the 1950s: much more in keeping are self-coloured fabrics woven with alternate matt and shiny stripes.

ORNAMENTS Gilded mirrors sound the appropriate note. A rectangular mirror over a fireplace is authentic for the time. Ornaments in the shape of obelisks or sphinxes help to set the scene. Porcelain and pottery richly decorated with colour and gilding, but with rather severe Neo-classical shapes, suit this style.

FINISHING TOUCHES A witty and much less expensive alternative to a large carpet is to paint a design directly onto smooth floorboards. Suggested music: Beethoven's *Piano Concerto No.5* ("Emperor") and *Violin Concerto*; Schubert's *Trout Quintet*.

1

This wonderful rich red in the music room of Richard Jenrette's house on the Hudson River is carefully matched to the original colour. This was certainly a period when no one was afraid of strong colours – it was a time of confidence and opulence, as we can see from the mirror, which once belonged to Madame Jumel of the Morris Jumel Mansion in New York. The window benches are reproductions of original benches now in the Brooklyn Museum. The carpet was designed to complement the wall colour and the gilding.

CREATING THE LOOK

2

2

Another view of the opulent music room. The sensational early 19thC furniture has quite a history. It was purchased in 1823 by the Donaldson family and shipped from North Carolina. The boat sank and the furniture lay underwater for three months. When it was brought to the surface, the only damage was water stains on the fabric.

The domestic and middle-class German and Austrian variant of the late Empire style, termed Biedermeier (after a popular fictional bourgeois character), flourished from around 1820 to 1860. Although its roots are firmly in the French Empire style, it was influenced also by the simpler middle-class English furniture of the Regency. A Biedermeier interior has none of the pomposity of the Empire. The emphasis is on function, simplicity and comfort.

Interest is centred low down in such rooms: furniture does not often extend above eye level.

Walls, ceilings and floors

Ceilings were usually white or pale grey as a foil for walls in clear, bright colours. Walls might be painted or covered with a wallpaper or fabric in a design of stripes or small flowers. Sometimes walls were hung with fabric or rooms were completely tented. Bare floors were quite usual – parquet or plain boards – with sometimes the addition of a simple rug.

Windows

Curtains and other draperies were most commonly white or a pale colour. Curtains were lightweight and hung on brass rods. Alternatively, a delicate fabric might be casually swathed over the curtain pole to decorate just the top of the window; or simple roller blinds might be chosen.

Furniture

Simplicity and clean lines gave furniture an unpretentious elegance. Angles were smoothed out, shapes were rounded and "swollen". Although mahogany was used for a lot of Biedermeier furniture, pale woods were also very popular – maple, cherry, apple, birch and ash. Ornaments such as pilasters, columns and palmettes were rather understated and used with discretion. Narrow strips of ebony inlay were often used to make a striking contrast with the pale woods.

Chairs had sabre or straight legs. Sofas were frequently rather square, although they might have a curved outline. Upholstery fabrics could be decorated with checks, stripes or fresh floral designs.

Circular or oval tables were often placed in front of sofas. Vitrines in which to display porcelain and glass were a characteristic feature.

Accessories

Watercolours, prints, family pictures and smaller oil paintings in simple frames were hung quite low down in a single or double row.

During this period the Berlin porcelain factory produced designs that complemented the Biedermeier furniture – tableware, vases, plates, icepails and other pieces painted with views of buildings in and around Berlin.

1

2

1 and 2

Grand Empire style was not in keeping with German taste. In Germany Biedermeier furniture – Classically inspired but along cleaner, simpler and more functional lines – was all the rage. This "new-look" soon spread to Scandinavia and into France. This Swedish Biedermeier dining room contains a very typical French Charles X chiffonier, c.1820-25, made from light-coloured elm root (1). The beautifully shaped chairs are Scandinavian. The room uses an interesting background colour to set off the light wood of the furniture. The porcelain is also Swedish from the same period, and the cherrywood table is Austrian.

3

— 3 —

A Biedermeier table and chairs fit perfectly with the long lean lines of modern seating units and give this room an immediate sense of period. Modern works of art (including an abstract painting by Deryck Healey over the sofa) provide an effective contrast.

4

5

— 4 —

Here, Biedermeier chairs blend perfectly with the much later Art Deco style. The table, which was made in 1925, is by Sveet Marc. Notice how the pale walls lend added impact to the furniture and paintings.

— 5 —

The Biedermeier chair out of context again, this time quite at home with the late 1930s table, the Lalique vase and a dramatic modern abstract by Deryck Healey.

VICTORIAN

1

Queen Victoria came to the British throne in 1837 and ruled until 1901. For the British middle classes, this was a time of extreme self-confidence: the self-made man was proud of his achievements and used his house as a vehicle to display the wealth gained by his industry. The family was paramount in the Victorian scale of values, and the home was important as a haven of comfort and family life.

1

Colour and pattern have dominant roles in the Victorian interior. This glimpse of a hallway shows just how evocative a busy patterned wallpaper and colourwashed lincrusta below dado level can be. Prints in gilt frames and the obligatory barometer add further credibility.

2, 3 and 4

A set-piece of Victorian style, designed by Jonathan Hudson, which depends for its considerable impact on a rich variety of colours, fabrics, plants and pictures. The mix of old and new fabrics works particularly well. The exuberant drapes have tremendous style and are typical of the age. The design of this room was based on the Linley Sambourne house, an authentic late Victorian villa in Stafford Terrace, London. The corner of the room shown in picture 3 shows the Victorian obsession with detail – the lacy lampshade, the fabric on the mantelpiece, the firescreen, the chair cover – all are absolutely authentic. Victorians had a basic aversion to light and air and were keen to bring greenery indoors where they could appreciate it in comfort. In picture 4 an excess of flowering plants cascade from a converted Victorian cellaret (wine cooler), and on the mantelpiece a credenza overflows with love-lies-bleeding (Amaranthus caudatus).

2

3

4

2

— 1 —

All the pictures on these two pages are of a house designed by Christophe Gollut. This drawing room has the womb-like atmosphere favoured by the Victorians. The first impression is of colour – from the aubergine cotton fabric on the walls to the terracotta marble paint finish on the cornice.

— 2 —

The paint finish is shown to best advantage on the architraves and skirting boards.

— 3 and 4 —

The Victorians were inveterate travellers and collectors of curios. The French Empire marble-topped commode (3) sports a collection of the kind one would expect of a Victorian gentleman. Over the Louis XV sofa (4), draped with oriental and European fabrics, hangs an oil painting depicting a procession in Ceylon.

3

THE VICTORIAN TOWNHOUSE, TO 1870

Eclecticism is a keynote of Victorian townhouse interiors. A number of different historical styles were popular simultaneously. Elizabethan and Gothic appealed to the Victorian sense of continuity with tradition, satisfying a deep sense of nostalgia. Even styles that were not truly indigenous, such as Rococo (Louis XV), enjoyed popularity. On the whole, these models were freely interpreted and indiscriminately mixed.

Mid-Victorian rooms were usually full of pattern in rich colours on carpet, walls and curtains. Walls would be divided into dado, infill and frieze, with perhaps a painted embossed paper on the dado and a patterned one above; the woodwork might be varnished a dark colour or grained. Windows were heavily draped and usually had lace curtains or blinds as well, making the rooms dark during the day. There was drapery everywhere; even the mantelpiece would be festooned with fabric.

A typical room of the period would be crammed full of furniture, much of it with luxuriously thick, well-sprung and deeply-buttoned upholstery. It was not considered necessary for furniture to be matched in suites. As well as an assortment of sofas and armchairs, there were any number of occasional chairs. Any space left over would be filled up with small tables and, of course, a whatnot or two.

4

1

Kelims, cushions, collections and yet more collections can give a Victorian feel to almost any room. The copper lustre ware on the mantelpiece was a particular favourite of the period.

2

A kelim covers a Victorian chesterfield laden with cushions made from pieces of tapestry and carpet. Leather-bound books are piled nonchalantly around the room. Blue and white porcelain and stoneware complete the collection.

3

Here the seating is modern, the oils and watercolours not all Victorian, but the sense of period is nonetheless evoked with the eclectic mix of fabrics, the clutter of frames on the side tables and the tight grouping of paintings.

1

4

A fresh look at Victorian style from the decorator Jane Churchill who has created a pleasing symmetry. The round tables can be bought at very little expense – many of them are just made of chipboard – but they do require good heavy fabric covers, interlined and often weighted down.

5

The Victorians had never heard of the dictum "Less is more". No surface was left bare. Here, a massing of oils, watercolours and miniatures, all in good frames, proves that the whole is greater than the parts.

Pictures and miniatures covered the walls, and every available surface would be crammed with trophies, souvenirs, lamps, vases, pottery figures, shell-covered boxes, needlework items, domed glass cases containing waxed flowers, and bric-à-brac of all sorts. No home would have been complete without a selection of the leafy green plants so beloved of the Victorians – ferns, trailing plants and aspidistras.

At night, when the curtains were drawn, the gas would be lit, filling the room with a warm glow which would reflect off ornaments and cut glass.

Walls

Although, early on, colour schemes were light with warm sunny colours (except for the library and the dining room, where red flock was fashionable), soon a preference for strong, rather gaudy colours became apparent. The fashion for dividing the wall into dado, infill and frieze came in strongly from about 1860.

Wallpaper Mass-produced from the 1840s, wallpaper was available in a wide range of qualities. Hand-printed papers were also produced but these were expensive. There was a wide range of patterns. In the 1860s white-and-gold designs became popular for drawing rooms furnished in the "Louis" styles (see page 128). A.W.N. Pugin, decorator of the Houses of Parliament, designed a number of papers with medieval motifs – stylized roses, fleur-de-lys, pineapples, geometric trellis – which suited Gothic interiors. Repeat patterns of flowers were fashionable, as were embossed papers used on both ceilings and walls and then painted over. William Morris and Co. started producing their famous wallpapers in the 1860s.

Paint Walls might be painted with coloured distemper. A room treated in this way might have a border of a repeat pattern, which might be either stencilled or painted freehand.

Woodwork This might be painted or grained and in Gothic interiors would frequently be dark-stained.

Windows

Heavy curtains helped to prevent carpets and upholstery from fading. The fashionable fabrics of the early 1860s are listed in *Cassell's Household Guide* as "all kinds of damask, moreen, and rep . . ." as well as a new fabric from France called Timbuctoo, which was ". . . striped horizontally in white, scarlet, black and yellow on a green, red or blue ground".

Draped pelmets were still fashionable in the early part of the period. Later on, an ornate type of flat pelmet, called a lambrequin, was popular: this had a shaped outline and extended some way down the sides of the curtains. Curtains were often hung on heavy brass poles.

Lace or muslin undercurtains were used next to the glass to keep dust and dirt out of the room. Roller blinds were quite common also and were often decorative; some "transparent" blinds were painted with designs of landscapes and other subjects.

The mantelpiece often had its own curtain to match the other furnishings. This took the form of a board covered with fabric with a flounce of material hanging down.

2

3

4

5

1

This room, designed by Jonathan Hudson, was inspired by an exceptional collection of Victorian paintings, many of them by Sir Lawrence Alma-Tadema whose work was popular around 1870-90. The strong wall colours, the soft pools of light, the indoor palms and the interesting mix of furniture styles are typical of this late Victorian period.

2

2

Not all Victorian interiors were dark and cluttered. Here, a simple Victorian chest, blue sponge effect wallpaper, an armchair covered in white calico and a small oriental rug conjure up the plainer aspects of Victorian decoration. The strong blue Nailsea glass flasks were greatly admired at the time.

Floors

Carpets with large patterns were popular, and it was fashionable for the border of floorboards left around the edges of the room to be stained, painted or perhaps marbled – or sometimes covered with felt. In a grand house the border might be of parquet. A canvas drugget was sometimes placed on top of the carpet to protect it from wear. Floorcloth, often elaborately patterned, was an economical form of floor covering.

Lighting

Oil table lamps were still a commonplace form of lighting until superseded by gas in the 1870s. Candles no longer played a major part in the lighting of interiors.

Furniture

Mahogany was the most popular Victorian wood. Later on, there was a vogue for walnut and satinwood.

Heavily carved, and often artificially blackened, oak was used for "Elizabethan" and "Gothic" pieces; craftsmen sometimes complained that pieces had to be ". . . stained to imitate old, and sold for old". In addition, antique furniture was often cannibalized to make new pieces. It was usually the ornament rather than the shape that distinguished a piece of Victorian Gothic furniture.

A material, little used before, that became very fashionable in the middle of the century was papier mâché. This was usually lacquered black and decorated with mother-of-pearl or "paste" inlay and/or painted flowers and fruit. A whole variety of charming small pieces was made – chairs, work boxes, trays, bedheads, small tables and the like. The best-known makers were Jennens and Bettridge of Birmingham.

Brass bedsteads were a Victorian innovation; the grander ones frequently had a half-tester construction.

The dining room was important both for eating and for family prayers. The sideboard was a massive affair, often surmounted by a large mirror. Although some shapes were quite simple, with fairly restrained ornament, there was a fashion for heavily carved pieces. Two exhibited at the International Exhibition of 1862 were the "Shakespeare" and "Robinson Crusoe" sideboards by Thomas Tweedy and his pupil Gerrard Robinson. Both are very detailed pieces; the former is covered with scenes and figures from many of Shakespeare's plays, the latter with incidents from Defoe's tale of the island castaway.

A dining table was usually rectangular, with square or rounded ends. It was solid in construction, with four bulbous turned legs, and could be extended with additional leaves. Tablecloths were used at mealtimes, and between meals the dining table would be covered with a baize, linen or velvet cloth. Although dining chairs – as well as tables, sideboards and so on – might be in Elizabethan or Gothic styles, the balloon-back shape was the most popular. It went out of fashion around 1870, although manufacture continued. Balloon-back dining room chairs had straight legs. The same style of chair was also made for the drawing room, but with cabriole legs from the 1850s.

Davenport desks were popular – small writing desks, usually with drawers at the side. Chiffoniers and oval or round tilt-top pedestal (or loo) tables were a feature of morning rooms in early and mid-Victorian upper-class houses, and of drawing rooms in middle-class ones. No home was complete without its whatnot – a piece of furniture with shelves for the display of knick-knacks.

An important piece of hall furniture was the stand to take coats, hats and umbrellas. This sometimes incorporated a seat; alternatively, it might include a table, but sometimes there would be a separate, narrow table for visitors' calling cards. An oak or mahogany longcase clock was a typical feature also, and there was usually a hall chair. Some hall furniture was made of cast iron.

By the 1830s springs for seat furniture were in general production in

1

1

A modern interpretation of the Victorian look, avoiding overdecoration but including some fine Victorian pieces. The rough plaster work is given added emphasis with a coloured edging which emphasizes the fact that the finish is intentional, not merely slapdash. The skirting board has been marbled and the floorboards colourwashed and then rubbed back to allow the pattern of the wood to show through.

2

Rich, red hues, a fine overmantel painting, a lattice wallpaper and shelves on which old and new rub shoulders are the ingredients here. The flower dome makes an evocative focus.

3

This elegant corner has been created in a small terraced cottage built c.1840 in Chelsea, London. The plain wooden fire surround has been marbelized, the solidly comfortable 19thC French chair has been upholstered in a suitable modern fabric and the corner table, with its pretty lace cloth, is adorned with tole vases, cranberry glass and a collection of porcelain.

4

A light and airy ground-floor flat in Brighton, England. It has a distinctly 19thC feel, with its Osborne and Little rag-rolled wallpaper, its stripped pine furniture and bare floorboards. The frieze at picture rail height seems to lower the ceiling.

5

The success of this room depends on its light touch, evoking Victorian comfort with a minimum of ostentation.

Birmingham, making possible the typically Victorian opulent, rounded shapes. Deep buttoning which accentuated the thickness and curvaceousness of the upholstery was very popular. Upholstered pieces included the circular or rectangular ottoman around which several people could sit, the chaise longue, various types of sofa, and novelty pieces such as the sociable (an S-shaped couch allowing the two occupants to face each other) or the *tête-à-tête*(rather like two armchairs joined by a single long seat with a small table fixed in the middle). Early in the period, chairs and sofas completely covered with upholstery were in vogue; later on, styles with exposed frames of polished mahogany or rosewood became popular.

There were innumerable kinds of occasional chair – typical are the spoon-back and the prie-dieu. The latter, with its low seat and tall T-shaped back, looks rather strange until you realize that instead of sitting on it you were intended to kneel on the seat and lean with your elbows on the upholstered top rail.

Accessories

Advances in mass production made silverware cheaper. Electroplating, the process patented in 1840 by Elkington, superseded Sheffield Plate: the process required less silver and worn articles could be easily re-plated.

Major Victorian developments in porcelain include Minton's *pâte sur pâte*(in white relief on a dark background) and the creamy-white, marble-like Parian ware introduced by Copeland and widely used for figurines, often of Classical subjects. Coalport favoured a Neo-rococo style. Large quantities of blue-and-white printed wares were made in Britain in imitation of Chinese export designs – these were far more ornate than Chinese taste would allow in wares for home consumption. Such pieces were cranked out by the thousands for the American and home markets.

Staffordshire pottery figures, whose naive charm is highly appealing, were made from around 1835 to 1895. Majolica pottery, with colourful glazes, was also popular. It was made, most notably, by Minton.

2

LATE VICTORIAN

By the last quarter of the 19th century there was also a nostalgic look back to the time of Queen Anne. A relaxed informality was the keynote of this style. Rooms with inglenooks and "cosy corners" were furnished with antiques, not necessarily of the Queen Anne period. A well-worn look was considered an advantage in such interiors. The "Queen Anne" style was in harmony with the rather bohemian mood of the Aesthetic Movement, on which it exerted a considerable influence.

An "Aesthetic" interior was less heavy, less eclectic and more casual than rooms in the mainstream Victorian tradition. There was an emphasis on asymmetry and on hand-crafted objects – mass production was considered "philistine", the antithesis of "aesthetic". In these rooms a lived-in look was a positive virtue: old pieces handed down from grandparents were mixed with Anglo-Japanese, often ebonized, rather angular furniture, and distinctive pieces made in bamboo.

Late Victorian also had a more formal side, giving rise to interiors decorated in a rather general "18th-century" style. These rooms were furnished with graceful, well-made reproduction pieces – "after Chippendale" and so-called "Queen Anne" (actually in the style of Adam, Sheraton and Hepplewhite). Satinwood was the favourite wood.

3

4

5

1

2

3

1

An opulent mid-19thC style has been created in this 1820s London house, lavishly decorated by Ian Lieber. The peach walls have been softened with a stipple, all the colours are muted and the magnificent mirror and elegant wall sconces all add to the light, glittering, regal style.

2

A carefully coordinated Victorian-style "designer" interior turns the wide bay window of this drawing room into a focal point with its extravagant use of chintz and tassels.

3

It is good to see a new breed of hotel paying close attention to period style. The Dorset Square Hotel in London is a good example. This well-coordinated room has an interesting stencilled cornice frieze from a Caroline Warrender stencil kit. The plain grey marble fireplace and overmantel mirror are warmed by the wall colour, the floral fabrics and the simple but effective drapes.

4

Feather-filled cushions line the window seat in this wonderfully relaxing corner of a bedroom in a house in Southport, Connecticut. The table behind the chaise longue is American cherrywood, c.1800, the table in the foreground is a reproduction and the chair, c.1835, is from the New York State Senate in Albany.

5

This good, strong Victorian drawing room has quite masculine overtones – although in fact it was designed by a woman. The colours, the drapes and the variety of fabrics give this rather stately room a warm and homely feeling.

6

A mixture of fabrics, patterns and rich strong colours give this room a cosy, Victorian feeling. Note how the proportions of the room are affected by the change of colour at dado height.

7

This is a wonderful example of a Victorian interior that is neither dark nor overbearing. The house belongs to Linda Gumb, a dealer in antique fabrics and furniture, and her drawing room houses some excellent examples of her wares. The magnificent chandelier is made of Venetian glass: there was a time when this could be picked up for a song – but alas, those days are long gone.

4

5

6

7

1

2

1

This grand Victorian mansion owned by Michael Wells could have been furnished by a wealthy Victorian collector. The 18thC marble bust sits happily with an 18thC French chair alongside a Victorian side table and celleret. The terracotta figures pick up the warm colour of the walls.

2

This is another view of the same dining room. The chairs are 19thC English oak Gothick style and the magnificent oil portrait that appears to be framed by the painted panel is by Lely.

1

1–5

An absolutely authentic Victorian kitchen/dining room, while visually appealing, would hardly be practical. The kitchens and eating areas on these pages present a happy compromise: modern appliances fitted into painted units, stripped pine dressers groaning with collections of pottery, a wonderful brick floor and an overhead hanging rail (an idea borrowed from the professional kitchen), an Aga fitted against a wall and fitted cupboards painted to look like an old French provincial armoire. All these rooms show an obvious enthusiasm for food and its preparation, and for the plates, pots, bowls and platters used for its presentation.

2

3

4

5

1

This is the New Orleans bedroom in the American Museum, Bath. The massive pieces of furniture are typical of the period – c.1850. They were adapted from the Louis XV style by a famous cabinetmaker called Prudent Mallard who moved from The Duncan Phyfe cabinet shop in New York to New Orleans in the late 1830s. The heaviness of the carved mahogany half-tester is softened by delicate use of white muslin and lace. The wallpaper, with its strong design, is absolutely in period.

2

The designer Melissa Wyndham has used a wonderful strong chintz fabric on the walls, windows and bed hangings, giving this room a distinctly 19thC flavour. When using such a fabric, a strong edging colour adds impact.

3

This 19thC American interior with its 19thC wrought-iron bed minimizes the impact of a sloping roof by using the same fabric all over – even over the light switches. The woodwork, including a very plain chest of drawers, is painted a complementary colour. The floorboards have been simply polished and a floral rug thrown over.

4

Clever use of fabric and some good Victorian furniture and pottery make for a stylish bedroom in the Dorset Square Hotel, London.

5

This bedroom in a 17thC house in Sussex has a distinctly Victorian feel, with a dash of French Empire. The exciting interior has many influences and this is the key to its success. The maple-framed bird-prints, the mix of fabrics, all exude a Victorian atmosphere.

1

6

This 18thC bed has been extravagantly but simply draped with a plain blue fabric – leaving a glimpse of an early crewelwork hanging behind. A treatment such as this requires nothing more than a bold touch and lots of fabric.

7

A truly theatrical bedroom in a New York State home, where the owner has taken out the ceiling and gone up into the roof space, making a minstrel gallery under the eaves. Hand-painted fabric decorates the walls, and the bold use of colours, plants and patterns turns this room into a dramatic stage-set.

8

A Victorian style in a very unVictorian bedroom. The vigorous lines of the bed and the collection of highly decorative Wemyss ware dominate this 17thC room. Wemyss ware, a great favourite of the present Queen Mother's, was produced in a Fife pottery from the 1880s.

9

This bedroom depends for its Victorian feel on the bedheads and bedside cupboard and mirror. The bedheads have painted floral decoration on a black-painted background with gilt lines. This finish could be applied to new wood. The lights are bunches of grapes – an amusing Victorian touch.

10

Although most of the furniture in this 17thC bedroom dates from the 17th, 18th and early 19thC, the room has an overall Victorian feel due to the confusion of fabrics, the way the prints are displayed, the porcelain collections and the groups of silver-topped scent bottles.

2

3

4

5

6

7

8

9

10

1

2

3

4

5

6

1

This light airy room shows how effective antique white linen – tablecloths and old sheets – can be when used as bedspreads and curtains. The lace contrasts well against stark mahogany furniture. Nothing matches exactly – for example, one pelmet is of satin ribbons and the other is a piece of tasselled, embroidered fabric. The painted effects on the wall, and particularly the painted cherubs, give the room a Romantic, feminine feel, accentuated by the heart-shaped chair-back and echoed by the dried flower wreath above the white-painted wrought-iron bed. A very sentimental, very Victorian room.

2

A light Victorian bedroom with a country feel in which diaphanous white muslin creates a Neo-medieval canopy.

3

This bedroom with its gleaming brass head and restful colours has been thoughtfully designed. The curtains are of machine-made lace over cotton – very effective and simple. The patchwork quilt ties in with the cotton rug, and the floorboards have been colourwashed and sanded back to let the wood grain show through.

4

This bedroom, feminine in mood, was designed by Jane Churchill. The features which make up this particular Victorian "designer" style are the complex pelmet design and flowing drapes, the old lace used under a glass top on the dressing table, and the coordinating bed-cover. The trompe l'oeil *panels add a delicate dimension to the same wall.*

5

This teenager's charming bedroom right under the eaves makes good use of boldly patterned fabric on the 19thC bed, tub armchair and drapes. The simple sprigged wallpaper and border is deliberately less dramatic. The dressing table, with its feminine flounces of fabric, could easily be a heavily disguised modern chest of drawers.

6

The centrepiece of this very feminine bedroom is an 18thC bed – many pieces of this kind are now reproduced by companies such as Heritage of Petworth, West Sussex. Here the fabric has been kept soft and light, and the colour of the room decided by the 19thC patchwork quilt. Many of the other drapes are actually old linen, tablecloths and sheets which have intricate embroidery: these can be found in many country auction rooms and specialist shops.

7

8

9

10

11

12

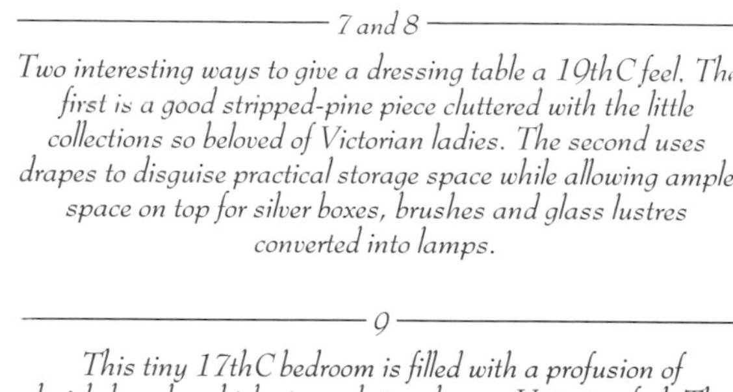

7 and 8

Two interesting ways to give a dressing table a 19thC feel. The first is a good stripped-pine piece cluttered with the little collections so beloved of Victorian ladies. The second uses drapes to disguise practical storage space while allowing ample space on top for silver boxes, brushes and glass lustres converted into lamps.

9

This tiny 17thC bedroom is filled with a profusion of knick-knacks which give a cluttered, cosy Victorian feel. The table in the foreground holds a collection of fairings: these highly collectable small pottery groups were sold as souvenirs at resorts and fairgrounds from c.1860 to c.1914. The earliest fairings came from Saxony.

10

This appealing child's room has a sweet, light simplicity. The bedspreads are made from tablecloths. In the hallway note the Lloyd loom chair which has been painted – these can still be acquired inexpensively – and a plain modern table completely covered in a patchwork quilt.

11

A comfortable wicker chair piled high with cushions, a pine chest of drawers and a small card table give a good Victorian country feel to this small corner.

12

This early Victorian four-poster is given a simple treatment in contrasting colours. The couch is an authentic touch.

1

2

5

1

A superb combined bath and shower unit.

2

Modern French bathroom fittings such as this double washbasin offer a 19thC look.

3

A period feel can be helped by tiles.

4

A touch of Victorian Gothic is achieved by cleverly shaped cornices in the alcoves.

5

A well-designed small bathroom built around an original Victorian vanity unit.

3

4

6

7

6

Late 19thC and early 20thC painted toilets and washbasins are sold as modern copies.

7

This small bathroom owes as much to the spartan setting as it does to the cast-iron bath.

8

Wooden panelling up to dado level creates a period mood by simple means.

9

Scatter rugs, sprigged muslin at the window, cascading fabric on the table, a day bed and a painted basket of dried flowers all reinforce the romantic mood.

8

9

1

2

3

4

1 and 2

This interior exudes American Gothic and contains many surprises, all collected by Lee Anderson. Most of the pieces in Lee's collection are by the master craftsmen of this period. The rooms are dark but not oppressive. Every detail is perfect – from the candlesticks to the cushions. Tiffany may seem an odd bedfellow to the earlier Gothic pieces but his designs are so derivative that his work has been called "the last expression of the American Gothic".

3 and 4

Gothic as a style has a strong identity which transcends both period and country. In picture 3 note the 19thC Gothic standing cupboard, the modern copy of an Italian frame chair and the painting in Gothic taste – all elements in total harmony with the Stuart Interiors pomegranate pattern fabric. Picture 4 shows a Strawberry Hill Gothick Windsor chair, c.1780, framed by a medieval stone arch and backed by a wool and linen pomegranate pattern which is based on a 17thC fabric. The iron candlestand was made by Stuart Interiors to a medieval design.

1 – 4, overleaf

In Lee Anderson's dining room in his New York Village home, the chairs and couch were made by Roux, the sideboard by Meeks in the 1830s, the table by A.J. Davis and the chairs by Crawford Riddell in Philadelphia in 1836. The lamps are by Tiffany. The whole effect depends upon the profusion of antiques from this period – some of high design, others mass-produced. In picture 2 we see exactly why Tiffany is often referred to in the same breath as American Gothic. The lamp seems to grow quite naturally from the table, which was probably made by Roux in New York c.1850. This table with its marble top and bronze heads and hooves shows the quality and integrity of design at this period. Picture 3 is the story of three chairs. The exquisitely carved example in the foreground was made by Joseph Meeks, c.1850, the chair by the door was by A.J. Davis for Itarrick Castle (note the wonderful deer feet, shown up on the light-coloured flooring) and the chair in the hallway is by Boudine, New York, c.1855. We are reminded by picture 4, that the American Gothic Revival was very much a Victorian phenomenon. This combination of paintings, glassware and furniture from the 1830s and 40s has an unmistakable Victorian stamp upon it.

1

2

3

4

5

A perfect American Gothic interior, again in Lee Anderson's home in New York's Village. The table on the right in a restrained taste which marks the transition from Classical to Gothic, the "hatbox" wallpaper (c.1820-30), the massive Gothic mirror by Roux, the collection of Gothic chairs – everything picks up the theme. The collection of parian figures (parian is an opaque white porcelain much loved by the Victorians), the sculpture and the small pieces of Gothic-influenced porcelain all blend in perfectly.
(for captions to 1–4, see page 199.)

This is a style from which you can take as much or as little as you wish. If you find the rather heavy, dark colours of a mid-Victorian room too oppressive, choose the lighter ones appropriate for the early period. You may not want a complete interior in this style, in which case you could put together a Victorian corner in a room that does not otherwise evoke a specific period.

COLOURS Dark, rich reds, greens, blues and browns are appropriate for a Victorian interior. Patterns can play an important role: if you are brave enough, try mixing various patterns in busy profusion.

WALLS Walls divided into dado, infill and frieze will carry the authentic stamp of the period. You could choose an embossed paper for the dado, painted or varnished, with one of the many authentic Victorian wallpaper designs above. Alternatively, you could paint the walls and add a wallpaper or stencilled border. Woodwork could be grained or painted olive green.

FURNITURE Rounded, deep-buttoned shapes are the obvious choice for sofas and armchairs. Mahogany is the most characteristic wood of the era, and there are numerous Victorian chairs and tables still to be found; balloon-back chairs are particularly apt.

SOFT FURNISHINGS Combine old or reproduction lace under-curtains with heavy velvet over-curtains and a draped and fringed pelmet. Match these up with a multi-layered round table with floor-length bottom cloth and one or more lace-edged cloths on top. As well as velvets and damasks, there is a whole range of suitable fabrics, from the ever-popular William Morris designs to Gothic patterns, and rose-strewn printed cottons. Needlework of various sorts can be used for cushions, and for covering chair seats and stools. Sofas and large ottomans, upholstered with kelims, will give a room a Victorian flavour. Oriental rugs are ideal for a Victorian room, reflecting an interest in exotic places. Paisleys, too, give an authentic touch.

LIGHTING There are many original gas lamps that have been converted in recent years to electricity. Reproduction Victorian lighting is also widely available. All too often, reproduction wall lights based on authentic gas fittings are installed upside-down: the ubiquitous flower-shaped shades would have had the opening facing the ceiling.

FLOORING Large carpets in a traditional pattern, perhaps the red and blue "Turkey" design or a pattern of flowers and leaves, convey the right mood. Parquet makes a good border, as do dark-stained, painted or marbled boards. If you prefer a fitted carpet, the same type of traditional pattern or a plain deep red, blue or green would work well. On top of a plain carpet you could place a flowery needlework rug.

ORNAMENTS Staffordshire figures are perhaps the single most evocative type of Victorian ornament, but there are numerous other items that would help to build up the picture – for example, shell boxes, needlework pictures, waxed flowers under glass domes, family photographs and, of course, sentimental pictures of animals and children. Collections of such bric-à-brac and art, arranged on draped tables, whatnots, chiffoniers and windowsills, as well as on walls, will capture the flavour of the age.

FINISHING TOUCHES An inexpensive feature can be created by making or buying a round chipboard table and covering it with a long, fringed cloth. Add one or more lace-edged cloths, a Paisley shawl, or even an Oriental rug, and arrange a collection of bric-à-brac on top. Help the ambience along with, for example, Wagner's *Siegfried Idyll* on the hi-fi, or Elgar's *Chanson du Matin*.

1

This cosy parlour with its simple sprigged wallpaper is typical of an early Victorian country home. The mood is conveyed by a tapestry-covered chair, a kelim thrown over the table, plain floorboards with a highly decorative rug, and a collection of Victorian Staffordshire figures – these, incidentally, are still relatively inexpensive, and even damaged pieces (which are even more easily affordable) can be used to great effect. A garland of garlic and herbs hung up to dry complete the ambience.

CREATING THE LOOK

2

2

A simple, warm beige fabric edged in a complementary braid provides a perfect background to an Italian table, c.1860, and a pair of Victorian chairs. Flowers and candles provide an authentic finishing touch.

1

2

3

4

5

6

7

1–8

The Victorians were great travellers and collectors and an instant feeling of nostalgia for the age can be achieved in a house of any period by building a collection around a fireplace, a convenient corner or against a suitable wall. Here, a collection of treen and Mauchline ware crowd a what-not beside a good Gothic chair (1). An interesting collection of luggage and sporting goods is randomly arranged in front of 15thC English carved panels (2). Fireplaces provide a good focal point for collections – for example, fine 18thC blue and white porcelain and 18thC English glassware (3). Picture 4 shows a selection of coloured glass from the 18th and 19thC, an amusing collection of mantel dogs and a wall covered with prints that are simply framed in black. Still more evocative is the wonderful inglenook covered with Victorian mugs, jugs, Toby jugs and teapots (5). Collections can certainly change the feel of a room: in picture 6, 19thC yellow and green majolica bring light and life to a 17thC interior. A collection of 18th, 19th and 20thC Chinese porcelain displayed on oriental boxes of different sizes gives an exotic feel to the hallway of Chilston Park, Kent (7). In picture 8, ivory inlaid tables and a coffer support exotic carvings, bronzes and a majolica jardinière.

8

1

2

3

4

5

1

Collections and individual pieces of interest can grace any kitchen wall. A pine spoon rack, hunting horn, 19thC spongeware and dried flowers have a warm, colourful, comfortable presence in this kitchen.

2

This stencilled wallpaper is an excellent substitute for hand-painted stencilling and makes a perfect backdrop for the stencilled box, display of country flowers and late 19thC wooden toy.

3 and 4

This bathroom in a terraced house in Tunbridge Wells has a good Victorian country feel about it, thanks to the interesting wall colour and frieze and the plentiful use of fabric, from the kelim-covered ottoman to the patchwork cushions and embroidered coverlets on the day bed.

5

The success of this corner is to do with the choice of matt colours, the way in which the pictures are displayed, the dried flowers and the eclectic selection of sundry items, including a rocking horse, fabric cat, 19thC jug and basket with soaps. No-one should be afraid to mix the serious with the frivolous.

1

1

This immensely feminine Victorian bedroom makes use of many different linens and textiles. The iron bedstead has been painted the same blue as the Lloyd loom chair. The bed coverings are old quilts, tablecloths and sheets. The curtain has been made from a lacy tablecloth. The round table, covered by a large Victorian crisp white linen tablecloth, has a collection of 19thC porcelain and scent bottles. Note how effective are the old-fashioned roses in the sucrier (sugar bowl).

2

3

2 and 3

Two methods of dealing with a sofa in a period interior. In the first instance (2), a ghastly beaten-up old sofa has been draped in a large quilt and comfortably covered in cushions. In the second (3), the choice has been a good modern sofa built on traditional lines and again covered with cushions.

CREATING THE LOOK

The Victorian country style is a lighter, simpler version of Victorian townhouse. It works particularly well in bedrooms, kitchens and bathrooms. There is less clutter and rooms have a cottagy, timeless quality, very different from the slightly claustrophobic feel of a room in a townhouse of the same period.

COLOURS White and pastel shades – varying in tone from pale to clear bright – should be offset by occasional touches of darker green, red, blue or black.

WALLS White or pastel colourwashed walls make a good background. You can introduce pattern with stencils. Flowery wallpapers, particularly roses, also work well.

FURNITURE The same rounded shapes are right for upholstery in town or country homes, but for the country look choose less opulent designs and fabrics. Slightly faded loose covers give a pleasant relaxed feel. Mahogany chairs and tables can work just as well in this more casual setting, provided that you choose the less grand designs. Alternatively, opt for plain painted pine cupboards and dressers, again perhaps decorated with stencils. Plainly shaped chairs and tables also look good when painted. If the paint is slightly scuffed, so much the better: a touch of shabbiness suits this style. Windsor chairs set just the right note. Iron or brass bedsteads are a good choice.

SOFT FURNISHINGS Simple muslin or floral-print curtains, sparkling white lace-trimmed tablecloths, crochet or knitted bedspreads, and patchwork quilts, set the airy mood of this style.

FLOORING Stripped, polished or stained floorboards with rag rugs on top are appropriate. A good alternative to rags would be striped cotton dhurries.

LIGHTING Oil lamps – real or electrified – are a better choice than reproduction gas-lamp styles. Choose candles for their decorative appeal and for lighting at mealtimes.

ORNAMENTS Bric-à-brac should be less sophisticated than in a townhouse room, and less abundant. Staffordshire figures, blue and white printed pottery, fairings (presents bought at a fair) and samplers would add the right note.

FINISHING TOUCHES Throw a patchwork quilt over an old comfortable armchair to blend it into a country room.

Look for authentic period fabrics in antique markets – scraps of old lace and pieces of linen. To take iron mould stains out of old cotton bedlinen and tablecloths soak them in Nappisan.

4

4

This relaxed feminine look has been achieved by covering an armchair with a quilt and cushions (do make sure that the quilt is in good condition) and by draping a table with fabric and the window with a linen tablecloth.

ARTS AND CRAFTS

1

1 and 2

Gustav Stickley (1857-1942) was one of the most important designers of the later Arts and Crafts style in the Eastern states of America. He not only produced good-quality Arts and Crafts furniture but between 1901 and 1916 edited the Craftsman Magazine. *His furniture is usually made of oak and he was known for his great belief in "simplicity of construction". Most pieces are stamped with the Stickley motto "Als Ik Kan" (All I can). This period of designer craftsmen harked back in some respects to the Shakers, but really had more to do with the English Arts and Crafts movement.*

William Morris, who hated mass production and insisted on truth to materials and honesty of design, laid the foundations for the English Arts and Crafts Movement of the 1880s and 90s. Artists, designers and craftsmen looked back to the Middle Ages as the golden age of craftsmanship and formed themselves into guilds on the medieval pattern. The movement found enthusiastic support in America, where it blossomed as the "Craftsman style".

The emphasis was on craftsmanship, quality of materials and the use of the right material for a specific purpose. Although inspired by the workmanship and sometimes the motifs of the Middle Ages, these designer/craftsmen were not aping medieval styles. The furniture and decorative articles they produced were true to a long English tradition; however, the style they created was totally original.

The Arts and Crafts Movement also produced a number of talented architects who worked in an English vernacular style, foreshadowed by Philip Webb who built William Morris' first home. Perhaps the most influential of this group was C.F.A. Voysey, who designed every detail of his houses, down to the pots and pans.

An Arts and Crafts room was light and spacious-looking, often painted all over in white or a pale colour, with natural-coloured wood floors covered with rugs. The furniture was plain and upright and usually made of oak decorated with simple cut-out motifs such as hearts or spear-heads. To complement the furniture there were articles in pewter, silver, brass and copper and needlework cushions, curtains and wallhangings executed in yarns coloured with natural vegetable dyes.

Decorative motifs were inspired by nature – birds, animals and flowers. The work of Arts and Crafts artists was to later inspire the Art Nouveau style, whose characteristic sinuous shapes were already beginning to be seen in Arts and Crafts designs, particularly illustration, wallpapers and fabrics.

Walls and windows

The treatment of walls was closely linked with their structure: features such as the fireplace played a decorative as well as functional role.

The whole wall surface (often with a picture rail or high plate shelf) might be painted a uniform pale colour, matching the ceiling. Alternatively, there might be a dado; or part of the wall might be covered with tongued-and-grooved boards, perhaps painted a restful green, to shoulder height. The fireplace surround would be incorporated into the wall treatment: for example, a typical room in Voysey's style would have a fireplace surround taken up to picture-rail height, with a mantelshelf at approximately shoulder level.

1

2

1 and 2

Andrew and Julie Wadsworth display their collection of Arts and Crafts furniture in a living room painted in four shades of eau de nil and carpeted in a deep blue. It is often argued that Arts and Crafts furniture is best displayed against a white background but this interesting colour choice certainly complements the oak and copper. The pieces, all made by designer-craftsmen, are very special, particularly the Liberty sideboard and the Viennese grandfather clock. The built-in units hold books but also conceal such appliances as hi-fi and TV. The desk and chair are Celtic Arts and Crafts.

3

This very typical Arts and Crafts beaten copper fireplace by George Walton was made in 1904. The grate is by the architect Charles Voysey. The picture above the fireplace, The Cloister and the World, *is by G. Sheridan Knowles, 1901: on its original beaten copper frame the title stands out in relief. The modern pottery ewer by Kate Wickham sits happily on the mantelpiece with an Arts and Crafts bowl and boxes and a pair of candlesticks by Christopher Dresser. One of the other interesting pieces in this room is the brass and steel smoking stand on the right by William Goburg. The lampshade is by Quentin Bell.*

Painted walls might be embellished with a hand-painted or stencilled frieze. Arts and Crafts artists such as Voysey and A.H. Macmurdo created wallpapers and fabrics. Window treatments would be of the simplest style, a wooden pole, a length of unlined fabric fluttering in the breeze.

Floors

Polished boards topped with rugs were a usual choice.

Furniture

Furniture shapes were plain and upright and made by traditional joinery techniques. Native woods were used, particularly oak, which would be waxed and allowed to mellow naturally. Sideboards, chests and the like were usually decorated in simple fashion, with cut-out shapes. Sometimes they were embellished with pewter, brass, ivory or leather.

Settles were a favourite style of seating, as were upright chairs with tall backs, again often decorated with cut-out motifs.

Accessories

Arts and Crafts Guilds included workers in silver, pewter, leather and brass who produced decorative articles by hand in designs inspired by Medieval motifs. One of the notable designers of silverware was C.R. Ashbee, who created some particularly attractive goblets, vases and other pieces set with semi-precious stones.

Typical of the style are mirror frames of beaten copper and candle sconces in brass, imposingly proportioned. Needlework in vegetable-dyed wools made up into table runners and cushions and used to trim curtains and door curtains would further embellish an Arts and Crafts interior.

AND THE WORLD

1

COLOURS The natural vegetable-dye colours associated with the Middle Ages are right for textiles and wallpapers. These reds, greens, blues, old roses and dull gold shades can be set against paintwork in a pale or muted colour – cream or ivory-white, or the duller, paler shades of green.

WALLS Panelling walls with tongued-and-grooved boards to above shoulder level, and finishing the top with a plate shelf, is an excellent way to set the scene. The boarding and woodwork can then be painted, or coated with coloured varnish – perhaps a greeny-blue – which allows the grain of the wood to show through. The light oak panelling often seen in houses of the late Victorian period and the first quarter of this century is perfect for this style.

FLOORS Seal and polish floorboards and top them with small rugs; handmade needlework ones in designs of stylized flowers and animals would be appropriate, or you could choose Morris-style patterns or old Oriental rugs. If you have a solid floor, cover with sisal or rush matting.

FURNITURE Oak is the material associated with this style. Look for upright chairs with straight backs, and sideboards, chests and settles constructed on straightforward, "honest" lines. Cut-out spearheads and hearts are often the only form of decoration, although larger pieces may have a relief decoration in copper or brass. Plain upright chairs and tables in oak made in the 1930s can be used in conjunction with authentic pieces. Or buy new furniture in the Arts and Crafts style.

SOFT FURNISHINGS Simple window treatments are best – pairs of curtains hung from wood or brass poles. For upholstery or curtains, choose fabrics by Morris, Voysey and their contemporaries with designs of birds, animals and flowers.

LIGHTING Concealed general lighting, with candles in pewter or brass candlesticks as the only visible light sources, would suit this style. Alternatively, use Victorian or Edwardian light fittings.

ORNAMENTS Pictures on Medieval themes in the Pre-Raphaelite manner work well. Look out too for illustrations by Walter Crane. Rectangular or oval mirror frames in beaten copper, sometimes ornamented with plain semi-precious stones, give an authentic touch. Blend these with pewter or slipware plate, saltglaze jugs and so on.

FINISHING TOUCHES Fix lengths of curtain pole around the walls of the room at a little above shoulder level and hang suitable fabric from them on rings to softly cover the walls. Appropriate sounds for this look might include Barber's *Adagio for Strings*, Mahler's Adagio from *Symphony No. 5*, or *Don Juan* by Richard Strauss.

2

CREATING THE LOOK

3

— 1 —

The crucial feature of this Arts and Crafts dining room is the choice of colour and the way in which the cream panels frame the mirror and paintings. The choice of floral decoration – blue thistles – is very appropriate for this style.

— 2 —

The eau de nil background and the deep matt blue in the foreground help to add warmth to the oak furniture in this room. Full, spiky, slightly medieval-looking flower arrangements reinforce the period touch. Underfoot is a copy of an 18thC marble floor.

— 3 —

A wonderful piece of stained glass in two tones of blue. Such panels can be bought or commissioned from a stained glass artist, and are certainly more striking and effective than net curtains.

EDWARDIAN AND ART NOUVEAU

1

While the various reforming movements were taking place in the homes of the avant garde, most Victorian citizens were still living in heavily draped, overfilled rooms. By the 1890s the fussiness and clutter was at its height. Everything was draped, and there were a lot of unnecessary pieces of furniture: it must have been quite difficult to cross a room without knocking over something.

By now even the traditionalists were beginning to react against such excesses. Gradually, the drapery became more simple, and furniture and bric-à-brac were reduced to manageable proportions. At last it was realized that lighter colours would create a less heavy, more spacious look. White or creamy painted woodwork came into fashion and in the first twenty years of this century became mandatory in any "tasteful" interior.

The lifestyle of the Edwardians was different from that of their parents. Even in fashionable circles, many people were now living in smaller houses

2

1

The strong green in this hallway, with a typical Art Nouveau lincrusta frieze, sets off a simple Art Nouveau table and Arts and Crafts chair. White lilies are an essential Art Nouveau prop.

2

The Art Nouveau style is typified by flowing lines within a linear frame. Here, the Art Nouveau display cabinet with pewter and silver boxes is surmounted by a W.S. Coleman print. The settee is part of an Irish Art Nouveau suite made in 1902, which has finer lines than some of its English counterparts. Few people have taken on Art Nouveau as a total period style. The more likely route is to take one or two strong Art Nouveau pieces and use them as keynotes.

3

This is an excellent example of how inexpensive Edwardian furniture can be used to good effect in a spare bedroom. The furniture is wonderfully functional, incorporating mirror, drawers and hanging space. The floral frieze sets the mood.

4

All the pine panelling in the bedrooms of Preston Manor, Brighton, has been painted white. This became fashionable in the late Victorian/Edwardian periods as contemporary writers on such issues warned against the distracting effect of patterned walls and ceilings to those confined to the sickbed. Brass beds were a feature of Victorian rooms and remained popular into the 20th C. The furniture in this room is a mixture of 18th and 19thC but the overall feel is certainly Edwardian.

and in apartments. The new built-in furniture – seats in niches and inglenooks, and fitted cupboards – helped to create an uncluttered look.

Freestanding furniture continued the tradition of "Queen Anne" styles, having a lightness and delicacy that contrasted with the solid bulk of most Victorian pieces. Satinwood was much used, but darker woods were also popular. A revival of interest in late 18th and early 19th-century Classical styles – Neo-classical and Regency – was reflected in the decoration of many rooms, as well as in the lines and ornamentation of furniture.

Walls

Pale colours predominated. In many rooms by the turn of the century the dado was absent (it remained in halls) and the whole wall was treated as one surface.

Wallpapers were produced in abundance, with a wide variety of patterns from which to choose. Art Nouveau, Adam patterns and pale Wedgwood blues and greens were fashionable.

Wallpaper borders were also popular, and might be used in conjunction with a paper of neutral self-coloured pattern, perhaps with the border taken above the skirting board and around the door.

3

4

Embossed papers and the heavier Lincrusta were often used for dados in halls; once painted, they provided a particularly robust surface. There were various designs, including curvilinear Art Nouveau motifs.

Woodwork

Creamy white woodwork was particularly fashionable, and combined with lighter walls to create a feeling of space. An Art Nouveau fashion was to paint flowers in the panels of doors.

Windows

As with everything else, window treatments were lighter to suit the more airy rooms – the Victorian mistrust of daylight seems to have been banished at last. Fabrics were less heavy and less ornamented with fringing and other trimmings.

Furniture

In general, Edwardian furniture was lighter and more delicate than previously. Sheraton-style pieces in satinwood were characteristic, but there were also graceful pieces in darker woods. Fragile-looking music cabinets, display cabinets and small tables with tapering legs made in mahogany with restrained inlay in pale colours to define the shape are typical of the time. Furniture was also sometimes painted, or might have painted decoration instead of inlay.

Lighting

By the turn of the century electric lighting was more general, but the shapes of the fittings usually reflected those of the past. Many looked much the same as gas fittings. There were also Adam-style brackets to suit Classically inspired rooms. Some of the most delightful light fittings of the time were those made in the Art Nouveau style – plant shapes with flower-shaped shades. Candlelight was usually preferred for dining rooms.

ART NOUVEAU DEFINED

Belgium, France, Spain, Italy, Germany and Austria all developed their own version of the sinuous style known as Art Nouveau, which grew out of the Arts and Crafts Movement and flourished in the 1890s and early 1900s. The Europeans enthusiastically created complete interiors – and often exteriors – in the style. Britain never wholeheartedly adopted it, although the characteristic motifs of stylized flowers and plants appeared in late-Victorian and Edwardian houses on tiles, textiles and wallcoverings, and plant and female forms were used for accessories such as lamps and photograph frames. In America Art Nouveau was disseminated by the influence of designers such as Louis Comfort Tiffany, best known for his art glass, lamps and jewelry.

Two distinct streams developed in Art Nouveau. At one end of the spectrum is the extravagant manner, with not a straight line among the waving forms, that typifies the work of Victor Horta in Brussels, Hector Guimard in Paris (famous for his ironwork Métro entrances) and Antoni Gaudi in Barcelona. In houses in this curvilinear version of Art Nouveau, the architecture is an integral part of the whole design. The same growing plant forms recur in staircases, plasterwork, painted decoration, fitted and freestanding furniture, light fittings, fabrics and small objects.

Substances that are shaped in a molten state – such as wrought iron and glass – lent themselves well to curving shapes. Staircases were a perfect vehicle for wrought iron, and there are some fine examples that epitomize the delicate writhings of the style. Glass vases and tall toadstool-like lamps by Emile Gallé in wonderful iridescent peacock colours look almost as though they are growing. More surprisingly, furniture made from wood was often just as voluptuously flowing in design, giving the impression that the wood had been melted and poured into a mould.

The other, much more severe extreme of Art Nouveau is represented by the work of Charles Rennie Mackintosh and the members of the Glasgow School. Among the influences on this group were Celtic art and Scottish baronial architecture. Mackintosh designs have strongly upright straight lines counterpointed by stylized flower forms – particularly the rose. It was the Mackintosh form of the style, more rectilinear in its shapes, that was taken up by artists of the Wiener Werkstätte, who produced a Viennese version of Art Nouveau known as the "Sezessionstil" or "Jugendstil".

1

1

The copper pans hanging from meat hooks, the highly efficient gas range, the pine butcher's block with drawers and the charming farming prints and carpet beaters give this efficient kitchen a country, turn of the century feel.

2

This pine display rack in the same kitchen as in picture 3 provides a perfect setting for a collection of late 19th and early 20thC ceramics. Art Deco ceramics can still be found at reasonable prices. Note the interesting collection of honey jars.

3

This practical kitchen with fitted pine dresser-type units derives its Edwardian feeling from the splashback of tiles, the wall lights (which would originally have been the other way up) and the profusion of dried hops and baskets.

2

3

1

2

3

4

COLOURS Colours in an Edwardian interior should be pale. White was very fashionable at this time, particularly for woodwork, offset by the pale mauves, pinks, greens, turquoises, blues and yellows of Art Nouveau.

WALLS These can be painted plain and have a stencilled, painted or wallpaper border, perhaps on an Art Nouveau theme. Instead of having the border at ceiling level or below the picture rail, you could run it above the skirting board and around door frames. Alternatively, cover the walls with an Art Nouveau wallpaper. There was a Neo-classical revival around the turn of the century, so Adam-style wallpaper designs are also correct for the period. Some Classically inspired friezes in Anaglypta paper reproduce late 19th-century designs. Dados are not so usual in Edwardian houses as they are in Victorian ones, except in the hall.

FURNITURE There are various styles of furniture of the period from which to choose, most of it lighter and more delicate than before – frequently in satinwood. Shapes were more upright. Sheraton styles were popular and would suit a Classical style of decoration. There are also full-blown Art Nouveau pieces of furniture with voluptuous curves. Built-in furniture – cupboards, seats and so on – suits an Edwardian room, provided that it is sufficiently craftsmanlike and convincingly styled.

FLOORS Opt for polished boards or parquet flooring topped with Oriental rugs or carpets: note that patterns and colourings should be restrained. If you wish to use a fitted carpet on the floor , choose a plain pale colour.

SOFT FURNISHINGS Keep rooms light and airy. Elegant swags and tails suit a formal room with large windows. If the windows are narrower, a more relaxed feel can be created by simply decorating the top of the window with a length of lace draped over a pole.

LIGHTING There are numerous reproductions of Art Nouveau ceiling pendants, wall lamps and table lamps. It is also possible to buy original designs. Adam-style brackets will suit Classically inspired rooms.

FINISHING TOUCHES Echo a stencilled border on plain walls with a similar design on the floor. For evocative music, try Delius' *Summer Night on the River* and *On Hearing the First Cuckoo in Spring*; Elgar's *Enigma Variations*; or Vaughan Williams' *Symphony No.2* ("London Symphony").

CREATING THE LOOK

5

1

The Voysey Room in the Geffrye Museum, East London, is an excellent example of the way things were at the turn of the century. The flowing lines and natural forms can be seen on the cast-iron chimney piece, c.1900. Voysey's furniture has been imitated and even mass-produced. The wallpaper in the room is another Voysey design.

2

This Edwardian radiator has been restored and is now an extremely practical heat source.

3

The Edwardians flavoured generous skirting boards and door architraves. The neutral colour on the dado and the wallpaper above were a common feature, as was half-panelling in the hallway.

4

The tile colours give this Edwardian washroom a friendly feel.

5

The epitome of Edwardian life – the billiard room with its fabric, books and rugs.

ART DECO

1

Art Deco is the style that swept through the most fashionable circles in the 1920s and 30s. The name is derived from the title of the Paris exhibition of 1925, the "Exposition des Arts Décoratifs". The look was luxurious and opulent, with blond woods, chrome, glass, leather, lacquer, sharkskin or ivory catching the eye. Instead of the twining, languorous curves and pale colours of Art Nouveau, we encounter the oranges, lime greens and mauves of Diaghilev's Ballets Russes – the current rage in Paris and London – and Egyptian motifs inspired by the opening of Tutankhamun's tomb in 1922. Other influences are Cubism, and the Mayan and Aztec art of Central America. (The stepped "ziggurat" shape of Aztec temples is a recurring motif).

Speed was another obsession: fast cars and trains, and the achievements of the early aviators, caught the general imagination and led to sleek, streamlined forms. Rounded corners were a feature of Art Deco buildings, inside and out, and furniture based on geometric shapes – the circle, semicircle, triangle, octagon and cube – was very popular. These same shapes decorate flooring, wallcoverings and fabrics, and also occur in pottery and light fittings.

Other typical motifs are sunrises, fans, stylized trees, flowers, fountains and animal forms, particularly the deer and ibex.

Walls

Pale backgrounds, particularly in off-white and shades of beige, were common in Art Deco rooms. In grand settings, walls might be lined with a luxurious light-coloured wood. More frequently they would be painted or

2

3

4

— 1 —

With Art Deco we move into an area of pure design. The style, which has been described as "domesticated cubism", was a reaction against decades of Classical restraint. Its practitioners believed that art and mass production were not mutually exclusive. Deryck Healey has succeeded here in creating a strong Art Deco preserve in the hall area of his London flat. The table, in characteristic pale wood and with unmistakable phallic conotations, is from the 1920s. It is surmounted by a French enamel vase of the same period and a pair of Liberty pewter candlesticks. The paintings above are by Deryck Healey.

— 2 —

This room, designed by Harry Schule, depends for much of its Art Deco impact on the widespread use of mirror glass. Art Deco is a distinctly dramatic style. The zebra skin rug, the 1940s table, the 1940s mirrored glass fire surround, the 1930s chair all reflected in mirrored glass add up to a classic Art Deco effect. The vases on the mantel shelf are by Villeroy and Boch.

— 3 —

This table was designed in 1979 by Ned Marshall in the style of Art Deco Regency. It is set in front of a 1940s American Mercury glass screen.

— 4 —

Reflection adds to the impact of this late 1930s rosewood and ivory man's dressing table by Leleu. Note also the collection of 1930s and 40s ivories.

1

2

papered. There were numerous wallpapers with the typical motifs, frequently in rather subdued shades. Painted walls might be stippled in two closely related colours: two shades of beige was a popular combination. The surface would then be finished with a painted or stencilled border of contemporary motifs.

Wallpaper borders were used on painted or papered walls. A simple border might be taken along each individual wall at ceiling or picture rail level, then extended part way down each side, the angles decorated with a complementary corner motif.

Floors

Polished woodblock or parquet flooring was fashionable. Rugs placed on top had bold geometric patterns. Linoleum was widely used in more modest houses and in kitchens.

Window treatments

Curtains, on the whole, were simply hung in pairs, and were often finished off with a pelmet, geometrically outlined.

Furniture

Developments in the technique of moulding plywood made it possible to make furniture with rounded outlines. Pale woods (sycamore, bird's eye maple, walnut and light oak), leather, lacquer, chrome and glass were fashionable for furniture. Pieces were often decorated with exotic materials

1

This rosewood commode with steel drawer handles was designed by Jules Leleu in the 1930s. Such pieces by designer craftsmen were always intended for the rich, but many copies of these designs exist. Primitive art was one of the sources of inspiration for Art Deco designers, hence the collection of African masks is quite correct.

2

This 1940s American hide-covered chair beside a linear-design book cabinet has as its backdrop a framed project for a French Post Office drawn in 1933 by J. Roger. Architectural drawings of this period can still be found in sale rooms and auction houses, and are often works of art in themselves.

3

4

3

It is interesting to see how well this Biedermeier (c.1815-1848) table fits into the Art Deco style. The French painted metal vases by Dericemo and paintings and sculpture by Deryck Healey give this wallscape a strong 20thC feel.

4

This pair of 1920s French painted metal tables with smoky mirrored glass tops set against a neutral background provided the perfect setting for a collection of modern pots by Fiona Salazar. The interesting point about Art Deco is how modern it looks today.

such as ivory, sharkskin and shagreen (imitation sharkskin). Off-white was a fashionable colour for upholstery. Mirror glass was used extensively.

Among the new pieces that appeared at this time were the cocktail cabinet and, of course, the coffee table.

Lighting

Light fittings typical of the era are chain-hung marbled bowl pendants, glass and chrome shell- and fan-shaped wall lights, table lamps with half-globe-shaped opaque glass shades on Perspex and chrome stands, and stylized female figures holding globes or supporting shades.

Accessories

Clocks, radios, vases, ornaments and tableware echoed the shapes and motifs of furniture, fabrics and rugs.

Memorable designers of tableware, vases and other pottery were Clarice Cliff and Susie Cooper (who is still designing today).

Cocktails were the "in drink", and a whole array of paraphernalia connected with preparing, serving and drinking them became fashionable.

Among the most charming ornaments were the graceful bronze figures – often of dancers – by Preiss, Chiparus and others.

An outstanding designer of glass objects, who worked in both Art Nouveau and Art Deco, was René Lalique. In the latter style he created bowls, lamps, statuettes, vases, perfume bottles and car mascots.

2

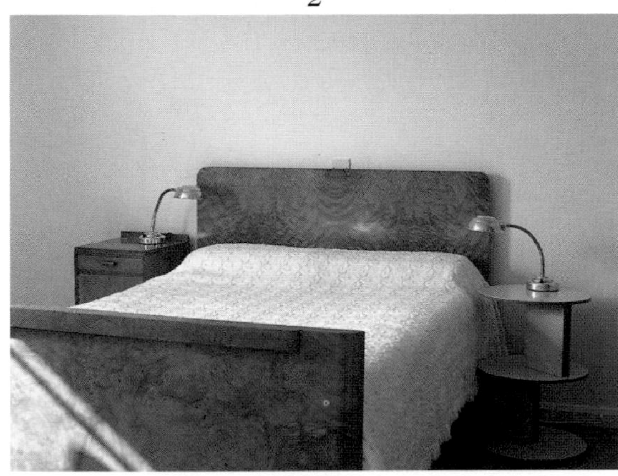

3

4

COLOURS Pale, neutral tones, particularly creams, beiges, warm golds, should be offset by touches of orange, mauve, lime green or turquoise.

WALLS These can be lined with a neutral, textured wallpaper, and painted plain, sponged or rag-rolled with two tones of a neutral colour. Decorating plainish walls with a wallpaper border is right for the period: the design might be of stylized leaves and flowers. Alternatively, design your own border with stencilled motifs.

FLOORS Polished parquet, pale sealed and polished boards, or linoleum, would all be correct. Use rugs with geometric patterns.

FURNITURE Choose pieces in pale woods such as bird's eye maple, walnut or light oak. Chrome and glass often do much to convey the mood. It is now possible to buy reproductions of well-known designs of the period, such as the round chrome-and-glass occasional tables with horseshoe feet, and circular-sided trolleys in the same materials. Upholstered pieces should either have curved back and sides or be made up of fat rectangular cushions. There is plenty of genuine 1920s and 30s furniture around today, ranging from luxurious pieces in exotic materials to squarish oak sideboards, tables and chairs with Art Deco detailing.

SOFT FURNISHINGS Simple window treatments complement the Art Deco style. Floor-length curtains in a fabric with an appropriate period pattern could be topped by a painted or fabric-covered pelmet ornamented with a central geometric motif and outlined in braid or paint. Alternatively, you could have venetian blinds: choose the sort with wide slats. Or hang curtains from a chrome pole, draping the fabric over in a loose "freehand" manner. Look for printed or woven fabrics with geometric motifs – squares, triangles, circles, semicircles – in muted pastel tones, beiges and browns, or bright oranges, mauves and lime greens. Animal-skin prints are also a good choice. Leather, uncut moquette or velvet are the best upholstery fabrics.

LIGHTING Reproduction Art Deco light fittings include shell-shaped, triangular and bowl-shaped wall-mounted uplighters in opaque glass, as well as chrome, round-topped table lamps and draped ladies holding illuminated globes. It is possible also to buy original fittings.

ACCESSORIES Choose large mirrors with ziggurat-shaped tops or the small angular ones with Art Deco detailing designed to hang on chains over a fireplace or sideboard in a suburban house. Look out for clocks, radios, glass fruit bowls, dressing table sets. Collect pottery in Art Deco shapes, decorated with brightly coloured stylized flowers, fruits and various geometric motifs.

1

This living room of the mid 1930s in the Geffrye Museum in London, shows some of the new styles and materials available. The items on display include a bakelite radio, a three-piece suite of 1928, a Shelley "Vogue" tea service and "Crocus" pottery by Clarice Cliff.

CREATING THE LOOK

5

2, 3, 4 and 5

All these views are of a fascinating hotel on Burgh Island off the Devon coast. The Art Deco building is furnished in period style using mainly mass-produced Art Deco furniture set against plain backgrounds.

CONTENTS

Interior Designers **p. 228**
Suppliers:
- *Fittings* **p. 228**
- *Floors and Carpets* **p. 229**
- *Furniture: Antique* **p. 229**
- *Furniture: Reproduction* **p. 230**
- *Lighting* **p. 231**
- *Paint finishes* **p. 232**
- *Textiles and Wallpapers* **p. 232**
- *Antique Textiles* **p. 233**
- *Florists* **p. 233**

Courses **p. 233**
Associations **p. 234**
Historic Houses and Museums **p. 234**
Places with style **p. 235**
Bibliography **p. 235**

INTERIOR DESIGNERS

Bennison
91 Pimlico Road
London SWl W 8PH
(01) 730 3370
Interior designers and fine art dealers, specializing in interesting antique furniture. They carry an imaginative stock of unusual pieces as well as making their own range of "antique" light fittings.

Jane Churchill Designs
81 Pimlico Road,
London SW1 8PH
(01) 730 8564
Designs combine an 18th or 19thC feel with a modern lightness of touch. Paintings and prints used imaginatively.

Colefax and Fowler
100 Fulham Road
London SW1
(01) 244 7427
Interior design service as well as practical advice on colour schemes, curtain treatment and upholstery. A wide selection of upholstered furniture, lighting and carpets as well as exclusive chintzes and wallpapers. Specially made accessories include lap and hearth rugs, flower holders, and a range of room fragrances.

The Country House Collection
The Tything
Preston Court,
Ledbury
Herefordshire HRB 2LL
(053184) 245
Interior designers refurbishing traditional English country homes, specializing in the Elizabethan period. They also produce their own fabrics in period styles.

Elizabeth Eaton
25a Basil Street
London SW3 1BB
(01) 589 0118
Offers a full decorator service of advice on interior use of period houses, services of a qualified architect renowned for work on period property, joinery and cabinetmaking to drawings, advice on painting and decorating, preferably executed by their own team of workmen. Period wallpapers and fabrics.

Paul Ferguson Workshop
Workshop 20
21 Wren Street
London WC1X OHF
(01) 278 8759
See under Furniture.

Christophe Gollut
116 Fulham Road
London SW3 6HU
(01) 370 4101
Furniture of the 18th and 19thC used in eclectic Continental-influenced interiors. Favours a rich, mellow mood.

Charles Hammond Ltd
2a Battersea Park Road
London SW8 5BJ
(01) 627 5566
Designers and suppliers of period fabric.

Helena Hood & Company
3 Margarets Buildings
Brock Street
Bath, Avon
(0225) 24438
Fabrics, small decorative pieces of furniture and lamps. Complete interior design service.

Jonathan Hudson Interior Decorations
16 Fitzjames Avenue
London W14 ORP
(01) 602 8829
Specializes in creating elegant interiors in period luxury.

Ian Lieber
Kingsmead House
250 Kings Road
London SW3 5UE
(01) 352 6422
International designer working in modern as well as traditional styles. Past projects include the Adam Room in the Lloyds Building, London.

London Interior Design Centre
1 Cringle Street
Battersea Park Road
London SW8 5BX
(01) 627 5566
Centre for architects, interior designers, specifiers and their clients. Display of merchandise from over 35 companies, including wide range of period fabrics from Charles Hammond and Pallu and Lake, reproduction and antique furniture from Arthur Brett and Sons of Norwich.

Mrs Monro Ltd
11 Montpelier Street
London SW7
(01) 589 5052
Specializes in the 18th-century English country house style. The company favours a simple, natural look, with an eye for strong colours. Uses both antique and good repro furniture.

Number Twelve Queen Street
12 Queen Street
Bath
Avon BA1 1NE
(0225) 62363
Provides a complete interior design service. Carries a selection of period decorative objects and 17th- and 18th-century oak and country furniture.

Anthony Paine Ltd
24 Highgate High St
London N6 5JG
(01) 340 4187
Architectural and interior design. Small multi-disciplinary practice, specializing in the sympathetic renovation of old and historic buildings.

Pavilion Designs
49 Pavilion Road
London SW1X 0HD
(01) 245 6788
Offers an interior design service and sells objets, pictures, small pieces of furniture, columns, candlestick lamps etc.

Simon Playle Ltd
6 Fulham Park Studios
Fulham Park Rd
London SW6 4LW
(01) 371 0131
Interior designers specializing in traditional English houses, using antiques from a wide range of periods, oriental influence, chinoiseries. Importers and suppliers of American wallpapers and fabrics.

Private Lives
The Old Parsonage
Church Street
Crondall, Near Farnham
Surrey GU10 5QQ
(0252) 850527
Flexible design service, with a range of traditional fabrics, antique bed treatments, repro furniture, panelling, period lighting, and tenting and walling with fabric.

Stuart Interiors
Barrington Court
Barrington, Ilminster
Somerset TA 19 0NQ
(0460) 42003
One of the country's leading specialist designers, recreating 16th- and 17th-century English interiors. They offer a complete design and furnishing service, including panelling, doors, staircases, stonework, furniture and accessories. There is an exclusive range of "early" fabrics, launched in conjunction with Tissunique. The company aims to promote interior design pre-1730 through the showrooms and with lectures and exhibitions.

Joanna Wood
Joanna Trading
7 Bunhouse Place
London SW1W 8HU
(01) 730 0693
English country house style, using antique furniture with old paintings and prints. Upholstery service available.

Melissa Wyndham
6 Sydney St
London SW3
(01) 352 2874
Every aspect of interior design from rebuilding structures to buying antiques. Colours, curtains, furnishings.

Design Associations

British Decorators Association
6 Haywra Street
Harrogate
North Yorkshire HG1 5BL
(0423) 67292
Over 1,000 members who specialize in the decoration of period homes.

British Institute of Interior Design
1c Devonshire Avenue
Beeston, Nottingham
NG9 1BS
(0602) 221255
Established in 1899 and now a leading organization in the interior design industry. Its objectives are to encourage better understanding, care and improvement of interior design. Has over 223 registered practices and about 1,500 members. A recommended shortlist is available.

Chartered Society of Industrial Artists and Designers (S.I.A.D.)
29 Bedford Square
London WC1B 3EG
(01) 631 1510
Association of professional interior designers. Will supply details of designers specializing in period houses.

Interior Decorators and Designers Association
Crest House
102-104 Church Rd
Teddington
Middlesex TW11 8PY
(01) 977 1105
Associations of interior decorators and designers.

FITTINGS

Architectural Components
(Locks and Handles)
4-10 Exhibition Road
London SW7 2HF
(01) 581 2401/(01) 584 6800
Three showrooms, near the South Kensington Museums, and Underground station, supply a large range of period fittings used in the renovation and furnishing of property. Over 6,000 different items in stock – door and cabinet fittings, bathroom accessories, all types of locks, window fittings, hinges, curtain hardware, door closers, grilles and vents, electrical switch plates, fireplace furniture.

Bailey's Architectural Antiques
The Engine Shed
Ashburton Industrial Estate
Ross-on-Wye
Herefordshire HE9 7BW
(0989) 63015
Bathroom fittings, fireplaces, light fittings, door accessories; antique and repro.

Beardmore Architectural Ironmongery
Field End Road
Ruislip
Middlesex HA4 0QG
(01) 864 6811
Also: 3-5 Percy Street, London W1P 0EJ
(01) 637 7041
Ornamental period-style brassware, ranging from electrical accessories to door furniture.

Brass Art Craft Birmingham Ltd
76 Atwood Street
Lye, Stourbridge West Midlands
(038482) 3346/4814
Period brass door and window fittings and electrical accessories. Catalogue available.

Brass Tacks Hardware Ltd
50-54 Clerkenwell Road
London EC1M 5PS
(01) 250 1971
Manufacturers and distributors of decorative brass door fittings and accessories, the range including locks, hinges and furniture, electrical accessories and bathroom fittings. The company also produces special items and decorative grilles for covering radiators, etc. Catalogues available.

Celmac Heatherley Ltd
Unit 3 Ferry Lane
Brentford, Middlesex
TW8 0BG
(01) 568 7963
English porcelain door furniture, English ceramic bathroom fittings, English natural wood bathroom fittings, toilet seats.

G. & H. Products Ltd
Unit 14 Gainsborough
Trading Estate
Rufford Road
Stourbridge
Worcestershire
(0384) 375321
Period electrical fittings.

Export Agency: A.D.N. Products
Radnor House
93-97 Regent Street,
London W1
Manufacturers and suppliers of electrical fittings, Georgian, Regency and Victorian, all complemented by a full range of door and cabinet fittings.

Charles Harden
14 Chiltern Street
London W1
(01) 935 2032
Specialists in brass, glass and china door furniture, bathroom fittings in brass, chrome and gold-plated finishes.

Hope Works Ltd
Pleck Road
Walsall WS2 9HH
(0922) 27175
Manufacturers of Lionheart decorative hardware in iron and brass. 16th to 19thC designs in door and window hardware.

Knobs and Knockers
36-40 York Way
London N1 9AB
(01) 833 0841
Brass radiator grills, door furniture, light fittings etc.

Leon Moodley's Fine Art Brass Co.
Unit 1b & 1c Langdon Rd
Industrial Estate
Langdon Rd
Bradworthy, Devon
(040924) 511
Castings used in restoration work.

Rothley Brass Ltd
Merridale House
Merridale Street
Wolverhampton WV3 0RB
(0902) 27532
Suppliers of brass door furniture and electrical fittings. A comprehensive collection including the Victorian Windsor, Georgian and China collection, also the Knockers and Numerals collection which covers ancient and traditional patterns.

A Touch of Brass Ltd
123 Kensington Church Street
London W8
(01) 221 9256
Solid brass shelf brackets, hooks, door knockers and drawer pulls. Brass radiator grills.

FLOORS AND CARPETS

Antique Carpet Gallery Ltd
The Mall
Beaconsfield
Bucks HP9 1QW
(04946) 2130
Specializes in the importing of antique, semi-antique and modern oriental carpets, rugs and kelims.

Bosanquet Ives Ltd
3 Court Lodge
48 Sloane Square
London SWI W8AT
(01) 730 6241
Design and produce carpets to interior designers' instructions. Also carry large stocks of coir and jute matting.

Brooke London Ltd
5 Sleaford Street
London SW8 5AB
(01) 622 9372
Flat weave dhurries based on Savonnerie designs of the 17th and 18th centuries. Available through Liberty and Co. and General Trading Company, 144 Sloane Street, London SW1 X 9BL (01 731 0411).

Crucial Trading Ltd
PO Box 689
London W2 4BX
(01) 727 3634
Floor coverings in natural materials — sea-grass, coir matting, sisal etc.

Fired Earth
Twyford Mill
Oxford Road
Adderbury
Oxon OX17 3HP
(0295) 812088
Handmade terracotta tiles, slate floors, encaustic floor tiles etc.

Arthur Goodwin
4 Devonshire Place
Exeter
Devon
(0392) 70943
Reproduces Victorian or Classical mosaics for walls and floors.

Harris Signs
116 Whyke Lane Chichester
West Sussex
(0243) 782578
Will undertake painted canvas floorcloths in the style of the 18th century.

Herez Carpets Ltd
110 New Bond Street
London WlY 9AA
(01) 235 7416
Antique carpets and tapestries.

Hometex Trading Ltd
Sedbergh Chambers
Chantry Drive
Ilkley
West Yorks. LS29 9HU
(0943) 608197
Floor coverings in natural materials — coir matting etc.

Naturestone Ltd
1 King's Ride Park
King's Ride
Ascot, Berks. SL5 8AR
(0990) 27617
Slate and stone flooring tiles.

Paris Ceramics
543 Battersea Park Rd
London SW11 3BL
(01) 228 5785
Unglazed decorated floor tiles, blue English limestone flagstones, antique terracotta tiles.

Dennis Ruabon Ltd
Hafod Tileries
Ruabon
Wrexham
Clwyd LL14 6ET
(0978) 843484
Quarry tile manufacturers. Polygon range of traditional patterns.

Saraband Furniture Co Ltd
Rooksmoor Mills
Bath Rd
Nr Stroud
Glos. GL5 5ND
Floor coverings in natural materials — coir matting etc.

Steeles Carpets
332 The Business Design Centre
52 Upper Street
London N1
(01) 288 6138

Stockwell, Riley, Hooley Ltd
Trade showroom and design service:
67a Great Titchfield Street
London W1P 7FL
(01) 580 5935
Wide range of carpet designs covering most periods, including Adam style, Victorian, William Morris, Machintosh, Art Nouveau, Art Deco, Pennsylvania-"Dutch". Savonnerie Collection of carpets inspired by classic pieces produced in France in the 18th and 19th centuries.

Thames Carpet Cleaners Ltd
48/56 Reading Road
Henley-on-Thames
Oxon RG9 1AG
(0491) 574676
Specialists in the cleaning and restoration of fine and rare oriental rugs, tapestries and silks.

Valerie Wade
108 Fulham Rd
London SW3
(01) 225 1414
19th-century style hand-made needlepoint carpets and cushions.

FURNITURE: *ANTIQUE*

Art Deco Furniture Centre
67 Camden Road
London NW1
(01) 267 3342
Specializes in dining, lounge and bedroom suites, cocktail cabinets, peach mirrors, lights, desks and tables.

Bizarre
24 Church Street
London NW8
(01) 724 1305
Art Deco.

J.W. Blanchard Ltd
12 Jewry Street
Winchester
Hants.
(0962) 54547
English period furniture.

John Bly
50 High Street
Tring
Herts.
(044) 282 3030
Fine English furniture.

Arthur Brett & Sons Ltd
40-44 St Giles Street
Norwich
(0603) 628171
Dealers in English 17th, 18th and 19thC, especially oak, treen and bygones.

Paul Cater Antiques
High Street
Moreton-in-the-Marsh
Glos.
(0608) 51888
Fine English period furniture.

Rupert Cavendish Antiques
610 Kings Road
London SW6 2DX
(01) 731 7041
Empire and Biedermeier furniture.

Cedar Antiques Ltd (Derek Green)
Hartley Wintney
Hants.
(025 126) 3252
Specialists in 17th and 18thC furniture, especially yew wood, walnut, fruit wood and oak.

Collins Antiques Ltd
Corner House
Wheathampstead
Herts.
(058 283) 3111
Fine oak, walnut and mahogany furniture.

Richard Davidson Antiques
Lombard Street
Petworth
West Sussex GU28 0AG
(0798) 42508
Fine period English and Continental furniture

Doveridge House Antiques
Neach Hill, Long Lane
Nr Shifnal
Shropshire
(090 722) 3131
Fine furniture and decorative antiques.

Brian Fielden
3 New Cavendish Street
London W1
(01) 935 6912
English walnut and mahogany furniture, mirrors and barometers.

Fron Furniture of Llanfynydd
Wrexham
Clwyd LL11 5HW
(0352) 770374
Specializes in traditional quality 17th and 18thC country furniture.

Heritage Restoration
Unit 5
Colhook Industrial Park
Petworth
W. Sussex
(0428) 78566
Restoration, conservation, cabinet-making.

Paul Hopwell
30 High Street
West Haddon
Northants.
(078 887) 636
Specialist in early English oak.

Huntington Antiques
The Old Forge
Church Street
Stow on the Wold
Glos.
(0451) 30842
Period oak, walnut and country furniture, medieval to 1740.

Jazzy Art Deco
67 Camden Road
London NW1
(01) 267 3342
Art Deco furniture and decorative items.

John Jesse and Irena Laski Ltd
160 Kensington Church Street
London W8
(01) 229 0312
Art Nouveau, Art Deco and decorative arts.

H.W. Keil Ltd
Tudor House
Broadway
Worcestershire
17th and 18thC furniture and works of art.

Lacy Gallery
38 Ledbury Road
London W11
(01) 229 9105
Antique picture frames.

Liberty and Co.
Regent Street
London W1
(01) 734 1234
Original Arts and Crafts pieces.

Mallet
2 Davies Street
Berkeley Square
London W1
(01) 629 2444
Fine English furniture and decorative items.

Trevor Micklem Antiques
Frogpool Farm
Moos Wood
Oakhill
Bath
Avon
(0749) 840754
Early English furniture and pottery.

Millers of Chelsea
Netherbrook House
86 Christchurch Road
Ringwood
Hants.
(0425) 472062
Fine English period furniture.

Old Bakery Antiques
St Davids Bridge
Cranbrook
Kent
Period oak and country furniture.

Angela and Bill Page Antiques
15 Cumberland Walk
Tunbridge Wells
Kent
(0892) 22217
Oak and country furniture, decorative items and folk art.

R.G.T Ratcliffe Ltd
Durwards Hall
Kelvedon
Essex
(0376) 70234
Fine decorative furniture.

Paul Reeves
32B Kensington Church Street
London W8
(01) 937 1594
Arts and Crafts.

Seventh Heaven
Chirk Mill
Chirk, Clwyd
(0691) 777622
Extensive collection of antique beds – mostly late 19thC.

M. & D. Seligmann
37 Kensington Church Street
London W8
(01) 937 0400
Early oak and country furniture including treen.

Keith Skeel Antiques
7-9 Elliott Place
London N1
(01) 226 7012
By appointment only. Interesting and unusual furniture, ornaments, panelling, small table lamps, chandeliers, small soft furnishings. Many eccentricities. Restoration service.

Stair and Co. Ltd
120 Mount Street
London W1
(01) 499 1784
Fine English period furniture.

Stuart Interiors (Antiques) Ltd
Barrington Court
Barrington
Ilminster
Somerset
(0460) 40349
Early oak furniture and accessories, interior design and architectural items including oak panelling.

Studio Antiques
Bourton-on-the-Water
Glos.
(0451) 20352
Period and contemporary furniture, porcelain and glass.

E.J.Tracy Ltd
4 Station Mews
Potters Bar, Herts.
(0707) 52144
Traditional techniques of french polishing used to restore furniture, on panelling, doors, staircases, floors etc.

Simon Tracy
18 Church Street
London NW8
(01) 724 5890
Arts and crafts furniture and accessories.

The Victorian Brass Bedstead Company
Hoe Copse
Cocking, Nr Midhurst
West Sussex
(073081) 2287
Wide selection of restored Victorian brass and iron bedsteads.

Anthony Welling
Broadway Barn
High Street
Ripley, Surrey
(0483) 225384
Specialist in 17th and 18thC oak and country furniture.

Robert Young
68 Battersea Bridge Road
London SW11
(01) 228 7847
Specialists in country furniture and folk art.

FURNITURE: *REPRODUCTION*

Artefact
36 Windmill Street
London W1P 1HF
(01) 580 4878
220 Battersea Park Rd
London SW11 1JL
(01) 720 7313
Manufactures a range of overmantel and decorative mirrors, mainly Regency.

Bevan Funnell Ltd
Reprodux House
Beach Rd, Newhaven
East Sussex BN9
(0273) 513762
Quality reproduction furniture in a variety of period styles, in mahogany, yew, oak and walnut.

Arthur Brett and Sons Ltd
Hellesdon Park Rd
Drayton High Rd
Norwich NR6 5DR
(0603) 486633
Manufacturers of fine English furniture of 18thC style. Will match antique originals and adapt designs to unusual sizes or finishes

British Antique Interiors
Queen Elizabeth Ave
Burgess Hill
West Sussex RH15 9RX
(04446) 45577
Period style furniture made from antique wood, including Georgian, Victorian, Queen Anne, William and Mary styles.

Rupert Brown
Dean Farm
Woodcutts
Nr Handley
Salisbury, Wilts.
SP5 5RT
(07255) 2438
A cabinetmaker with a thorough knowledge of all period styles and construction, and with a strong personal sense of design, enabling him to cope with the most exacting situations.

Château
36 Cathcart Rd
London SW10 9NN
(01) 352 0447
High-quality copies of French period furniture, mirrors and lighting. Also Art Deco designs.

Ray Denney
4 Kennard Close
Borstal, Rochester
Kent ME1 3LH
(0634) 402722
Cabinetmaker who undertakes quality work to order. Copies of antique pieces.

Martin Dodge Interiors
Showrooms:
15/16 Broad Street
Bath BA1 5LJ
(0225) 62202
Cabinet works:
Southgate, Wincanton
Somerset BA9 9EB
Manufacturers of English furniture in 18th and 19thC styles.

Duresta Upholstery Ltd,
Leopold Street
Long Eaton
Nottingham NG10 4QJ
(0602) 732246
National Trust Collection – upholstery designs based on pieces of different periods.

English Antiques Portfolio
55 Grove Park Gardens
London W4 3RY
(01) 747 4017
Cast copies of existing antique furniture, especially elaborately carved pieces, mainly Gothic. Cast Gothic radiator casings.

Environment Design
Heath Hall, Heath
Wakefield WF1 5SL
(0924) 366446
UK distributors for Cassina who reproduce furniture designs by Charles Rennie Mackintosh and Frank Lloyd Wright.

Paul Ferguson Workshop
Workshop 20
21 Wren Street
London WC1X 0HF
(01) 278 8759
Specializes in English and European styling, 1670-1820. High-quality reproductions, antiques, antique restoration, new furniture to the client's designs, designing to specification, pattern making for casting, period picture frames to specification or designs, styling advisory service.

Gostin of Liverpool Ltd
Portway, off 2a Higher Road
Halewood
Liverpool L25 0QQ
(051) 486 1703
Specialists in reproductions of English 17th and 18thC furniture in mahogany, oak and walnut.

Simon Horn
117-121 Wandsworth Bridge Road
London SW6 2TP
(01) 731 1279
French and classic wooden beds.

E.G.Hudson (UK) Ltd
Faraday Close
Worthing
West Sussex BN133PN
(0903) 692211
Quality handmade traditional furniture in mahogany, yewtree, rosewood and walnut. The inspiration for many designs comes from the 18thC.

Intermobel
Ward Street
Guildford
Surrey GUl 4LH
(0483) 302111
"Medea" range of Art Nouveau-style seating.

G. & A. Kelly Ltd
Unit 4
Heliport Estate
40 Lombard Rd
London SW11
(01) 228 9812
Traditionally upholstered, hand-sprung furniture.

Kingcome Ltd
304 Fulham Rd
London SW10 9EP
(01) 351 1444
Quality traditional upholstery.

Liberty and Co.
Regent Street
London Wl
(01) 734 1234
"Liberty Guild" furniture inspired by Arts and Crafts.

Stewart Linford
Kitchener Works
Kitchener Rd
High Wycombe
Bucks.
HP11 2SJ
(0494) 40408
Windsor chair maker; classic chairs in yew and English hardwoods.

Lion House Antiques
16 New Street
Chipping Norton
Oxon
(0608) 3294
Hand-built copies of 18thC period furniture in oak, pine and mahogany.

William Maclean Ltd
Wenstrom House
Hollingbury Industrial Estate
Carden Avenue
Brighton BN1
(0273) 565441
Manufacturers of quality furniture and upholstery. Ranges include – Country Chippendale collection, Brighton Regency collection, Georgian Drawing Room collection, 18thC Classic chair collection.

Meubles Français Ltd
27 Wigmore Street
London W1 Y 9LD
(01) 499 0206
Specialists in reproduction French-style Classical furniture re-created from authentic period designs.

The Old Bakery
Punnetts Town
Nr Heathfield
East Sussex TN21 9DS
(0435) 830608
Traditional upholsterers. Hand-built horsehair chairs and sofa, antique chairs and sofas, fine furnishing fabrics and co-ordinated wallpapers, curtains, loose covers, carpets, lamps.

Overmantels
66 Battersea Bridge Rd
London SW11 3AG
(01) 924 2283
Victorian-style archtop mirrors in a wide variety of styles and sizes, from ornamental gilt to classic pine and mahogany.

Kevin Pope
Queens Post Workshop
Bryants Puddle
Bere Regis
Dorchester, Dorset
(0929) 4771153
Hand-crafted reproductions of period furniture made to order.

G.T.Rackstraw Ltd
Hampton Lovett Ind Est
Droitwich
Worcs. WR9 0NX
(0905) 795050
Reproduction ranges in mahogany, oak and yew, mostly Georgian and Regency styles.

Restall Brown and Clennell Ltd
Cosgrove Hall
Cosgrove
Bucks. MK19 7JB
(01908) 565888
Fine-quality reproduction furniture; emphasis on more unusual decorative and inlaid pieces. Empire collection based on original Neo-classical designs in the French Empire style, with Egyptian and Roman influence.

David Seyfried
759 Fulham Road
London SW6 5UU
(01) 731 4230
Range of Victorian-style stools on turned mahogany legs.

Sinclair Melson Designs Ltd
Unit 5
Hampton Farm Ind Est
Bolney Way
Hampton Road West
Feltham, Middlesex TW13 6DB
(01) 894 1041
Hand-tied traditionally made sofas and other upholstery.

Stuart Interiors
Barrington Court
Barrington
Ilminster
Somerset TA19 0Q
See Interior Designers.

Sudeley Design
The Penthouse
130 Jermyn Street
London SW1 Y 4UL
(01) 828 8200
Specializes in hand-painted furniture and decorative items – particularly small pieces – to suit interiors of different historical periods; many designs based on original pieces from Sudeley Castle.

Swan Galleries
57 The High
Oxford
OX1 4AS
(0865) 242748
Hand-built furniture and panelled interiors.

William Tillman
Crouch Lane
Borough Green, Nr Sevenoaks
Kent
(0732) 883278
Fine reproductions of 18th- and 19th-century furniture for the dining room – especially known for tables.

Titchmarsh and Goodwin
Trinity Works, Back Hamlet
Ipswich IP3 8AL
(0473) 52158
Fine reproduction furniture covering the periods from the 16th to the 18thC.

Whale and Martin
2a Bradbourne Road
Sevenoaks
Kent
(0732) 451460
Furniture makers and restorers. Fine and decorative woodwork maintenance, eg panelling.

LIGHTING

Ampersand
62 Park Road
Baker Street
London W1
(01) 262 5444
Antique lamps, mostly late 19th- and early 20th-century. Fine silk and card lampshades made to order. Lamp conversions.

Best & Lloyd Ltd
William Street West
Smetherwick, Warley
West Midlands B66 2NX
(021) 558 1191
Produce brass light fittings including traditional candle sticks, wall sconces after Adam and Hepplewhite, and Victorian pendants.

The Birmingham Glass Studios Ltd
Unit 5, 102 Edwardes Road
Balsall Heath,
Birmingham B11 3SA
(0274) 721129
Tiffany-style lampshades. Also, suppliers of all stained-glass materials, coloured and antique glass, manufacturers of leaded lights.

R.J. Chelsom & Co. Ltd
Squires Gates Industrial Estate
Blackpool
Lancashire FY4 3RN
(0253) 46324
Specialize in period reproduction lighting. They market Flemish, Georgian, Regency, Adam, Louis XV and XVI light fittings in polished brass. Other ranges include Classical English, Victorian, period American and exterior lighting. Available from stockists nationwide.

Clare House Ltd
35 Elizabeth Street
London SW1
Specialist in making lampshades in silk, also repair and rewire light fittings. Range of antique lamps stocked.

Classic Reproductions
404 The Highway
London E14 8DZ
(01) 790 5203
Manufacturers of replica antique exterior and interior decorative lighting in copper and brass, covering the particular period 1780-1900.

Delomosne & Son Ltd
3 Campden Hill Road
London W8 7 DU
(01) 937 1804
Antique dealers specializing in 18th- and 19thC English glass chandeliers and candelabra.

Dernier & Hamlyn Ltd
17 Lydden Road
Wandsworth
London SW18 4LT
(01) 870 0011/2
Manufacturers of decorative light fittings of the 18th and 19th centuries. More than 200 different fittings, all available in eight different finishes. Also specialize in the restoration of light fittings.

End of Day Lighting Co. Ltd
51 Mill Lane
London NW6
(01) 435 8091
Specializes in Victorian, Edwardian and Deco lighting. over 40 designs available. Most of them in solid brass from original castings.

David Fileman Antiques
Squirrels, Bayards
Horsham Road, Steyning
West Sussex, BNA 3AA
(0903) 813229
Period lighting, chandeliers, candelabra and wall lights bought and sold. Restoration.

Fritz Fryer Decorative Antique Lighting
12 Brook End Street
Ross on Wye
Hertfordshire HR9 7EG
(0989) 67416
Specialists in all forms of decorative antique lighting from Georgian to Art Deco. Main period 1850-1920. Advisory, planning and fitting service available.

Greywell Interior Accessories
3 Dorchester Way, Greywell
Basingstoke
Hampshire RG25 1BX
Answerphone: (025671) 2802
Custom-made, hand-turned wooden lamps in classic designs.

H.L.C.Lighting
Unit 44a Moor End
Eaton Bray, Nr Dunstable
Bedfordshire LU6 2HN
(0525) 220068
Lighting manufacturers to customers' requirements.

David Hunt Lighting Ltd
Tilemans Lane
Shipston on Stour
Warwickshire CV36 4HP
(0608) 61590/62836
Manufacture light fittings for domestic and contractural use. Also, restoration and conversion of period lighting.

Illumin Glass Studio
82 Bond Street
Macclesfield
Cheshire SK11 6QS
(0625) 613600
Makers of stained glass lighting and windows. Renovation of antique light fittings, and a selection of original fittings in stock.

Jones (Lighting)
194 Westbourne Grove
London W11
(01) 229 6866
The largest selection of individual original lighting in Europe, c.1860-1960.

Liberty and Co.
Regent Street
London W1
(01) 734 1234
Original Art Nouveau lighting.

Leon Moodley's Fine Art Brass Co.
Unit 1b & 1c Langdon Rd
Industrial Estate
Langdon Rd
Bradworthy
Devon
(040924) 511
Column lamps in Ionic and Corinthian styles.

Planet Shades Ltd
P.O.Box 118
Lampard Grove
London N16 6XB
(01) 806 1013
Manufacturers of silk and fabric lamp shades, hand polished and antique brass chandeliers and wall brackets, glass shades and pendants, chandeliers and wall brackets.

Stair & Co Ltd
120 Mount Street
London W1Y 5HB
(01) 499 1784
Antique glass chandeliers, restoration, advice on decoration.

Starlite Chandeliers Ltd
127 Harris Way
Windmill Road
Sunbury-on-Thames
TW 16 7EL
(09327) 88686
Manufacture crystal light fittings, including chandeliers and wall brackets in Empire, Louis XV, Regency, Edwardian styles.

Stuart Interiors
Barrington Court
Barrington
Ilminster
Somerset TA19 0NQ
(0460) 42003
See Interior Designers.

Sugg Lighting Ltd
65 Gatwick Rd
Crawley
Sussex RH10 2YU
(0293) 540111
Manufacturers of gas and electric lighting for exterior and interior use in traditional Victorian and Edwardian styles. Manufacturers of replica lamp columns and specialist lighting fittings. Refurbishment of light fittings and mountings.

Sussex Brassware Ltd
Napier Road
Castleham Industrial Estate
St Leonards-on-Sea
East Sussex TN38 9NY
(0424) 440734
Full range of brass electrical accessories in four traditional designs: Georgian, Victorian, Regency and Adam gilt. Finishes available are wrought iron, satin brass, polished chrome, gold-plated and silver-plated.

Wilchester County
Stable Cottage
Vicarage Lane
Steeple Aston
Trowbridge
Wiltshire
(0380) 870764
Manufacturers of primitive lighting copied from original American designs, available in candle or electrified form.

Christopher Wray Lighting Emporium
600 Kings Road
London SW6 2DX
(01) 736 8434
Branches:
Birmingham (020 233 3364);
Bournmouth (0202 22660);
Bristol (0272 279537);
Leeds (0532 782653);
Manchester (061 832 5221);
Nottingham (0602 475494)
Repro and period-style lighting.

Yardstick Designs
51 Kinnerton Street
London SW1 X 8ED
(01) 235 9091
Period-style designs.

PAINT FINISHES

Christopher Boulter
43 Goodrich Road
London SE22 9EQ
(01) 299 2219
Experienced muralist, frieze painter and designer, with a knowledge of most decorative styles including trompe l'oeil, Egyptian and Baroque.

Cole and Son Ltd
P.O. Box 4BU
18 Mortimer Street
London W1A 4BU
(01) 580 5368
Special paints, including "Georgian Grey" and "Queen Anne White".

Crown Restorations
53 Miriam Road
London SE18
(01) 317 8753
Specialized wood finishing, all interior and exterior woodwork, French and wax polishing, metallic colouring, lacquered finishes, oak lining, bleaching. Comprehensive furniture restoration service.

Denney and Parker
54B Deptford High Street
London SE8 4RT
(01) 469 3218
Decorative paint effects, trompe l'oeil, murals. They also run courses.

Gentle and Davies
65 Pennard Road
London W12 8DW
(01) 749 1119
Quality decorating, including decorative paint effects.

Harris Signs
116 Whyke Lane
Chichester, West Sussex
(0243) 782578
Painted canvas floors in the style of the 18th century.

Sara Jane Longlands
17 St Patricks Rd South
Lythan St Annes
Lancs FY8 1XP
(0253) 22451 ext. 3
Trompe l'oeil paintings, screens, firescreens, chimney boards.

Jackie Lowe Interiors
Church Terrace Cottage
Laxfield, Woodbridge
Suffolk,
IP13 8DL
(098) 683 464
Rag rolling, marbling, etc.

Notting Dale Joinery Company
13 Hewer Street
London W10 6DU
(01) 960 9233
Wood graining, turning, stencilling, antique restoration, gilding, walling with fabric etc.

Sally Singer
21 Bristol Road
Kemptown, Brighton
Sussex
(0273) 600895 (workshop) and 773437 (home)
Marbling, graining, murals, gilding and all broken colour work. Restoration of antique painted furniture.

Jean Whitwell
98 Forburg Road
London N16 6HT
(01) 806 2489
Decorator offering specialist paint finishes of all types.

TEXTILES AND WALLPAPERS

Alexander Beauchamp
One Church Street
Douglas
Isle of Man
(0624) 27443
Design and hand print wallpapers for any particular need, including exact character reproductions of historical designs and colourings. The Archibald Knox collection consists of designs by Knox for Liberty & Co. around the turn of the century. Many 19th-century dado papers.

G.P. and J. Baker Ltd
PO Box 30
West End Road
High Wycombe
Bucks HP11 2QD
(0494) 22301
Wide selection of period fabrics taken from original documents, mainly 18th- and 19th-century designs. Collections include The National Trust Country House Collection and English Toile Collection.

Percy Bass
188 Walton Street
London SW3
(01) 589 4853
Upholstery, re-upholstery and restoration. Curtains, blinds, pelmets, bedspreads and bedheads made to order, and tenting and walling with fabric undertaken. Also stocks wide range of fabrics and wallpapers and offers an interior design service.

Cole and Son (Wallpapers) Ltd
P.O. Box 4BU
18 Mortimer Street
London W1A 4BU
(01) 580 5368 (pattern department)
Wallpapers, borders and fabrics. Extensive archive of wallpaper designs from the 18th century onwards – around 3,000 woodblocks dating from the 1780s. Facsimiles of late Victorian dado papers.

Colefax and Fowler
39 Brook Street
London W1
(01) 493 2231
Traditional English chintzes and wallpapers, mainly 18th- and 19th-century designs. Also trompe l'oeil wallpaper borders, gimps, braids, ropes, gothic braids etc.

Belinda Coote
29 Holland Street
London W8 4NA
(01) 937 3924
Reproduction of 18th-century and medieval tapestry designs and tapestry fabrics. Occasionally have antique pieces.

Crown Decorative Products
Belgrave Mills
Belgrave Rd, Darwen
Lancs. BB3 2RR
(0254) 74988
Lincrusta dado panels in original late 19th-century designs, also Anaglypta friezes from a similar period.

The Design Archive
79 Walton Street
London SW3 2HP
(01) 581 3968
Furnishing wholesalers recently set up by Courtaulds, now reproducing some fine old chintzes. Specialities are late 18th- and early 19th-century designs.

Hannerle Dehn
The Studio Centre
Studio 7
Ranelagh Gardens
London SW7
(01) 736 5171
Specializes in hand-painted fabrics and paint finishes.

Distinctive Trimmings
17 Kensington Church St
London W8 4LF
(01) 937 6174
Specialists in furnishing trimmings.

J.W.B.Drennan Ltd
Unit 67
Abbey Business Centre
15-16 Ingate Place
London SW8
(01) 622 1044
Curtain makers, re-upholsterers and soft furnishers. Historic projects, pattern cutting and customized drapery. Carpentry, poles and tracking systems.

Anna French Fabrics & Wallpapers
108 Shakespeare Rd
London SE24 0QQ
(01) 737 6555
Cotton lace panels, many of which are developed from Victorian designs.

The Gainsborough Silk Weaving Co. Ltd
Alexandra Road
Sudbury
Suffolk CO10 6XH
(0787) 72081
Quality jacquard fabrics, including damasks, brocatelles, tabourettes, plain satins, stripes and taffetas.

Gibbs and Dodd
66 Ledbury Rd
London W11
Trompe l'oeil balusters, columns, niches etc.

Hamilton Weston Wallpapers
11 Townshend Road
Richmond
Surrey TW9 1XH
(01) 940 4850
Specialists in documentary reproductions of wallpapers of the 18th and early 19thC. Also Fillet Borders – flexible gilt and leather effect fillet borders – and embossed ribbon borders. St James Collection of late-Victorian wallpapers.

The Charles Hammond Shop
253 Fulham Road
London SW3
(01) 376 5599
Sells Charles Hammond and Pallu and Lake fabrics covering a wide range of periods.

Liberty and Co.
Regent Street
London W1
(01) 734 1234
Art Nouveau, Arts and Crafts, William Morris textiles.

John Oliver Ltd
33 Pembridge Road
London W11 3HG
(01) 221 6466
Will reproduce wallpapers from client's own sample or design. Also De Havilland Papiers Peints de Paris, trompe l'oeil urns, columns, capitals, balustrading.

Ornamenta
23 South Terrace
London SW7 2TB
(01) 584 3857
Pre-cut hand-printed paper decorations with which to create trompe l'oeil effects without paint, including 18th-century designs. Silk garlands, ropes, knots and tassels.

Pilgrim Payne Ltd
Latimer Place
London W10 6QU
(01) 960 5656
Cleaners of fine carpets and tapestries, curtain relining service or new curtains made, curtains taken down, cleaned and rehung.

H.A. Percheron Ltd
97-99 Cleveland Street
London W1P 5PN
(01) 580 1192
Importers of furnishing fabrics and trimmings. Traditional damasks, brocades, velours. Trimmings of all kinds.

Ramm Son & Crocker Ltd
13-14 Treadaway Tech Centre
Treadaway Hill
Loudwater, High Wycombe
Bucks. HP10 9PE
(06285) 29373
Specialize in the reproduction of original documents, mainly of the 19th century.

Arthur Sanderson and Sons Ltd
Berners Street
London W1
(01) 635 7800
Hand-printed papers from original documents, including many by William Morris. Also dado papers.

Neil Shepherd
9 The Frame
Basildon
Essex SS15 5JZ
(0268) 417444
Soft furnishing specialist. Swags and tails, scarf drapes, lambrequins, coronas, covered laths.

The Silk Shop
31A Rivers Street
Bath
(0225) 311641
Wide selection of braids, cords, fringes, gimps and tassels; will match lampshades and fabrics with toning trimmings in a variety of yarns and will dye to match.

Stuart Interiors
Barrington Court
Barrington
Ilminster
Somerset TA19 ONQ
(0460) 42003
See Interior Designers.

Tempus Stet Ltd
Trinity Business Centre
305-309 Rotherhithe Street
London SE16 1EY
(01) 231 0955
Extensive range of curtain accessories – tie-backs, coronas etc. Wide range of decorative mirrors, furniture and lighting.

Textiles (FCD) Ltd
16 Berners Street
London W1P 3DD
(01) 636 3461
Classical and traditional damasks.

Tissunique Ltd
10 Princes Street
Hanover Square
London W1R 7RD
(01) 491 3386
Wholesalers and importers of high-class furnishing fabrics and wallpapers, braids and trim-

mings. Collections cover many periods. Specialists in historic house reproduction work, Lyons silks, traditional chintzes.

Today Interiors Ltd
Hollis Rd
Grantham
Lincs.
NG31 7QH
(0476) 74401
Broderie collection of fabrics, wallpapers and borders, inspired by antique botanical prints, and studies of 18th-century lace panels and trimmings.

Top Layer Ltd
5 Egerton Terrace
London SW3 2BX
(01) 581 1019
Wallpapers and fabrics from any age or period.

Turnell and Gigon Ltd
Room G/04
250 Kings Rd
London SW3 5UE
(01) 351 5142
Excellent range of trimmings in a wide range of colours by Passementerie Ile de France.

Warner and Sons Ltd
7-11 Noel Street
London W1V 4AL
(01) 439 2411
Reproductions of period wallpapers and printed fabrics, mainly from the early 1800s. Damasks and woven fabrics dating from 16thC onwards, in traditional designs.

Watts and Co.
7 Tufton Street
Westminister
London SW1P 3QE
(01) 222 2893
Hoar Cross Collection of hand-printed Victorian Gothic wall-coverings designed by A.W.N. Pugin and G.F. Bodley. Also woven damasks and tapestries, stamped velvets.

Zoffany Ltd
63 South Audley Street
London W1
(01) 629 9262
Manufacturers of Document wallpapers, including the hand-printed Temple Newsam Collection. Designs range from mid- and late-18th century to Art Deco.

ANTIQUE TEXTILES

The Antique Textile Company
100 Portland Road
London W11 4LQ
(01) 221 7730
Stock includes Regency Chintz quilts, Toiles de Jouy and printed cottons, Kashmir and Paisley shawls, oriental textiles.

The Gallery of Antique Costumes and Textiles
2 Church Street
London NW8 8ED
(01) 723 9981

Linda Gumb
9 Camden Passage
London N1
(01) 354 1184
Antique textiles, cushions, curtains and other soft furnishings; specializes in 1700-1900, mainly European styles. Aubusson carpets and portières, tapestries.

Gwyneth Antiques
56 Ebury Street
London SW1 W9QD
(01) 730 2513
Specialize in antique textiles, mostly 1700-1900.

Hand in Hand
3 North West Circus Place
Edinburgh EH3 6ST
(031) 226 3598
Embroidered and Paisley shawls, fine embroidered bed and table linen, velvet and brocade curtains, quilts, antique lace and period costumes and accessories.

Danielle Hartwright at Liberty
Regent Street
London W1
(01) 734 1234
Retail outlet for antique and decorative textiles, tapestry, needlework, carpets and cushions. Full cleaning and restoration service for these and for Oriental carpets and textiles. Brokers for tapestries and carpets. Full interior design service.

Herez
25 Motcomb Street
London SW1X 8JU
(01) 245 9497
Specialize in cushions made from antique textiles. New Paisley shawls. Occasionally have old pieces of fabric.

Paul Jones
Chenil Galleries
183 King's Rd
London SW3 5EB
(01) 351 2005
Fine antique European textiles. Tapestry, curtains etc.

Richard and Pamela Nadin
5 Woolley Street
Bradford-on-Avon
Wilts BA15 1AD
(02216) 2476
Country house furniture, textiles, carpets and furnishings.

Punch Antiques
31 Georgian Village
Camden Passage
London N1
(01) 359 5863
Painted furniture, decorative objects and furnishings, samplers and decorative textiles.

Janet Shand Kydd
The Green Room
2 Church Street
Framlingham
Woodbridge
Suffolk IP13 9BE
(0728) 723009
17th, 18th, 19th and early 20thC textiles, quilts, curtains, etc.

Catherine Shinn
7 Suffolk Parade
Cheltenham
(0242) 520163
All types of antique textiles, embroidery, cushions etc.

Ron Simpson Textiles
Gray's Antique Market
138 Portobello Road
London W11
(01) 727 0983
Antique textiles including North American and European patchwork quilts, Kashmir and European "Paisley" shawls.

Toynbee-Clarke Interiors Ltd
95 Mount Street
London W1
(01) 499 4472
Specialists in the restoration and installation of antique wallpapers, including 18th and 19thC hand-painted Chinese papers and French hand block printed papers.

Advice from:

The Silk Museum
Roe Street
Macclesfield
Cheshire SK11 6UT
(0625) 613210

The Victoria and Albert Museum
Textiles Department
Exhibition Road
London SW7 2RL
(01) 589 6371
Offers an advisory service on Tuesday and Thursday afternoons, and on Saturday by appointment.

FLORISTS

Liz Wallace Flowers
37 Winchester Street
Salisbury, Wilts
(0722) 2559

The Flowersmith
34 Shelton Street
London WC2
(01) 240 6688

Kenneth Turner Flowers
Brook Manor
35 Brook Street
London W1Y 1AJ
(01) 499 4952/3

Pulbrook & Gould Ltd
181 Sloane Street
London SW7
(01) 235 3920

Robin Day
49 Cheyne Walk
London SW3
(01) 352 1455

Stephen Crisp
London
(01) 262 9183

COURSES

Brick Kiln Farm Craft Centre
West Tisted, Nr Arlesford
Hampshire
(073088) 353
One-day course in a variety of crafts including soft furnishings and decorative paint finishes.

The Country House Course
Holmstall, Mayfield
East Sussex TN20 6NJ
(0435) 872275
Full-time study in Interior Design, The Decorative Arts, History of Art and Architecture. One-year Diploma and GCE A level Course, and shorter courses.

Country Restorations
Weavers Workshops
Uley, Glos.
(0453) 46846
Courses in antique restoration.

Denney and Parker
54B Deptford High St
London SE8 4RT
(01) 469 3218
One-day courses (in Kent) in Paint Techniques – rag rolling, dragging, sponging, stencilling, tortoiseshelling, marbling.

The Ivy House
Rode, Bath BA3 6NZ
(0373) 830013
Four-day Interior Design courses.

The Inchbald School of Design
7 Eaton Gate
London SW1W 9BA
(01) 730 5508
Courses in history and practice of Interior and Garden Design, lasting from 5 days to 1 year.

KLC Interior Design Course
5 Blythe Mews, Blythe Road
London W14
(01) 602 8592
30-week, 4-week and 1- and 3-day courses in Interior Design.

Lyn Le Grice Stencil Design Ltd
Bread Street
Penzance TR18 2EQ
(0736) 69881
One-day stencilling courses in London and one-week courses in Falmouth.

Montgomery College
Llanidloes Road
Newtown
Powys SY16 1BE
(0686) 622722
5-day residential courses in traditional upholstering.

Roger Newton School of Decorative Finishes
27 The Tailina Centre
Bagley's Lane
London SW6 2BW
(01) 736 1658
5-day courses on gilding and furniture painting.

"On Course"
Draycott Farm
Draycott, Nr Yeovil
Somerset
(0935) 840171
Courses in rag rolling, dragging, marbling, stencilling and designer curtaining.

The Palladio Academy
10 Kendall Place
London W1H 3AH
(01) 486 1050
Range of specialized courses in many areas including, Interior Design, Interior Design Drawing and Presentation, History of Architectural and Interior Decoration, The Fine and Decorative Arts

Rhodec International
Dept GW,
50 West Street
Brighton
Sussex BN1 2RA
(0273) 27476
Home study course in Interior Design leading to a Diploma Degree.

Sotheby's Educational Studies
Box 84,
30 Oxford Street
London W1R 1RE
(01) 408 1100
Courses ranging from one week to one year in the Decorative Arts.

Stuart Walton
The Dons,
Leggatts Park
Potters Bar
Herts. EN6 1NZ
(0707) 58561
One-day stencilling courses.

Peta Weston and Julia Roberts
The Farmhouse
Letchmore Heath
Nr Radlett
Herts. WD2 8ES
(01) 624 2504 and (09276) 3655
One-week courses in decorative paint finishes and stencilling.

Victoria and Albert Museum
Education Dept
London SW7 2RL
(01) 938 8638
Run a range of courses and lectures on different aspects of the Decorative and Fine Arts.

West Dean College
West Dean
Chichester
West Sussex
PO18 0QZ
(0243) 63 301
Short courses in a wide variety of skills including stencilling, caring for antique furniture, upholstery. Lecture courses and seminars on art, architecture etc. One-, two- and three-year courses in antique restoration.

ASSOCIATIONS

Art Workers Guild
6 Queen Square
London WC1N 3AR
(01) 837 3474
Guild of artists, architects, craftsmen and others engaged in the design and practice of the arts.

The Assocation of British Laundry, Cleaning and Rental Services
7 Churchill Court
58 Station Rd
North Harrow
Middlesex
HA2 7SA
(01) 863 7755
Can supply addresses of specialists in cleaning and re-glazing old chintz, and cleaning fine linen and antique lace.

English Heritage
25 Savile Row
London W1X 2BT
(01) 734 6010
Secures the preservation of the country's architectural and archaeological heritage and promotes the public's enjoyment and knowledge of this through the management of more than 350 historic properties in its care.

The Georgian Group
37 Spital Square
London E1 6DY
(01) 377 1722
Gives advice on repair and restoration to owners of Georgian buildings.

The Guild of Master Craftsmen
166 High Street,
Lewes
East Sussex
(0273) 477374
Trade association helping to put prospective clients in touch with experienced craftsmen able to carry out restoration work. Also publish Guide to Restoration Experts.

Historic Homes of Britain
21 Pembroke Square
London W8
(01) 937 2402

Historic Houses Association
38 Ebury Street
London SW1
(01) 730 9419

Charles Rennie Mackintosh Society
Queen's Cross
870 Garscube Road
Glasgow
G20 7EL
(041) 946 6600
Information centre open Tues, Thurs, Fri 12-5.30, Sun 2.30-5pm.

National Association of Decorative and Fine Arts Societies
38 Ebury Street
London SW1 0LU
(01) 730 3041

The National Trust
36 Queen Anne's Gate
London SW1H 9AS
(01) 222 9251

The National Trust for Scotland
5 Charlotte Square
Edinburgh
EH2 4DU
London office:
15 Queen Anne's Gate
London SW1
(01) 222 4856

The Victorian Society
1 Priory Gardens,
Bedford Park
London W4 1TT
(01) 994 1019
A conservation amenity group dedicated to the preservation of Victorian and Edwardian buildings.

The Wallpaper History Society
Victoria and Albert Museum
London SW7 2RL
(01) 938 8638

HISTORIC HOUSES AND MUSEUMS

American Museum
Claverton Manor,
Bath
(0225) 60503
Late 17th to mid-19thC American rooms.

Arbury Hall
Nuneaton
Warwickshire
(0203) 382804
Georgian Gothick interiors.

Athelhampton
Dorset
(030 584) 363
Fine medieval house, medieval, Tudor and 18thC rooms.

Barrington Court
Ilminster
Somerset
(0460) 41480
Tudor house.

Belton House
Nr Grantham
Lincs.
(0476) 66116
Restoration house, Grinling Gibbons school carvings.

Boughton Monchelsea Place
Nr Maidstone
Kent
(0622) 43120
Elizabethan house, interior partly remodelled in the Regency period.

Burghley House
Stamford
Lincs.
(0780) 52451
Fine late Elizabethan house.

Calke Abbey
Ticknall
Nr. Melbourne
Derbyshire
(0332) 863822
House built 1701-03, contains treasure trove of Victoriana.

Cardiff Castle
Cardiff
South Glamorgan
Gothick dining room.

Castle Coole
Co. Fermanagh
N. Ireland
(0365) 22690
Regency.

Charleston Farmhouse
Lewes
East Sussex
1930s Bloomsbury.

Chettle House,
Chettle
Blandford
Dorset
(0258) 89 209)
Queen Anne House with interiors re-modelled in the 19thC.

Church Farm House Museum
Greyhound Hill
London NW4
(01) 203 0130
Mainly 19thC domestic material, with two period furnished rooms, the kitchen c.1820 and the dining room c.1850.

Claydon House
Middle Claydon
Nr Winslow
Bucks.
(029673) 349
Georgian Rococo and chinoiserie rooms.

Cragside House
Rothbury
Northumbria
(0669) 20333
House designed by Norman Shaw, Aesthetic interiors, first house in the world to be lit by electricity generated by water power.

Doddington Hall
Doddington
Lincs.
(0522) 694308
Elizabethan mansion.

Forde Abbey
Nr Chard
Dorset
(0460) 20231
Cromwellian country house.

Dorney Court
Windsor
Berks.
(062) 86 4638
Elizabethan manor house.

18 Folgate Street
Spitalfields
London
(01) 247 4013
House built in 1724 with rooms furnished and decorated in styles from 1724 to the early 20thC. Tours available.

25 Fournier Street
Spitalfields
London E1
(01) 377 9312
House open for dinner served "in the manner of the 18thC".

Geffrye Museum
Kingsland Road
London E2
(01) 739 8368
Series of Georgian rooms.

Hagley Hall
Nr Stourbridge
West Midlands
(0562) 882408
Georgian Rococo decoration.

Hardwick Hall
Nr Chesterfield
Derbys.
(0246) 850430
Elizabethan house.

Hatfield House
Hatfield, Herts.
(07072) 62823
Fine Jacobean house.

Holkham Hall
Norfolk
Fine Palladian mansion.

Houghton Hall
Kings Lynn,
Norfolk
(048) 522 569
Palladian, interior by William Kent.

Kedleston Hall
Nr Derby
(0332) 842191
House designed by Robert Adam.

Kelmscott Manor
Nr Lechlade, Glos.
Cotswold manor of the 16th and 17thC. Summer home of William Morris. Original Morris possessions and designs.

Knole Park
Sevenoaks, Kent
(0732) 450608
Splendid Jacobean interior.

Lacock Abbey
Nr Chippenham
Wilts.
(0294) 73 227
Georgian Gothick interiors.

Layer Marney Tower
Nr Colchester
Essex
(0206) 330202
Tudor house.

Linley Sambourne House
18 Stafford Terrace
London W8
(01) 994 1019
Aesthetic interior.

Longthorpe Tower
Cambs.
(0733) 268482
Most complete example of early 14thC wall painting.

The Mackintosh House
Hunterian Art Gallery
University of Glasgow
82 Hillhead Street
Glasgow G12 8QQ
(041) 339 8855 ext. 7431.
Reconstruction of main interiors of Charles Rennie Mackintosh's home.

Marble Hill House
Twickenham
Middlesex
(01) 892 5115
Palladian villa.

Medieval Merchant's House
French Street
Southampton
House built in 1290, recently restored and furnished in appropriate style.

Number 1, Royal Crescent
Bath
(0225) 28126
Restored Georgian house, furnished as an 18thC home.

The Old Hall
Gainsborough,
Lincs.
(0427) 2669
15th and 16thC manor house with medieval, Tudor and later rooms.

Osterley Park House
Osterley
Middlesex
(01) 560 3918
Fine Adam interiors.

Pallant House
9 North Pallant
Chichester
West Sussex PO19 1TJ
(0243) 774557
Queen Anne merchant's house.

Parham House
Pulborough
West Sussex
(090 66) 2021
Elizabethan house.

Pattyndene Manor
Goudhurst
Kent
(0508) 211361
15thC manor house, open by appointment only for parties of ten or more.

Petworth House
Petworth
West Sussex
(0798) 42207
William and Mary house, Grinling Gibbons school carvings.

Preston Manor
Preston Park
Brighton
East Sussex
(0273) 603005
Edwardian interiors.

Queen's House
Greenwich
London SE10
Designed by Inigo Jones.

The Red House
Bexley, Kent
(01) 303 8808
House built by Philip Webb for William Morris – open by appointment only.

Rokeby Park
Nr Barnard Castle
Durham
Palladian house. exceptional collection of 18thC needlework pictures.

Saltram House
Plymouth, Devon
(0752) 336546
George II house with two fine Adam rooms.

St Fagans
Nr Cardiff
South Glamorgan
(0222) 499441
Welsh folk museum. Collection of furnished farmhouses, cottages and barns and an Elizabethan Great House.

Saint Mary's
Bramber
West Sussex
(0903) 816205
Medieval house with excellent Elizabethan painted room.

Sandford Orcas Manor House
Sandford Orcas
Sherborne
Dorset
(096) 322 206
Tudor manor house.

Sezincote
Glos.
Late Georgian house in "Indian" style inspired by Royal Pavillion, Brighton.

Shrubland Park
Suffolk
Regency "Tent Dressing Room".

Sir John Soane's Museum
13 Lincoln's Inn Fields
London WC2
(01) 405 2107
Regency house built by Sir John Soane. (Monk's Parlour is a Gothick spoof.)

Squerryes Court
Westerham
Kent
(0959) 62345
William and Mary manor house.

Standen
East Grinstead
West Sussex
(0342) 23029
Aesthetic interiors.

Stourhead
Stourton
Nr Mere
Wilts.
(0747) 840348
Palladian house, designed by Colen Campbell.

Strawberry Hill
Twickenham
Middlesex
Best-known Gothick house, by appointment only with St Mary's College (01 892 0051).

Syon House
Brentford
Middlesex
(01) 560 0881
Fine Adam interiors.

Victoria and Albert Museum
London SW7
(01) 938 8638
Rooms of different periods including Haynes Grange room designed by Inigo Jones.

Waddesdon Manor
Nr Aylesbury
Bucks.
(0296) 651211
Late 19thC house in French Renaissance style, Re-creations of French rooms of different periods.

Wilton House
Salisbury
Wilts.
State rooms by Inigo Jones, including famous double- and single-cube rooms.

PLACES WITH STYLE

Bodysgallen Hall
Llandudno
Gwynedd LL30 IRS
(0494) 84466
An imposing 17thC mansion. Stone-mullioned and stained-glass windows, ornately carved fireplaces and mellow oak panelling. Edwardian-style bathrooms.

Burgh Island
Bigbury on Sea
South Devon TQ7 4AU
(0548) 810514
Hotel recently restored to its original 1929 Art Deco design. Accessible on foot at low tide.

Chilston Park
Sandway, Maidstone
Kent ME17 2BE
(0622) 859803
Extensively restored 17thC house with a treasure trove of antiques from Chippendale to Jacobean. Renaissance hall with Tudor panelling. Roaring open fires. Four-poster beds.

Clifton Hotel
Viewfield Street
Highlands
Nairn IV12 4HW
(0667) 53119
Creeper-clad Victorian house crammed full of antiques, objets d'art, paintings, artefacts and books.

The Crown
High Street
Southwold
Suffolk IP18 6DP
(0502) 7222275
A town centre inn furnished in solid country style with a variety of antiques.

Dorset Square Hotel
39-40 Dorset Square
London NW1 6QN
(01) 723 7874
The main architectural features of the 1815 residences have been retained. The interior features and decor are a clever mix of old and repro which works well.

Ettington Park Hotel
Alderminster
Stratford-upon-Avon
CV37 8BS
(0789) 740740
A splendid Victorian Gothic mansion, parts of which date back to the Middle Ages. Exquisite drawing room with gilded ceilings and grand piano. Fine antiques and original paintings.

Julian Humfrey
25 Fournier Street
London E1
(01) 377 9312
Mr Humfrey offers 18thC style dinner parties in his home.

Hunstrete House
Hunstrete
Chelwood, Bristol
Avon BS18 4NS
(076) 18 578
Handsome Georgian stone mansion with the feel of an English country house. Italianate courtyard, fine antiques, paintings and objets d'art. Open fires.

Inverlochy Castle
Torlundy
Fort William PH33 6SN
(0397) 2177
A magnificent castle much admired by Queen Victoria. Crystal chandeliers, frescoed ceiling in the great hall, antiques and paintings.

Middlethorpe Hall
Bishopthorpe Road
York YO12 1QP
(0904) 641241
An elegant 17thC country house which has been skilfully converted into a sumptuous hotel. Period-style bedrooms. Furnishings and fine paintings consistent with the period.

Priory Hotel
Weston Road
Bath Avon BA1 2QT
(0225) 447928
Elegant Georgian hotel with period furnishings.

Sharrow Bay Hotel
Ullswater
Nr Penrith
Cumbria CA10 2LZ
(085) 36301
Greystone hotel with a profusion of antiques of all periods.

Dennis Severs
18 Folgate Street
London E1
(01) 247 4013
A 3-hour period experience.

Ston Easton Park
Ston Easton
Chewton Mendip
Nr Bath
Somerset BA3 4DF
(076 121) 631
A fine Palladian mansion with magnificent 18thC interiors. Trompe l'oeil murals, fine antiques, paintings, period bedrooms with four-poster beds.

Thornbury Castle Hotel
Thornbury, Nr Bristol
Avon BS12 1HH
(0454) 418511
A fairytale castle built by the 3rd Duke of Buckingham and seized by Henry VIII. Mullioned windows, stone fireplaces, grandly proportioned public rooms, panelled dining room, antiques, tapestries, paintings.

BIBLIOGRAPHY

The Antiques Directory: Furniture, Judith and Martin Miller (Gen. Ed.), Mitchell Beazley, 1985

Authentic Decor – The Domestic Interior 1620-1920, Peter Thornton, Weidenfeld, 1985

The Curtain Book, Caroline Clifton-Mogg and Melanie Paine, Mitchell Beazley, 1988

Displaying Pictures, Caroline Clifton-Mogg and Piers Feetham, Mitchell Beazley, 1988

English Country Houses – Caroline 1625-1685, Oliver Hill and John Cornforth, Antique Collectors Club, 1985

English Country Houses – Baroque 1685-1715, James Lees-Milne, Antique Collectors Club, 1986

English Country Houses – Early Georgian 1715-1760; Mid Georgian 1760-1800; Late Georgian 1800-1840, Christopher Hussey, Antique Collectors Club, boxed set 1988

The English Mediaeval House, Margaret Wood, Ferndale Editions, 1981

E.W. Godwin, Furniture and Interior Decoration, Elizabeth Aslin, John Murray, 1986

The History of Interior Decoration, Charles McCorquodale, Phaidon Press, 1983

Charles Rennie Mackintosh, The Complete Furniture, Furniture Drawings and Interior Design, Roger Billcliffe, John Murray, 1986

The Penguin Dictionary of Decorative Arts, John Fleming and Hugh Honour, 1979

Miller's Pocket Antiques Fact File, Judith and Martin Miller, Mitchell Beazley, 1988

The Penguin Dictionary of Architecture, John Fleming, Hugh Honour, Nikolaus Pevsner, 1966

Period Details, Judith and Martin Miller, Mitchell Beazley, 1986

The Potterton Book of Curtain and Drapery Designs, Potterton Books, Sessay, North Yorks.

Victorian Furniture, R.W.Symonds and B.B.Whineray, Studio Editions, 1987

GLOSSARY

Acanthus Leaf motif, originally used on Greek architecture.

Balloon-back A type of chair with a hooped back, typical of the later 19thC.

Baroque A theatrical exuberant style, originating in 17thC Italy.

Bird's eye maple Wood of the sugar maple with a distinctive pattern created by aborted buds.

Blue and white A style of underglaze ceramics decoration, originating in China.

Bombé A term applied to the outswelling curves of furniture in the Rococo style.

Bonheur du jour A small writing table on tall legs.

Boulle Marquetry in tortoiseshell and brass.

Brocade A rich fabric with an embossed design, originally in gold or silver. The term has come to mean any flowered fabric with a raised pattern.

Brocatelle A brocade-like fabric, usually of silk or wool.

Cabriole leg A leg, particularly a chair leg, that curves in a shallow S.

Carver A dining chair with arms.

Ceiling rose A circular moulding in the centre of a ceiling, from which a chandelier might be hung.

Chiffonier A low or side cupboard, the upper part having one or two shelves.

Chinoiserie The use of pseudo-Chinese motifs in fabrics, furniture etc.

Chintz A cotton fabric, usually glazed, printed in colourful patterns of flowers, fruit and birds. The term was originally applied to painted calico from India.

Classical Orders A repertoire of treatments for columns and the entablatures that surmount them. Derived from Ancient Greek temples, the Orders have had a major influence on architecture, furniture and interiors in Europe and North America.

Commode A chest of drawers in the French style.

Console table A table on a large bracket, set against a wall.

Corinthian One of the Classical Orders. The capitals are bell-shaped, with acanthus leaves.

Cornice A decorative moulding at the top of a wall, just below the ceiling.

Court cupboard A cupboard with the lower stage open.

Crewelwork Designs in worsted on a cloth or linen ground.

Dado The lower few feet of a wall, when treated differently from the area of wall above.

Damask A silk or linen fabric with a woven textural pattern.

Delft Tin-glazed earthenware from Holland, usually blue-and-white. When used without a capital initial, the word applies to English earthenware in the same style.

Dentil A small moulding in the shape of a block.

Doric The plainest of the Classical Orders.

Ebonized A term applied to light-coloured wood stained to the colour of ebony.

Egg-and-dart A form of architectural moulding.

Entablature Decorative band above a row of columns, made up of architrave, frieze and cornice.

Faux finish A surface finish intended to imitate a material such as wood or marble.

Frieze A band across the upper part of a wall, just below the cornice. Also, the middle part of an entablature.

Galloon Narrow close-woven braid.

Girandole A circular wall mirror in a carved gilt frame.

Gothick Pseudo-Medieval style of the 18th and 19thC.

Greek key pattern A band of geometric ornament, in a maze-like design.

Half-tester A rectangular canopy above a bed, extending part-way down the bed from the headboard.

Infill The area of a wall between the dado and frieze.

Inlay The setting of one material (especially a wood) in or over another. Marquetry is one type of inlay.

Ionic One of the Classical Orders. The columns are fluted and the capitals have scrolls, or volutes.

Japanning A Western imitation of oriental lacquering.

Kelim A Middle-Eastern tapestry-woven rug.

Lambrequin A stiff, shaped surround to a window, like an extended pelmet.

Majolica Victorian earthenware with a thick, coloured glaze.

Marquetry See inlay.

Mullions Uprights dividing a window into sections.

Ormolu Any mount, sconce or other article that is gilt or at least gold-coloured.

Ottoman A cushioned seat like a sofa without arms.

Palladian An architectural style derived from that of Andrea Palladio, the 16thC Italian architect.

Parquet Flooring made up of pieces of wood in a geometrical pattern.

Pediment A gabled top over a portico, door or piece of furniture.

Pembroke table A small table with short drop leaves.

Pilaster A shallow pier or column set against a wall.

Press cupboard A cupboard with upper and lower section both closed by doors.

Rococo A lively, delicate 18thC style, often asymmetrical, with S-shaped curves.

Satinwood An exotic close-grained hardwood, yellow to golden in colour.

Sconce Wall light with candle-holders.

Stencilling A method of decoration, usually to make a repeated pattern, in which paint is brushed over a cut-out design.

Strapwork Decoration of interlaced bands and forms similar to cut leather.

Ticking Stout striped material of linen or cotton.

Toile de Jouys A fabric with pictorial scenes printed in one colour on a cream background.

Treen Small objects made of wood.

Turkeywork Upholstery, cushions, etc, knotted in the manner of Near Eastern rugs.

Wainscot Wood panelling on an internal wall.

Whatnot A stand with three or more shelves.

Windsor chair A country-style chair with a spindled back.

Worsted Closely woven fabric made from a woollen yarn.

Page reference in *italics* refer to captions of illustrations.

A

Adam, Robert 81, 85, 152
  styles *89*, 102, 218
"Aesthetic" interiors 185
Aga cookers *107*, *108*, *190*
Albrizzi table *87*
Alma-Tadema, Sir L. *183*
American Museum, Bath *101*, *103*, *108*, *127*, *192*
American styles
  17thC Country House 52
  William and Mary 63
  Queen Anne 66
  Federal 100-3
  Colonial *18*, 110-21
  Empire 161, *161*
  Greek Revival 100, 161, 162
  Gothic *8*, 10, *199-200*
Anaglypta paper 220
Anderson, Lee 10, *199*, *200*
Architectural drawings *224*
Argand lamps 162
Art Deco *12*, *15*, *20*, 35, *80*, *175*, *222-7*
Art Nouveau 210, 217, 218-21
Arts and Crafts Movement 18, *19*, *30*, 35, 210-15
Ashbee, C.R. 212
Aubusson carpets *140*, *142*, *151*, 162
Axminster carpets 74, 82

B

Back-stools 40
Bahouth, Candace 30
Balloon-back chairs 180
Banister-back chairs *114*, *116*
Barley-twist legs 65
Barometers *176*
Baroque styles 60-5, 128-47
Bateman, Richard Latrobe *30*, *33*
Bathrooms *94*, *159*, *196*, *197*, *207*
Bauhaus furniture 71
Beds/bedrooms 16, 21
  medieval 33, *33*
  Elizabethan/Jacobean 40, *43*, *56*
  17thC Country House 51, *56*
  Queen Anne *66*, *67*
  Georgian *79*, *94*
  American Federal 103, *103*, *166*
  American Colonial 110, *116*, *117*, 121
  Shaker *125*, *127*
  Baroque/Rococo *134*
  Regency *152*
  Empire *94*, *192*
  Victorian *94*, 180, *192*, *194*, *195*, *209*
  Edwardian/Art Nouveau *217*
Bell, Quentin *212*
Bellarmines (flagons) *30*
Bench tables 43
Benches 33, 40, 52, 121, 122
Berlin porcelain 174
Biedermeier styles *169*, 174-5, *225*
Billiard rooms *221*
Blackamoor figures *24*, *138*
Black Basaltware 81-2, 85
Blinds 121, *130*, *144*, 159, 173, 179, 180
Blue and white wares *10*, 24, *25*, 65
Blue John stone 85
Bonheurs du jour 85
Bookcases *15*, *87*, *100*, *162*
Boucher, François 130
Boulle, André-Charles 130, *142*
Boulton, Matthew 85
Brackets, wall *64*, *140*, 147
Bramber, Sussex *40*
Brass 33, 51, 66, 180, 210
Brewster armchairs 52
Bric-à-brac 180, *195*, 216
Bronze 33, *59*, *138*, 159, *184*, *192*, *225*
Brussels carpets 150, 162
Buffets 36, 51
Bureaux *64*, 71
Burgh Island, Devon *227*

C

Cabinets 14, 24, *155*, 217, *217*, *224*
Cabriole legs 66, 71, 77, 180
Candelabra *77*, 102, 130, *138*
Candles/candlesticks 12
  medieval *27*, *29*, *30*, 33, 35
  17thC Country House *46*, *49*, 51, 59
  English Baroque *60*, 63, 65
  Queen Anne *69*, 71, *71*
  American Federal 102
  American Colonial *117*
  Shaker *125*
  Baroque/Rococo 14, *147*
  Regency 152
  Empire 159
  Victorian *14*, 209
  Arts and Crafts *30*, *212*, 215
  Edwardian/Art Nouveau 218
  Art Deco *223*
Candlestands *27*, 159, *166*, *199*
Carl Johan style *148*
Carpets 36, *54*
  English Baroque 63
  Georgian 72, 82, *91*
  American Federal 100
  18thC Country 104
  Baroque/Rococo *140*, 149
  Regency 150, *155*, *162*
  American Empire *161*
  Victorian 180, 202
  Edwardian/Art Nouveau 220
Carver chairs 52
Ceilings
  medieval 28
  Elizabethan/Jacobean 40
  17thC Country House 49
  English Baroque 60
  Georgian 74, 81
  American Federal 100
  American Colonial *116*, *121*
  Regency 148, 150, *155*
  Biedermeier 174
  Arts and Crafts 210
Celtic Arts and Crafts *212*
Chair rails *125*, 127
Chairs
  medieval *28*, *29*, *30*, *33*
  17thC Country House *46*, 51, *51*
  Elizabethan/Jacobean *38*, 40, *40*, 43, *43*
  17thC American 52, *52*
  English Baroque *60*, *62*, *64*, 65
  Queen Anne *69*, 71
  Georgian 77, *77*, *78*, *82*, *85*, 85, 89, *89*, *91*, *94*, *96*
  American Federal *100*, *101*, 102, *103*
  18thC Country 104, *108*
  American Colonial 110, *114*, *116*
  Shaker 122, *123*, *125*, *127*
  Baroque/Rococo *130*, *132*, 133, *134*, 134, *136*, *140*, *142*, *144*
  Regency *43*, *138*, *148*, *151*, 152, *152*, *155*, *157*, *162*, *165*, *170*
  Empire *159*, 159
  American Empire 161, *166*
  Biedermeier *166*, *174*, 174
  Victorian *14*, 179-80, *182*, *185*, 184, *189*, *194*, *195*, *199*, 202, *205*, 209, *209*
  Arts and Crafts 215, *217*
  Art Deco *223*, *224*, *227*
  modern *64*, *82*
Chaises longues *151*, 159, 184, *186*
Chandeliers *38*, *56*, 71, *78*, 89
  English Baroque 63, 65
  American Federal *100*, 102
  American Colonial 110, *121*
  Baroque/Rococo *136*, *138*
  Empire *159*
  Victorian *186*
Chelsea porcelain 84
Chests 43
  medieval 33
  Elizabethan/Jacobean 43
  17thC Country House *49*, *64*
  17thC American 52
  Georgian *94*
  American Colonial *117*, 121
  Shaker *123*
  American Empire *170*
  Victorian *183*
  Arts and Crafts 212
Chests-of-drawers 51, 71, *94*, 121, *195*
Chests-on-stands *67*
Chiffoniers 14, *14*, 82, 152, *174*, 183
Chilston Park Hotel, Kent *134*, *205*
Chimney pieces *221*
"Chinese Chippendale" *80*
Chinese porcelain *51*, *59*, 65, *65*, *66*, *67*, *100*
Chinoiserie 21, 46, *62*, 65, 72, 74, 89, 130, 148
Chiparus 225
Chippendale, Thomas 75, 79, *80*, 85, 87, 89, 185
Chrome 224, 227
Churchill, Jane *180*, *194*
Cliff, Clarice *225*, *227*
Clocks 43, 130, *142*, *156*, *170*, 183, *212*
Coalport 152, 184
Cocktails 225
Coffee tables 14, *17*, *59*, *90*
Coffers *30*, 33, *33*, *40*, *144*
Colbert, Jean Baptiste 130
Colefax and Fowler wallpapers *142*
Collections 24, *25*, *207*
Colour 18, *19*
  medieval 18, 35
  17thC Country House *46*, *54*, 59
  English Baroque *62*
  Queen Anne *67*, 71, *71*
  Georgian 72, *80*, 81, *82*, *87*, *89*, *90-8*
  18thC Country *108*
  American Colonial 110, *110*, *112*, *114*, *116*, 121
  Shaker *123*, 127
  Baroque/Rococo *134*, *140*, 149
  Regency 148, *155*, *156*
  American Empire *166*, *170*
  Victorian 18, *176*, *179*, 180, *182*, *186*, 202, *207*, 209
  Arts and Crafts 210, *212*, *215*, *215*
  Edwardian/Art Nouveau 217, 220
  Art Deco *225*, *227*
Commodes 85, *103*, *132*, 133, *138*, *159*, *179*, *224*
Concealment of modern equipment 14, *14*, *15*, *117*, *144*
Console tables 72, *75*
Cooper, Susie 225
Copeland porcelain 184
Copenhagen porcelain *96*
Copper *180*, 210
Country House style (17thC) 46-59
Country styles 21, *54*, *194*, *207*
  18thC 104-27
  early 19thC American *166*
  Victorian 209
Court cupboards 36, 43, 52
"Craftsman Style" (America) 210
Crane, Walter 215
Crapaud chairs 134
Creamware *82*, 85
Crewelwork *30*, *43*, *56*, *67*, *192*
"Cromwellian" chairs 52
Cupboards 14, *15*
  medieval 33, 36, 43
  17thC Country House 51, 52
  American William and Mary 63
  Queen Anne 71
  American Federal *100*
  American Colonial 110
  Shaker 122, *125*
  Biedermeier *166*
  Victorian *199*
Curtains 21, 35
  17thC Country House 49
  English Baroque 63, 65
  Queen Anne/Early Georgian 71
  Georgian 74, *80*, 82, 89, *92*
  American Federal *101*, *103*
  18thC Country *106*
  American Colonial 110, *116*, 121
  Shaker 127
  Regency 21, *155*
  Empire 21, 159
  Biedermeier 174
  19thC Classicism *134*, 134
  American Empire *166*
  Victorian 179, 180, *194*, 202
  Arts and Crafts 210
  Art Deco 224, *227*
Cushions 26, 35, 43, *52*, *52*

D

Dados 71, 89, 159, 179, 180, 210, 217, *221*
Davenport desks 183
David, Jacques Louis 133
Davis, A.J. *199*
Day-beds 159
Dehn, Hannerle *147*
Delftware *52*, *59*, 60, *62*, 65, 66, *74*
Derby porcelain 85, 152
Dericemo metal vases *225*
Desks 110, *116*
Distressed finishes 65, 121
Dornix fabrics 47
Dorset Square Hotel, London *186*, *192*
"Dragged" effects 18, 71, 121, *196*
Drapes *see* Curtains; Fabrics
Dresser, Christopher *212*
Dressers *49*, *54*, *56*, *59*, 104, *107*, *108*, 121, *190*
Dressing tables 51, *194*, *195*
Druggets 180
Duchesse brise *144*
Ducks, decoy *110*, 121, *121*

E

Edwardian style 12, 216-21
Egyptian influences 148, *152*, 159, 161, 222
"Egyptian matting" 28
Electroplating 184
Elizabethan styles 6, 21, 36-45, 179, 180
"Elizabethan" (Victorian) furniture 65
Elkington plate 184
Elm furniture *30*, *33*
Embroideries *see* Needlework
Embroidery frames 35
Empire styles *8*, 21, 159-75
Encoignures 133
Engravings *142*
Etruscan style 81, 149

F

Fabrics *20*, 21, *43*
  medieval 21, 26, 28, *28*, *30*, *33*, 35
  Elizabethan/Jacobean 21, *37*, 40, *43*
  17thC Country House 47, 59
  17thC American 52
  English Baroque *62*
  Queen Anne *66*, *67*, *69*, 71
  Georgian 71, 74, *77*, *87*, *96*
  18thC Country 104, *106*
  American Colonial 110, *121*

INDEX

Baroque/Rococo *130*, *136*, 147, *147*
Regency 148, 150
Empire 159, *159*, *165*
American Empire 162
Biedermeier 174
Victorian *14*, *176*, 179, *179*, *180*, *184*, *186*, *192*, *194*, *195*, *197*, *199*, 202, *207*, 209, *209*
Arts and Crafts 215
Edwardian/Art Nouveau 216, 220, *221*
Art Deco 227
Fairings *195*
"Farthingale" chair 43
Faux finishes 65, *125*, 150, *155*, *157*, *159*
Fire implements *138*
Fireplaces
Georgian 14, *74*, *87*
18thC Country *106*
American Colonial 110, *110*, *117*
Baroque/Rococo *128*, *138*
Regency *155*, *156*
American Empire 162, *166*
Arts and Crafts 210, *212*
Firescreens *176*
Flagons *30*
Flamestitch 47, 62
Floorcloth 71, 74, 82, *85*, 100, 104
Floors
medieval 28, *28*, *30*, 35, *35*
Elizabethan *37-8*, 40
17thC Country House 49, *51*, 52, 59
English Baroque 63
Queen Anne 71
Georgian 71, 72, 74, 82, *87*, *98*
American Federal 100, *100*, *101*
18thC Country *104*, 104, *108*
American Colonial 110, *110*, *114*, *116*, *117*, 121, *121*
Shaker 127
Baroque/Rococo *140*
Regency 150, *155*, *157*, *162*
American Empire *166*
Biedermeier 174
Victorian *14*, 180, *184*, *190*, *192*, *202*, 209
Arts and Crafts 212, 215
Edwardian/Art Nouveau 220
Art Deco 224, 227
Flowers *14*, *22*, *23*, *46*, *59*, *114*, *121*, *127*, *136*, *147*, *148*, *162*, *170*, *176*, *207*, *209*, *217*
Fortuny *130*, 147
Friezes *54*, 89, 148, 179, *184*, *186*, *207*, 212, *217*
Fruit *22*, *46*, *59*
Furniture 14, 16
medieval *26*, *28-30*, 33, *33*, 35
Elizabethan/Jacobean 36, *38*, 40, *40*, 43, *43*
17thC Country House 49, *49*, 51, *51*, *56*, *69*
17thC American Country House 52, *52*
English Baroque *62*, 63, 65
American William and Mary 63
Queen Anne 66, *69*, 71
Georgian *69*, 74, 75, *80*, 81, 82, 85, *85*, *87*, 89, *89*, *92*, *94*, *217*
American Federal *101*, 102, *165*
18thC Country *104*, 104
American Colonial 110, *110*, *112*, *114*, *117*, 121, *121*
Shaker 127
Baroque/Rococo *128*, 130, *132*, *140*, *144*, 149
Regency 148, 150, *152*, *155*
Empire 159
Biedermeier 174, *174*
19thC Classical 133-4, 149
American Empire 161, *161*, 162, *165*
Victorian 65, 179, 180, *182*, *184*, *192*, *199*, 202, 209, *217*
Arts and Crafts 210, *210*, 212, *212*, 215
Edwardian/Art Nouveau 14, *217*, 217-18, 220
Art Deco 224-5, 227

G

Gallé, Emile 218
Gaslighting 180
Gateleg tables *77*
Gaudí, Antoni 218
Geffrye Museum, London *92*, *221*, *227*
Georgian style *8*, 71-99
"German carpets" 63
Gibbons, Grinling 60
Girondoles 89
Glasgow School 218
Glass/glassware *130*, *140*, *170*, *182*, *184*, *205*, *227*
Elizabethan 43
English Baroque 63
Georgian *96*
Biedermeier 174
Victorian *183*, *199*
Gobelins tapestries 130
Goblets 33
Goburg, William *212*
Gollut, Christophe *179*
Gothic Court furniture *30*
Gothick styles 14, 74, 148, 179. 180, *189*, *196*, *199-200*, 202, *205*
Greek influences 100, 133, 148, 159, 161, 162
Greek Revival 100, 161, 162
Guéridons 159
Guimard, Hector 218
Gumb, Linda *186*

H

Hall-stands 183
Hallways *49*
Georgian *98*
American Federal *100*
American Colonial *112*
Baroque/Rococo *130*, *138*
Regency *148*, *155*, *162*
American Empire *166*, *170*
Victorian *176*, *195*
Hangings, wall *see* Wall hangings
Hart Room (New York Metropolitan Museum of Art) 52
"Hatbox" wallpaper *200*
Haynes Grange Room (Victoria and Albert Museum) 47
Healey, Deryck *175*, *223*, *225*
Hepplewhite furniture 85, 102, 152
Hi-fi systems 14, *212*
Highboys 110
Hockin, Kenneth *170*
Hogarth, William 71
Horn beakers *52*
Horta, Victor 218
Hudson, Jonathan *176*, *183*
Hudson River School *100*, *101*

I

Imari ware *140*
"Indian Styles" 46
"Ingrain" carpeting 100
Islamic influences 47
Ivory *223*

J

Jacob, Georges *132*
Jacobean styles 21, 36-45
Japanning 47, 102
Jasperware 85
Jennens and Bettridge 180
Jenrette, Richard *161*, *162*, *165*, *166*
Jones, Inigo 46, 47, 72
"Jugendstil" 218
Jumel, Madame *173*

K

Kangxi porcelain *65*, *140*
Kauffmann, Angelica 82
Kelims *56*, *91*, *180*, *199*, *207*
Kitchens *15*, 16
18thC Country 104, *104*, *107*, *108*
American Colonial *114*, *117*, 121
Victorian *190*, *207*
Edwardian/Art Nouveau *219*
modern 14
Knifeboxes *96*
Knowles, G.Sheridan *212*

L

Lace 21
Lacquerwork 47, 59, 63, 65, 130, *144*, *152*, *227*
Ladderback chairs 104, *106*, *107*, *108*, *116*, 121, *122*, *123*, *125*
Lalique, René *174*, 225
Lambrequins 180
Lampshades *176*, *212*
Lanterns *117*, 121
Laura Ashley Designer Collection 130
Le Brun, Charles 130
Leather 36, *59*, 60, 224, 227
Lee, Ann 122, *127*
Leleu, Jules *223*, *224*
Lely, Sir Peter *189*
Liberty designs *212*, *223*
Lieber, Ian *186*
Light switches 12, *15*, 16
Lighting 12, *60*
medieval 35
Elizabethan/Jacobean *39*
17thC Country House 51
English Baroque 63
Queen Anne/Georgian 71
American Colonial 110, 121
Baroque/Rococo *130*
Regency 148, *151*, 152
Empire 159
American Empire 162
Victorian 180, *192*, 202, 209
Edwardian/Art Nouveau 218, 220
Art Deco 225, 227
modern *89*
Lincrusta (embossed wallpaper) *176*, 217, *217*
Linley Sambourne House *176*
Linoleum 224
Lloyd Loom chairs *209*
Lolling chairs 102
Loo tables 152, 183
Loudspeakers 14
Louis XIV styles 128, 130, *142*
Louis XV styles 130, 133, *144*, *145*, 149, 179, *179*, 180, *192*
Louis XVI styles 133-4, *136*, 149
Lowboys *51*
Lustres *101*, *138*
Lyre-back chairs *103*, *195*

M

Mack, Stephen *114*
Mackintosh, Charles Rennie 218
Mahogany 71, 72, 75, 85, 162, 180
Majolica *25*, 184, *205*
Mallard, Prudent *192*
Mantelpiece displays *72*, *74*, *75*, *205*
Marc, Sveet *174*
Marquetry *28*
Marshall, Ned *223*
Martha Washington chairs 102
Mary II, Queen 60
Mary Queen of Scots needlework *43*
Matting *30*, 35, *38*, 59, 71, *144*
Mauchline ware *205*
McAlpine, Lord and Lady *25*
Medieval styles 26-35, 180, *194*, 210
Meeks, Joseph *199*
Meissen figures 84, 130
Minton porcelain 184
Mirrors *101*, *223*, *227*
Queen Anne 71
Georgian 89
American Federal *101*
Baroque/Rococo *128*, 130, *130*, *134*, *136*, *138*, 149
Regency 152, *152*, *155*, *156*, *162*, *170*
American Empire *166*
Victorian 180, *186*, *192*
Arts and Crafts 212
Art Deco *223*, *227*
Moorcroft pottery *30*
Moorfields carpets 82
Moquette *20*, 227
Morris, William 18, 35, 180, 202, 210, 215
Mortlake tapestries *128*
Mouldings 72, *80*, 89, 133, *155*
Music 35, 59, 65, 89, 121, 149, 173, 202, 215, 220

N

Nailsea glass *183*
Naïve paintings *49*, *56*, *92*, *100*, *101*, 121, *125*
Napoleon I 159
"Napoleonic Bee" design 159, *159*, *165*
Needlework 36, *43*, *69*, 210, 212, 215
Neo-Classicism 81, 100, 133

O

Oak *30*, 35, *38*, 40, 71, 104, 180, 210, 215
Oil lamps 152, 159, 162, 180, 209
Ormolu 152, *156*, 162
Osborne and Little wallpapers 104, *184*
Osterley Park, Middlesex 81
Ottomans 184, 202
Oudry, Jean-Baptiste 130

P

Paintings 24, *60*
17thC Country House 47, *49*, *51*, *56*
Queen Anne/Georgian 71, *72*, *77*, *92*
American Federal *100*, *101*
American Colonial 110, *112*, *114*, 121
Shaker *125*
Baroque/Rococo *132*
Regency *165*
Empire *148*
American Empire *170*
Biedermeier 174
Victorian *179*, 180, *180*, *182*, *189*, *199*, 202, *207*
Arts and Crafts *212*, 215
Art Deco *223*
modern *140*, *174*
Paintwork 14, *54*, *75*, 89
medieval 26, *27*, 28
Elizabethan *37*, 40
17thC Country House 47, *52*
English Baroque *60*, *62*, 65
Queen Anne *69*
Georgian *77*, *78*, *79*, *85*, *89*, *92*
American Federal *101*, 102, *103*
18thC Country *104*
American Colonial *114*, *116*, *117*, 121
Shaker 122, *125*
Baroque/Rococo *134*, *136*, *140*
Regency 148, 150, *155*, *165*
American Empire *166*
Victorian *179*, 180, *190*, *192*, *195*
Arts and Crafts *212*
Edwardian/Art Nouveau 216, 217, *217*, 218

  Art Deco 222, 224
  modern 18
Paisleys 202
Palladian style 66, *72*, 82
Panelling 16, 18, *19*, *38*
  medieval 28, *205*
  Elizabethan/Jacobean 36, *37*, *38*, 40
  17thC Country House *46*, 47, *54*
  English Baroque 60, *60*, *62*, 65
  18thC American *52*
  Queen Anne *69*, 71
  Georgian 71, *75*, *77*, *82*, *85*, 89, *92*
  American Federal *101*
  18thC Country 104
  American Colonial 110, *110*, *116*
  Regency *152*
  American Empire *166*
  Victorian *197*
  Arts and Crafts 210, 215
Edwardian/Art Nouveau *217*, *221*
Papier mâché 180, *192*
Parham House, W.Sussex *37*, *43*, *156*
Parian 184, *200*
Parquet 40, 63, 134, 202, 220, 224, *227*
Patchwork 52, *56*, *103*, *166*, *194*, *195*, 209
Pavilion Designs *192*
Pedestal tables 152, *155*, 183
Pedestals 85
Pelmets 63, 65, 71, *80*, 82, 89, 100, 180, *194*, 202, 224
Pembroke tables 85, *94*, *101*
Pennsylvania Dutch 52, *108*
Persian carpets 63, *155*, *162*
"Petticoat tables *162*
Pewter 36, *40*, 43, *46*, 52, *127*, 210, *223*
Photographs 202
Phyfe, Duncan *165*
Pierce, Edward 60
Pine 121
Plants 22
Plas Teg, N.Wales *142*, *151*, *152*
Plasterwork 49, 60, *60*, *72*, 81, 104, *110*, *121*, *184*
Pompadour, Madame de 130
Porcelain 24, *205*
  17thC Country House *51*, *59*
  English Baroque 65, *65*
  Georgian 81, *82*, 85, *94*, *96*
  Queen Anne *66*, *67*, 71, *71*
  American Federal 100, *100*, 102
  18thC Country *107*
  Baroque/Rococo *132*, 133, *136*, *140*, 149
  Regency *155*
  Empire 159
  Biedermeier 174, *174*
  Victorian *180*, 184, *184*, *192*, *209*
Pottery
  medieval *30*, 33
  Elizabethan 43
  17thC 52, *59*
  English Baroque 63
  Queen Anne/Georgian 71, 81
  American Colonial *114*
  Victorian *108*, *190*, *192*, *195*, 202, *205*
  Edwardian/Art Nouveau *219*
  Art Deco *223*, *227*, *227*
  modern *108*, *174*, *212*, *224*
Preiss 225
Presses (cupboards) 43, 52
Preston Manor, Brighton *217*
Prie-dieux 184
Prints 24, *79*, 89, *92-4*, *170*, 174, *176*, *192*, *205*, *217*, *219*, *224*
Pugin, A.W.N. 35, 180

Q

Qianlong porcelain *51*, *65*
Queen Anne styles 66-71, *101*, *166*
"Queen Anne" 185, 217
Quilts *103*, *116*, 121

R

Radiators 14, *14*, *144*, *157*, *159*, *221*
Radios *227*
Rag rolling 18
Régence styles 130, 133
Regency styles 21, 148-58
Restoration styles 60-5
Riddell, Crawford *199*
Robertson, Vanessa *33*
Robinson, Gerrard 180
"Robinson Crusoe" sideboards 180
Rococo styles 21, 72, 74, 89, 121, 128-47, 179, *192*
Rosewood furniture 152
Roux designs *199*, *200*
Rugs
  17thC Country House 49, 59, *59*
  Queen Anne/Georgian 71, 74, *77*
  American Federal *103*
  American Colonial *117*, *121*
  Shaker 127
  Regency *162*
  Victorian *14*, *182*, *197*, 202
  Arts and Crafts 215
  Edwardian/Art Nouveau 220
  Art Deco *223*
Rush lights *38*, *56*
Rush matting 28, 49, *106*, 121, 215
Rushes 10, 28, 35, *38*

S

Salazar, Fiona *225*
Saltglaze *59*
Samplers *56*
Sash windows 49
Satinwood 82, 180, 185, 217
Savonnerie carpets 63, 65, 74
Scagliola 75
Schule, Harry *12*, *223*
"Scotch" carpets 74, 100
Screens 24, *30*, *49*, 63
Settees *51*, *100*, *140*
Settles 212
Severs, Dennis *6*, *60*, *62*, *72*
Sèvres porcelain 84, *96*, 147, 159
"Sezessionstil" 218
Shaker style 122-7
"Shakespeare" sideboards 180
Sheffield Plate 184
Shelving 14, *15*
Sheraton 85, *100*, *101*, 102, 152, *165*, *166*, 217, 221
Shutters *77*, *78*, *85*
Sideboards 14, 85, *96*, 104, 180, *199*, 212, *212*, 227
Silver furniture *69*, 130
Silverware 51, 63, 65, 66, *69*, 102, 133, 183, 212, *217*
Singerie 130
Smoking stands *212*
Sociables (sofas) 184
Sofa tables 152
Sofas 16, 35, 71, 89, *94*, *134*, *144*, *170*, *209*
  Empire *159*, *179*
  American Empire 161, *166*
  Biedermeier 174
  Victorian 184, 202, *209*
Soft furnishings *see* Fabrics
Southport, Connecticut *101*
Spinning wheels 35
Spode ware 152
"Sponged" effects 18, *104*
Spongeware *54*, *56*, *207*
Spoon-back chairs 184
Staffordshire figures 24, *25*, 184, 202, 209
Stained glass *215*
Staircases *112*, *162*, 218
Stencilling *19*, *103*, *107*, 110, 173, *207*, *209*, 221, 224
Stickley, Gustav *210*
Stoneware *180*
Stonnington, Connecticut *121*
Stools 40, 52, *82*, *142*, *147*, 159
Stoves *106*
Strapwork 36, 40
Strawberry Hill Gothick *199*
Stuart Interiors *30*, *199*
Stucco 60, 74
Suites, three-piece *227*
Swedish Biedermeier style *174*
Swedish Empire style *148*, *159*

T

Table lamps 89
Tables
  medieval 26, 28, *28*, 33
  Elizabethan/Jacobean *38*, 43
  17thC Country House *46*, *49*, 51, *65*
  17thC American 52
  Queen Anne *69*, 71
  Georgian 75, 77, 85, *87*, *89*, *91*, *94*
  American Federal *100*, *101*
  18thC Country *108*
  American Colonial 121
  Shaker 122
  Baroque/Rococo *136*, *138*, *142*, *144*
  Regency 14, 148, *148*, *151*, 152, *152*, *155*, *157*, *162*
  American Empire 161, *166*, *170*
  Biedermeier *174*, *224*
  Victorian *14*, 180, *180*, *184*, *186*, *199*, *200*, 202, *205*, 209, *209*
  Arts and Crafts 215
  Edwardian/Art Nouveau *77*, 217
  Art Deco *174*, *223*, *227*
  modern 14, 51, *59*, *195*
Tambour desks 102
Tapestries 28, 36, *37*, 40, *43*, 47, 49, *59*, *128*, 130
Tea caddies 77
Tented rooms 159, 173
Tête-à-têtes 184
Textiles *see* Fabrics
Thomire, Pierre-Philippe 159
Ticking 71, 104
Tiffany, Louis Comfort *199*, 218
Tiger maple *125*, *127*
Tiles 28, 35, *35*, 66, 104, *107*, 121, *142*
  vinyl *51*, *138*
Toile de Jouys fabrics 147
Tole ware *25*, *108*, *184*
Topiary *22*
Torchères *128*, 152
"Trafalgar" chairs 152
Treen 24, 127, *157*, *205*
Trenchers 33
Trompe l'oeil 19, *40*, *82*, 89, *194*
Turkeywork 36, 49, 63
Turkish carpets 63, 202
Turner, Kenneth *136*
TV sets 14, *15*, *212*
Tweedy, Thomas 180

U

Upholstery 43, 184
Urns 85, *130*, *142*, *147*, *148*, *151*, *161*, *166*

V

Velvets 71, 74, 202, 227
Venetian blinds 82, 227
Versailles 130
Victorian styles *10*, 18, 176-99, 216
Vinyl *51*, *138*, *155*
Voysey, C.F.A. 210, *212*, 215, *221*

W

Wadsworth, A. and J. *212*
Wainscot chairs 52
Wall hangings *30*, *33*, 36, *37*, 40, *43*, 47, *56*, 60, 63
Wallpapers
  Elizabethan/Jacobean 40
  17thC Country House 47
  English Baroque 63
  Georgian 74, 89
  American Federal 100, *100*, 162
  18thC Country *104*, *107*, *108*
  Baroque/Rococo 134, *142*
  Regency *155*
  Empire 159
  19thC Classicism 134, *142*
  Biedermeier 174
  Victorian *35*, *176*, 180, *183*, *184*, *192*, *194*, *200*, 202, *207*, 209
  Edwardian/Art Nouveau *14*, 217, 220, *221*
  Art Deco 224, 227
  modern *104*
Walls
  medieval 26, *27*, 28, *28*, *33*, 35, *35*
  Elizabethan/Jacobean 36, *37*, *38*, 40, *43*
  17thC Country House 47, 49, 59
  17thC American Country House 52, *52*
  English Baroque 60, *62*, 63, 65, *65*
  Queen Anne *67*, 71
  Georgian 72, *72*, 74, *74*, *77*, 78, 81-2, *89*, *91*, *92*, *98*
  American Federal 100, *101*
  18thC Country 104, *106*
  American Colonial 110, *110*, *114*, *116*, 121, *121*
  Shaker *125*
  Baroque/Rococo *140*, *142*, *147*
  Regency 148, 150, *151*, *155*, *159*, *165*
  Empire *148*, 159
  American Empire *170*, *174*
  Biedermeier 174
  Victorian 179, 180, *186*, *192*, 202, *207*, 209
  Arts and Crafts 210, 215
  Edwardian/Art Nouveau 217, 220
  Art Deco 222, 224, *224*, *227*
Walnut 63, 65, 71, 75, 180
Walton, George *212*
Warrender, Caroline *186*
Watercolours *69*, 174, *180*
Watteau, Jean Antoine 130
Webb, Philip 210
Wedgwood, Josiah 81-2, 85
  Pottery 102, 152, 217
Wells, Michael *189*
Wemyss ware *192*
Whatnots 24, 180, 183, *205*
Wickham, Kate *212*
Wiener Werkstätte 218
William and Mary style 60, *62*, 63, *64*, 65
Willow pattern 184
Windows
  17thC Country House 49
  English Baroque 63
  Queen Anne/Early Georgian 71
  Georgian 74, 82, *92*
  American Federal 100
  18thC Country 104
  American Colonial 121
  Shaker 127
  Baroque/Rococo *130*, 134, 149
  Regency 150
  Empire 159
  Biedermeier 174
  Victorian 179, 180, *186*, *192*
  Arts and Crafts 210, 215
Edwardian/Art Nouveau 217
Windsor chairs 121, *199*, 209
Wing chairs 77
Worcester porcelain 85
Wyndham, Melissa *192*

Z

Zoffany wallpapers *19*, *138*

ACKNOWLEDGMENTS

The Authors and Publishers would like to thank the following house-owners, interior designers, antique dealers, museums and hotels for allowing special photography for this book. The page number on which a photograph appears is followed, after an oblique stroke, by the picture number.

The American Museum in Britain, Claverton Manor, Bath BA2 7BD (0225) 60503 *52/1, 53/2, 82/1, 101/3, 102/1, 109/7, 126/1, 192/1*
Candace Bahouth 30/2
Richard Latrobe Bateman *30/1, 32/1*
Cornelia Bayley, Plas Teg, Nr Mold, N. Wales (0352) 771335 *8/1, 20/1, 42/4, 142/2, 150/1, 151/2, 151/3, 152/1, 152/2, 152/3, 152/4, 153/5, 157/4, 193/6, 196/1, 196/7*
Burgh Island Hotel, Bigbury on Sea, S. Devon (0548) 810514 *12/5, 20/4, 227/2, 227/3, 227/4, 227/5*
Rupert Cavendish Antiques, 610 Kings Road, London SW6 2DX (01) 731 7041 *149/2, 158/1, 174/1, 174/2*
Charleston Farmhouse, Firle, Lewes, E. Sussex (032 183) 265 *14/4*
Chilston Park, Lenham, Nr Maidstone, Kent (0622) 859803 *10/2, 17/16, 22/6, 23/15, 23/13, 135/5, 136/3, 142/1, 204/2, 205/7*
Jane Churchill Designs Ltd, 81 Pimlico Road, London SW1 W8PH (01) 730 8564 *15/8, 16/2, 20/2, 20/3, 20/9, 20/10, 86/1, 92/1, 97/6, 139/2, 181/4, 186/2, 194/4, 194/5*
Arnold Copper, 872 Madison Avenue, New York, NY 10021, USA (0101) (212) 737 5213 *93/5, 93/6, 103/2, 110/1, 111/2, 112/1, 113/2, 116/1, 120/1, 121/2, 166/1, 166/2, 166/3*
Stephen Crisp (01) 262 9183 *22/6, 23/13, 23/15*
Richard Davidson Antiques, Lombard Street, Petworth, W. Sussex (0798) 42508 *4/1, 17/13, 46/2, 48/1, 49/2, 49/3, 49/4, 49/5, 59/2, 59/3, 62/1, 136/4*
Hannerle Dehn, 30 Holland Park Road, London W14 (01) 602 2244 *14/2, 105/3, 130/1, 134/1, 135/6, 146/1, 147/2*
Dorney Court, Windsor, Berkshire (06286) 4638 *6/2, 6/3, 19/13, 42/2, 60/1, 69/7, 193/8*
Dorset Square Hotel, Dorset Square, London NW1 (01) 723 7874 *4/2, 14/3, 19/20, 97/4, 186/3, 193/3*
Geffrye Museum, Kingsland Road, London E2 (01) 739 8363 *6/4, 10/1, 39/2, 39/4, 39/5, 85/3, 92/2, 220/1, 226/1*
Christophe Gollut, 116 Fulham Road, London SW3 6HU (01) 370 4101 *16/3, 145/4, 178/1, 179/2, 179/3, 179/4, 196/5*
Linda Gumb, 9 Camden Passage, London N1 (01) 354 1184 *14/6, 21/16, 187/7, 190/1, 190/2, 191/5, 194/1*
Kenneth Hockin, 247 West 10th Street, New York, NY 10014, USA (212) 463 8163 *8/5, 170/1, 170/2, 170/3, 170/4, 171/5*
Jonathan Hudson Interior Designs, 16 Fitzjames Avenue, London W14 ORP (01) 602 8829 *14/1, 18/1, 18/2, 23/16, 176/1, 176/2, 177/3, 177/4, 182/1*
Humphrey Antiques, North Street, Petworth, W. Sussex (0798) 43053 *47/2, 59/2, 59/3*
Julian Humphreys, 25 Fournier Street, London E1 (01) 377 9312 *75/5, 77/2, 77/3, 77/4, 78/2, 79/4*
Richard Hampton Jenrette, Duchess County, New York State *101/6, 160/1, 161/2, 162/1, 162/2, 163/3, 164/1, 165/2, 165/3, 167/4, 172/1, 173/2*
John Jesse and Irina Lasky, 160 Kensington Church Street, London W8 (01) 229 0312 *12/2, 12/4, 12/12, 15/12, 15/9, 216/2*
Erik Karlsen, Jane Churchill Ltd, Ellis House, 118-120 Garratt Lane, London SW18 4EF (01) 877 0600 *33/2, 69/6, 87/2, 87/3, 97/5*
Ian Lieber, Kingsmead House, 250 Kings Road, London SW3 5UE (01) 352 6422 *15/11, 20/5, 33/3, 50/1, 51/2, 51/3, 51/4, 64/4, 65/5, 96/1, 132/1, 181/3, 185/3, 185/5, 186/1*
Stephen Mack Associates, Chase Hill Farm, Ashaway, Rhode Island 02804, USA (0101) (401) 377 8041 *18/3, 22/5, 113/3, 114/1, 114/2, 115/3, 117/2, 117/3, 118/1, 118/2, 118/3, 118/4, 119/5*
Marshall/Schule Associates Inc., 1065 Madison Avenue, New York, NY USA (0101) (212) 772 1230 *13/7, 18/4, 18/5, 80/1, 80/2, 99/3, 168/1, 222/2, 223/3, 223/4, 224/1, 224/2*

In creating a book like Period Style, *so much depends on visual stimulation. If the book succeeds in stimulating, this must be due to the photographs taken by James Merrell and the art direction of Jacqui Small. Thanks are due, too, to Tommy Candler who, as always, was at hand when I was short on inspiration. And, of course, to all those whose homes are the real statement of* Period Style.

Joan Elaine Mazzola, New York and Green Farms *10/4, 103/4, 135/3, 143/3*
Angela and Bill Page, Tunbridge Wells, Kent (0892) 22217 *19/19, 54/1, 54/2, 55/3, 55/4, 56/1, 56/2, 57/3, 206/1, 206/2, 206/3, 206/4, 207/5*
Parham House, Pulborough, W. Sussex (09066) 2021 *36/1, 37/2, 37/3, 42/1, 42/3, 44/1, 45/2, 156/1*
Pavilion Designs, 49 Pavilion Road, London SW1 (01) 245 6788 *185/2, 203/2*
Preston Manor, Preston Park, Brighton, Sussex (0273) 603005 *8/6, 10/4, 217/4*
Vanessa Robertson *32/1*
Saint Mary's, Bramber, Sussex (0903) 816205 *41/2, 43/5, 204/1*
Dennis Severs, 18 Folgate Street, London E1 (01) 247 4013 *1/1, 7/5, 25/8, 61/2, 62/3, 66/1, 67/2, 67/3, 68/1, 70/1, 71/2, 72/1, 73/2, 74/1, 74/2, 74/3, 75/4, 154/2*
Shaker Museum, Shaker Museum Road, Old Chatham, New York (0101) (518) 794 9100 *122/1, 123/2, 124/2, 125/4, 127/2, 127/3*
Catherine Shinn, 7 Suffolk Parade, Cheltenham, Glos. (0242) 520163 *180/1, 181/2, 205/6*
Keith Skeel Antiques, Islington High Street, London N1 (01) 226 7012 14/7, *15/10, 15/15, 17/7, 17/8, 17/10, 17/11, 17/15, 21/12, 24/4, 69/4, 87/4, 108/2, 136/1, 136/2, 139/5, 144/1, 145/3, 156/3, 191/4, 192/9, 196/2, 196/3, 196/4, 196/6, 205/8, 218/1*
Sqerryes Court Westerham, Kent (0959) 62345 *24/3, 69/3, 87/5*
Henry and Irene Stewart, New York *132/2, 133/3, 133/4, 133/5*
Michael Strauss Ltd, 49 The Drive, Hove, Sussex (0273) 734438 *104/1, 185/4, 194/2*
Stuart Interiors, Barrington Court, Barrington, Ilminster, Somerset (0460) 40349 *31/5, 31/6, 40/1, 64/3, 199/3, 199/4*
Teneyck-Emerich Antiques, 351 Pequot Avenue, Southport, Conn., USA (203) 259 2559 *15/13, 100/2, 101/4, 101/5, 169/4, 186/4*
Kenneth Turner, Brook Manor, 35 Brook Street, London W1Y 1AJ (01) 499 4952 *11/7, 17/9, 20/8, 22/2, 22/7, 23/10, 23/12, 137/5, 190/3, 202/1*
Michael Wells, Frankham, E. Sussex *24/5, 128/1, 129/2, 188/1, 189/2*
Melissa Wyndham, 6 Sydney Street, London SW3 (01) 352 2874 *20/7, 25/14, 181/5, 186/6, 193/2*

The following people kindly allowed us to photograph their homes:
Rosie and Michael Addison, Lee Anderson, Jane Baigent, John and Rebecca Barratt, David Cockburn and Anthony Shaw, Anne Cockerell, Coline Covington, Dan and Vikki Cruickshank, Jane Cumberbach and Alastair Brown, Richard and Deirdre Davidson, Louis de Wet, John and Caroline Evetts, Ruth and Peter Fane, Piers and Caroline Feetham, Vera and Murray Gordon, Mr and Mrs Richard Gray, Deryck Healey, Charles and Maggie Jencks, Mr and Mrs Michael Keehan, Wendy Kidd, Georgia and David Langton, Ira Levy, Angela Lucas, Anna and Tony Mansi, Sue March, Christopher and Heidi Marchant-Lane, Sarah and David McElwee, Lord and Lady McAlpine of West Green, Walter and Jacqui Meyer, Freda and Jack Parker, Jo Peters, Jacinth Rhodes, Mr and Mrs Espirito Santo Silva, Elspeth Riley-Smith, Dick Snyder, Anna Simonde, Mr and Mrs D.Spearing, Sarah van Gerbig, Andrew and Julie Wadsworth, Julia Walker, Michael B. White.

Music suggestions: Ambient Music Co.

Textiles by Candace Bahouth and Vanessa Robertson, and furniture by Richard Latrobe Bateman, are available via the Crafts Council, 1 Oxendon Street, London SW1Y 4AT.